STRENGTH
FOR TODAY

STRENGTH FOR TODAY

*Daily Devotions
for the Chronically Ill*

Sharon Broyles

HarperSanFrancisco
A Division of HarperCollins*Publishers*

FIRST EDITION

Library of Congress Cataloging-in-Publication Data

Broyles, Sharon.
    Strength for today / Sharon Broyles. —1st ed.
        p.   cm.
    Includes indexes.
    ISBN 0–06–061066–2 (pbk.)
    1. Chronically ill—Prayer books and devotions—English.
I. Title.
BV4910.B76   1993
242'.4—dc20   92–54537
                                                        CIP

93 94 95 96 97 98 ❖ MAL 8 7 6 5 4 3 2 1

This edition is printed on acid-free paper that meets the American National Standards Institute Z39.48 Standard.

To Marvin
for his persistent portrayal of
Ephesians 5:25

Preface

Being chronically ill means learning one of life's central lessons: the choice to live day by day under painful and frustrating circumstances is an ongoing act of courage and faith.

The society of the chronically ill is not exclusive. Forty-four million Americans suffer with long-term physical disabilities. Nearly forty-three million others contend with heart disease. Forty million cope with arthritis, and over ten million have diabetes. More than thirteen million endure asthma. Over half a million have lupus. And upwards of a quarter million suffer from multiple sclerosis. Add to these numbers those with severe allergies, emphysema and other lung conditions, endometriosis, Chronic Fatigue Syndrome, Parkinson's disease, Tourette's syndrome, debilitating premenstrual syndrome, and various internal disorders, migraine headaches and other chronic pain, and recurrent mental illness. And this is not a complete listing of the chronic health problems that plague tens of millions.

Depression has dogged me most of my adult life. I understand the frustration of not being able to find definitive answers or solutions in a culture where technological breakthroughs occur every day and information reigns supreme. I also feel the guilt and confusion of a Christian who is embarrassed to admit her condition to other Christians. Sometimes I mistakenly conclude that if I were a better person, a stronger Christian, I wouldn't have the health problems I do (which include escalating food and environmental allergies that manifest themselves in brutal headaches). But God has a way of penetrating the spirits of those He loves, especially when they suffer. In my life, God has been faithful beyond measure.

But what does a careful reader of Scripture in particular and the Christian community in general do with committed believers who continue to suffer from chronic pain, unending sickness, or unhealed disease? Although this issue is addressed, it is not this book's intention to provide answers, but to introduce the suffering reader to the Answer Himself. Whatever the problem, dilemma, or need, God is more than able to supply us with the power and promise we so desperately crave.

Over the coming year, you will meet four remarkable women who agreed to share their physical and emotional pain with you.

Carol Kelly has Ménière's disease. The unpredictable and infrequent attacks of vertigo, head full of noisy reverberations, and accompanying nausea can be intense. What's worse, no one can tell Carol why this happens. Even so, like millions of others with chronic health problems, she continues to live a satisfying life.

When Glenna Hadley reported to work as a school crossing guard one morning six years ago, she was thrust into a violent encounter with chronic illness. An unforeseen seizure knocked her to the ground, where she sustained a concussion. The episode left her balance impaired for months; unrelenting tests, procedures, and experiments with different drugs and dosages followed. Her system was found to be highly sensitive to many medications, including those used to treat other maladies.

Nancy Browning is plagued by chronic asthma. It frustrates her attempts to be the active and involved wife, daughter, homemaker, church member, and mother to two young children she wants to be.

Jackie Poor suffers from lupus, a chronic illness involving dysfunction of her body's immune system. Joint pain, stomach distress, extreme fatigue, cognitive difficulties, and memory loss are her daily companions. Jackie's chronic, intimate contact with lupus means incessant doctor visits, perpetual testing, and an absence of explanations for herself or her concerned grown children.

This book is for people like Jackie and Nancy and Glenna and Carol. For people like you and me—people who wrestle fear, loss, and pain every day. Those who feel alone and ignored, who many times may appear perfectly healthy on the outside. The ones who face an exhausting day in–day out effort to reach some kind of physical, emotional, and spiritual balance in life. Those who ask, "Does anyone truly understand how I feel?"

As I and each of these women have experienced, the answer is a resounding Yes! God understands. And in His merciful identification with us, God not only imparts strength for today, but hope for tomorrow as well.

Acknowledgments

"Gee whiz," my husband whined with a twinkle in his eye, "we'll never get this book finished!"

We? How many hours had *he* spent bent over a word processor or poring over reference material under the pressure of a deadline? But he was right, of course. He had spent hours standing over a hot iron or beside a hot stove so that I could write. He logged miles on the car making pizza runs for dinner instead of enjoying home-fried chicken. While following cooking and laundering instructions, without committing too many blunders, my three children expanded their understandings of patience and respect. No project, especially a book, makes it to completion without employing "we."

Christian author Joyce Landorf calls them stretcher-bearers. They're the people who do for me what I cannot do for myself—like the four men in Mark 2 who lowered their paralyzed friend through the roof to Jesus. When I was paralyzed with fear that I'd never find enough words to write an entire book, or weighed down with depression over my lack of creativity, or assailed by guilt for neglecting my family, my stretcher-bearers encouraged me, did my chores, and prayed with and for me.

Without Jackie Poor's question, "Why isn't there a Christian book for chronically ill people like me?" this book would never have come to be. She fed me ideas and invited me to her lupus support group meetings. She shared all her pain and collaborated with me by testing the authenticity and relevance of every word. For more than ten years, Carol Kelly has shared her considerable knowledge of Scripture with me. And, in the writing of this book, she helped me to streamline my theology. Glenna Hadley and Nancy Browning, like Jackie and Carol, shared their lives, their painful places, and the supreme gift of their cherished friendships.

My artists' support group and St. David's Christian Writers' Association stimulated and strengthened me. I am most grateful, however, for each and every prayer my family, friends, and extended church and Emmaus families prayed on behalf of this book.

While writing, I read and listened extensively to the words of Eugene Peterson and Brennan Manning. The influence of their insights is unmistakable throughout the book. I also bow to Henry Gariepy for his discerning thoughts on Job and to Dr. Lloyd John Ogilvie for his exposition on the Beatitudes.

Ron Klug of Harper San Francisco, with his wise and gentle spirit, was an open and caring editor. He fine-tuned and expertly crafted my phrasing and theology, all the while maintaining respect for me, for the work, and for you, the chronically ill reader.

I will also be forever obliged to all the other people at Harper San Francisco who offered their support and assistance.

STRENGTH
FOR TODAY

JANUARY 1   ❧   *The Light in My Darkness*

You are my lamp, O Lord; the Lord turns my darkness
into light.   2 *Samuel* 22:29

A wise woman, Mary Gardiner Brainard, has said, "I would
rather walk with God in the dark than go alone in the
light." Like other people, I can't see in the dark. Trying to
find the bathroom away from home during the night can
be a comedy of errors unless I turn on a light. So it is with
my illness. I'm living in unfamiliar territory, unable to see
clearly and groping for direction. If, out of ignorance, I
make an error in judgment concerning my illness, I may
wind up with worse than a stubbed toe from taking a
wrong turn in strange surroundings. But God says He will
shed light on any confusion I may have. His presence is a
lamp in my darkness so that I can see what He's doing and
where I'm going. He assures me of His continuing guidance along the way.

Together He and I will travel by the light of a lamp of
love that cannot burn out. With God, I'll never be lost in
the darkness of illness.

Lord, please turn on Your lamp of love in my life
today. Sometimes it's just too dark for me even to
find the switch.   ❧

Here is my servant whom I have chosen, the one I
love, in whom I delight.   *Matthew 12:18*

A newspaper cartoon depicts two little girls playing with
their dolls. One of the girls tells the other, "My doll doesn't
do anything. She just soaks up love."

Being ill and physically unable to do many things may
cause me to feel useless and unimportant. Because of the
society in which I live, where people are valued for what
they do instead of who they are, illness may also cause me
to feel unloved. But God wants me to know that no matter
what I can do or cannot do, His love for me is unending.
God loves me when I feel well, and God loves me when I
don't. He delights in me when I complete a task, and He
delights in me when I can't even attempt one.

Paul Tillich defines faith as "the courage to accept my
acceptance." What would life be like if I were bold enough
to plop right down in the middle of God's love and start
soaking?

O God, I need courage to accept Your complete
and total acceptance of me. Today I want to know
the depth, breadth, and height of Your love for me.
May I delight in You, just as You delight in me.   ❧

Therefore we do not lose heart. Though outwardly
we are wasting away, yet inwardly we are being
renewed day by day. . . . So we fix our eyes not
on what is seen, but on what is unseen.
2 Corinthians 4:16, 18

Some years ago a friend gave me a geode. This ordinary-
looking rock is precious to me and sits on my shelf like a
trophy. Geodes are volcanic rocks that appear common
enough on the outside. But cracking one open exposes a
hollow center lined with sparkling colored crystals. No
two geodes are alike; each one is fascinatingly unique. The
breathtaking interior is created by monumental volcanic
force—extreme heat, intense pressure, explosive power.
One day the geode becomes part of the magma flowing
down a mountainside. Then it waits to be discovered and
broken open, that its inner artistry might be enjoyed.

Because of my illness, I may feel spiritually nauseated
from the upheaval in my life, as if I am living inside a vol-
cano waiting for an eruption. I may think my mental and
spiritual growth has ended. But, I cannot see what God
sees—the beauty of a beginning, not the end.

Thank You, Lord, for the beautiful person I am
becoming. Today I need eyes to envision unseen
beginnings. ❧

> Moses answered, "What if they do not believe me
> or listen to me and say, 'The Lord did not appear to
> you'?" *Exodus 4:1*

When I spoke out of turn as a child, I was disciplined with
pepper or soap on my tongue. It stung, but the sting of humiliation was much worse. I was also often chastised for
spilling what my family considered a "pot of private beans."
It didn't take me long to identify with Moses. I thought
anything that came out of my mouth was bad, that I had
nothing to say that anyone would care to hear.

Moses was not a great orator, and he was terrified to
plead the Hebrews' case to Pharaoh. But God employed
that very weakness to free millions. God is also now using
me in the area of my greatest fear and weakness—trying
to communicate with words after having been shot down
for the same thing so many times before. Illness can be that
weakness for others. I may feel physically devitalized and
spiritually impotent, no longer useful. But, if God can mobilize a doubting Moses and empower a hurting child like
me, He can utilize anyone—even in illness.

Lord, sometimes I use my illness as an excuse not to
try new things. Help me to understand that today
You still work best through doubting, hurting
people just like me.   ✉

Love is patient, love is kind. It does not envy, it does
not boast, it is not proud. It is not rude, it is not self-
seeking, it is not easily angered, it keeps no record
of wrongs. Love does not delight in evil but rejoices
with the truth. It always protects, always trusts,
always hopes, always perseveres. Love never fails.
1 Corinthians 13:4—8

In geometry class I learn that if $a = b$ and $b = c$, then a also
equals c. In the Bible, I learn that God is love or God equals
love. Then God must also equal the long list of attributes in
1 Corinthians 13.

God is patient with me and kind to me. God does not
envy my accomplishments or boast when I accomplish
nothing. God is not overbearing or rude with me. God
does not insist on His own way, nor is He easily angered.
God does not keep a list of all my failures. God does not
delight when I am sick, rather He rejoices when I look to
Him as the source of all truth and wholeness. God always
protects me, always trusts and believes in me, always hopes
for me, always perseveres with me. God's love for me will
never fail.

O God, thank You for the refreshing reminder of
the remarkable quality of Your love. Today, when I
fail to act lovingly toward myself, I will remember
that love originates with You and not with me. 🐦

The star they had seen in the east went ahead of
them until it stopped over the place where the child
was. When they saw the star, they were overjoyed.
Matthew 2:9–10

This day in the Church year is known as Epiphany, a com-
memoration of the day God surprised the three Wise Men
with a baby King.

God has always been full of surprises. He surprised old
Abraham with a son and Noah's neighbors with rain. He
surprised Mary in her youth and the Pharisees in their self-
righteousness. He surprised the woman at the well and
Peter at the cross. He surprised Thomas in the upper room
and Paul on the road to Damascus. Preacher and writer
John Claypool has said that "God's other name is always
Surprise."

The word *epiphany* has taken on the meaning of a sudden or surprising perception, as in "I had an epiphany"—an
"Ah!" experience. Just as the Wise Men never expected to
see God in the form of a human infant living in humble
quarters, I may not expect to see God in my pain and confusion. But even in illness, maybe especially in illness, I can
expect God's surprises.

O God, I confess that at times I become so bogged
down in the circumstances of my illness that I fail
to see Your star of hope. Lord, surprise me today
with overflowing joy.   ❧

Pleasant words are a honeycomb, sweet to the soul
and healing to the bones.   *Proverbs 16:24*

"I keep asking God to heal me," said Nancy, referring to
her asthma. "He hasn't, so I guess that means He doesn't
love me."

This was Nancy's attitude immediately before a retreat
weekend at a time when her body required eight different
medications to withstand the assault of living with asthma.
She prayed and pleaded for physical healing, for the
asthma to disappear.

Instead, the ears of her heart were opened to the sweetest sounds, words of love from Another. Her soul was filled
with more of God's love than she ever thought possible.
Finding herself enveloped by the love of Almighty God,
Nancy was healed—not of asthma, but of the obsessive
need to have her illness removed.

Nancy still has asthma, but she needs considerably less
medication since that time. And she is becoming more
content to allow an all-loving God take charge of her illness and her life.

O passionate Father, may my ears be attuned to the
echo of Your healing love around me and within
me today. Permeate my very bones with Your
wonderful words of warmth. Today I will love
You back.   ❧

Blessed are the poor in spirit, for theirs is the
kingdom of heaven.   *Matthew 5:3*

Look up *blessed* in a Bible dictionary and the definition is *"See
happy."* The words are interchangeable. In his book, *Con-
gratulations—God Believes in You!*, Dr. Lloyd John Ogilvie
comments on this first of Jesus' teachings from the Sermon
on the Mount. "Unhappiness," writes Ogilvie, "is always
caused by self-sufficiency which arrogantly demands our
making it on our own strength."

It's so easy to adopt a mind-set of self-sufficiency. Remember the old television commercial "Mother! I'd rather
do it myself!"? How often I take that attitude with God. *I
can handle this illness by myself, God. Then, when I'm better, I'll be able
to do great things for you.* I may even believe that if I'm sick and
ask for help, I'm letting God down. But the truth is, the
closer I get to God, the more I need Him. The poor in
spirit realize that they cannot do anything without God.

Happy am I when I recognize and admit my need of
God, for then God Himself dwells within me.

O Lord, please nurture in me today the joy
of discovering Your sufficiency through my
illness.   ☿

He also warms himself and says, "Ah! I am warm; I see the fire." From the rest he makes a god, his idol; He bows down to it and worships. He prays to it and says, "Save me; you are my god." *Isaiah 44:16–17*

Ever hear the expression "it's a three-dog night"? During long, cold frontier nights, a man might have his little house dog lie on his feet to keep them warm. If it was very cold, the two of them would snuggle up next to a larger dog, maybe a collie at the man's back. If the night was bitterly cold, an even larger third dog was needed to keep the man warm while he slept. Hence, a three-dog night bears out what nineteenth-century naturalist John Burroughs once said, "Winter, like poverty, makes us acquainted with strange bedfellows."

Illness, like winter, can do the same thing. I may be tempted to lie down with the strange bedfellows of alcohol, food, drugs, spending, or anything else that promises to keep me warm within the winter of illness. But only in the God of the burning bush and the pillar of fire will I find the comforting and healing warmth I seek. Only His loving glow will save me in the ongoing winter of chronic illness.

Most loving God, You Whose fire perfects as well as comforts, keep me from the trap of praying to other fires. Only You can—and will—preserve me through this winter. Today I stretch out my hands to absorb the only warmth that saves. ⊛

How can we sing the songs of the Lord while in a
foreign land?   *Psalm 137:4*

God's people, the Israelites, were living as captive slaves.
Taunted by their kidnappers, they were forced to remember home and sing happy songs about life in Jerusalem.

Living each day with illness can be much like dwelling
in a foreign land. When I'm most vulnerable—a sick alien
in a strange land at the mercy of others—I may feel threatened by the unfamiliarity. I must now learn a new language,
one of doctors and medicines and treatments.

My own thoughts often torment me with memories of
what it was like to be healthy and well. And God, it seems,
insists I sing songs of Zion, melodies of happiness and joy,
just when I feel most alone and afraid.

The Israelites had no choices. As slaves, it was sing or
die. But when they did sing, when they remembered God's
faithfulness, they were comforted. They discovered a
refuge in their turmoil and felt less alone.

Today, Lord, I will praise You even as I dwell in the
foreign land of illness. Today I will choose You as
my refuge.   &

Hallelujah! For our Lord God Almighty reigns.
Let us rejoice and be glad and give him glory!
Revelation 19:6–7

Coping with recurring illness can mean missing some exciting things—like parties. I may plan and look forward to special times, but all too often my body lets me down. Symptoms flare up and disappointments set in. I am left feeling either sick and alone or guilty that my illness ruined someone else's good time.

There is one great party, though, I can count on attending. It won't matter how sick my body is because it will already have been made well and whole. I won't have to worry about what to wear because the Host will be giving out fine, new clothes to all who come. Never again will I dress in a sickroom gown. The decorations will be spectacular—a sparkling sea of glass under a canopy of rainbows surrounded by flaming, golden torches. The aroma of incense will fill the air as the fanfare of trumpets fills my ears. What sublime pleasure there will be in cheering the One who brought everyone here!

O God of forever, the One Who was and is and is yet to come, thank You for painting me a picture of hope today. How good it feels to be able to look forward to tomorrow.

> I am going there to prepare a place for you. And if
> I go and prepare a place for you, I will come back
> and take you to be with me that you also may be
> where I am. *John 14:2–3*

A friend tells of an airplane trip home for Thanksgiving. There were endless delays, culminating in a four-hour wait in the plane on the runway. While they were waiting, a small child seated in front of her kept asking, "Are we there yet, Daddy?" Like that child, I want to get to where I am going. The waiting can be interminable, even more so when I have an unending illness.

Jamie Buckingham, the late pastor, author, and Christian leader, once wrote, "God is no longer preparing a dwelling place for His people. Now He is preparing a people for His dwelling place." In living a life of preparation, it is easy to grow impatient. Jackie, who has lupus, awakens many mornings with the same thought: "Why am I still alive?" Her symptoms vary from joint aches to stomach pain to mental dullness. Each day brings new symptoms or the awful repetition of the same ones. Or, in their absence, the dread of their return. Her pain and suffering are ever with her.

Are we there yet, Daddy?

Today, Lord, I will leave the trip in Your hands—
the driving, the timing, the speed, the stops, the
detours. Even though I yearn to reach our final
destination, today I will relax and let You drive. ❧

> But those who hope in the Lord will renew their
> strength. They will soar on wings like eagles.
> *Isaiah* 40:31

Modern culture demands speed: fast cars, fast food, novels and newspapers condensed into *Reader's Digest* and *USA Today*. We consume our scraps of literature and information the way we gulp instant coffee and munch microwave popcorn. The superhero we want to become is faster than a speeding bullet.

For one who suffers, though, waiting is not just a lost art to be regained. It is essential equipment for the journey.

Eagles know how to wait. They perch themselves on a cliff or treetop, patiently anticipating the right updraft before opening their broad wings. We don't imagine eagles muttering, "C'mon wind," or, "Will this traffic light never change?" or, "I'm tired of being sick, God. When will this end?" When the wind lifts and carries them, their flight is almost effortless.

Waiting can bring the sweetest rewards. With it come the updrafts of life, with which God will carry me if I'll let Him.

Just for today, Lord, help me to stop flapping my wings of impatience long enough to allow You to give me what I need to soar above my illness.   ☙

JANUARY 14 ❧ *A Weightless Burden*

For my yoke is easy and my burden is light.
Matthew 11:30

A children's picture book holds a two-page drawing of a youngster yoked to a gigantic, powerful ox. Together they are pulling a wooden cart overflowing with rocks and boulders. The cart is so large it takes up almost all of one page. The child's face is strained and the caption reads, "I'm as strong as an ox."

During Jesus' time, it was common to yoke a young, inexperienced ox to one much older, stronger, and tougher. At first, the weaker ox might waste energy trying to get out from under the heavy wooden yoke. Or he might mistakenly believe he was to pull the whole load and exhaust himself. But eventually he caught on. When the younger ox relaxed, the older one would do the work.

My illness can be like a cartful of rocks, so heavy that it saps my strength trying to haul it along. But Jesus says if I take on His yoke, the work will be easy and the burden will be light. He will provide the power needed to carry anything.

Today, God, I will say, "I'm as strong as Jesus Christ, to Whom I am yoked." ❧

> When Peter saw him, he asked, "Lord, what about
> him?" Jesus answered, "If I want him to remain
> alive until I return, what is that to you? You must
> follow me."   *John 21:21–23*

We are all at different stages of illness and recovery. Some have just been diagnosed and are dealing with a mixture of shock and panic. Others have had years to assimilate information and symptoms and are adjusting to the daily struggle. Still others find that their mental and emotional outlooks improve even as their physical conditions worsen. Illnesses are as individual as the people and bodies they inhabit.

A well-meaning friend may remind me of someone who was healed of her condition during a worship service. I may read a personal testimony of another being cured of a fatal disease. Overseas missionaries may tell stories of the dead being raised. And I may think, "Look at me, God! Why don't You heal me?"

It is useless to compare my life to others. Jesus says to leave the comparisons to Him. When I am looking at another person and back at myself, Jesus is left out. When I turn my gaze to Him, I see Someone who suffered much more than I ever will. In comparing myself to Jesus, I always fall short.

Lord, forgive me for questioning You. If I must compare my suffering to anyone else's, may I today be reminded of Yours, chosen and endured for me.   ℬ

I lift up my eyes to the hills—where does my help
come from? My help comes from the Lord, the Maker
of heaven and earth.   *Psalm 121:1–2*

When David wrote this psalm, many people worshiped
pagan gods that were believed to dwell in temples on the
mountains surrounding Jerusalem. Male and female prostitutes plied their trade there, and pagan sacrifices were offered.

David says looking to the hills, or to the gods of men, is
futile. Rather, he will look beyond the hills to the God
Who made the hills themselves.

In my illness, it can be tempting to replace God with
human experts—doctors and specialists and technicians.
But each one, no matter how well-educated or experienced
or caring, is fallible. I can be grateful that God has given
me talented practitioners and effective medications, but
these people and things cannot take the place of God Himself. Instead of looking to man's god—modern medicine—
for wholeness, I must look instead to the God Who created
each drug and empowers each doctor.

O God, without realizing it, I often set my sights
on the hills. Today help me lift my eyes higher that
I may call on You, the Creator of heaven and earth
and everything in it.   ❖

> Therefore do not worry about tomorrow, for
> tomorrow will worry about itself.   *Matthew 6:34*

Four months after the Persian Gulf War, a young Kuwaiti man told an American journalist of being captured and tortured by the occupying Iraqis. But the worst, he said, was being forced to bury Kuwait's dead. Mutilated corpses, some without body parts, came to him at the local cemetery. He even had to bury his own brother. The fear of what might happen to him began to possess this man. But he survived the war, and now it was over. He was on his way back to graduate school in America.

I may look around me and see the sometimes devastating effects that illness has on others. Some people suffering the same disease I have must bear almost constant pain or loneliness. No matter where I look, chances are I can find someone with worse war stories than mine.

I can live in fear of what might happen to me tomorrow. Or I can choose to live in, and enjoy, today.

> Today, Lord, I give You all my anxieties about
> tomorrow. I will remember that all the things that
> might happen haven't happened yet.   ❧

Then he said to them, "My soul is overwhelmed with sorrow to the point of death."   *Matthew* 26:38

Dr. Archibald Hart of Fuller Theological Seminary believes that depression is not only normal, but necessary. Its purpose is to help me come to terms with loss: the loss of a loved one to death or of a reputation to gossip, the loss of belongings to thieves or of energy to illness.

Depression's mission, Dr. Hart says, is to "bring us to a place where we are willing to let go of the object we prize." He holds that depression must be allowed to do its work, to bring me to that point of letting go.

Chronic illness involves many losses: the loss of expectations and dreams, perhaps of physical beauty or mental acuity, and a certain loss of freedom. Jesus understands loss. He lost everything so that I could gain every thing. Depressed in Gethsemane, Jesus faced the greatest of all losses. He was "overwhelmed . . . to the point of death." When I am depressed, Jesus understands.

Dear Jesus, help me identify the deeper losses in my life, those things I am unwilling to let go into Your hand today. Thank You for understanding and not condemning my feelings.   🕊

> In the same way, the Spirit helps us in our weakness.
> We do not know what we ought to pray for, but the
> Spirit himself intercedes for us with groans that words
> cannot express.   *Romans 8:26*

When illness and pain become a daily part of living, it is easy to give up on prayer. "It never works anyway," I may say to myself. I may think I don't know how to pray or that it takes too much energy. Perhaps I think I don't know all the right words. But the Bible tells me that God's Spirit translates my awkward phrases and misguided requests of God.

My friend Judy knows this. When she's overwhelmed by the circumstances of an unhappy marriage and doesn't know what or how to pray, sometimes all she can manage is "Ba-a-a!" She imagines herself a little lamb, with God as her Shepherd and the Holy Spirit her Interpreter. The Spirit tenderly delivers and translates that whimper to the heavenly throne of God. Even Jesus as He hung on the cross in pain and desolation, could only pray, "My God, why have you forsaken me?" His prayer was painfully simple, but His Father heard and understood.

God, I don't have words eloquent or expressive enough to thank You for all You have done and will do in, for, and through me. Thank You for Your Spirit, Who delivers my groans of both pain and joy. Today my heart will praise You. ❧

This is love: not that we loved God, but that he loved
us and sent his Son as an atoning sacrifice for our sins.
1 John 4:10

At times I may feel that my illness is a punishment from
God—that God is getting back at me for all the times I
haven't lived up to His standard of loving. For all the times
I could have said or done a kinder thing and didn't. For all
the times I intentionally hurt myself or someone else.

These feelings of uncertainty can lie just beneath my
consciousness, waiting to accuse me. That's where the
worst damage is done, below the surface of my mind,
where guilt eats away at me, silently and lethally eroding
my love for God and my belief in God's love for me.

For the same reasons, I may feel that I don't deserve
God's love. I have broken His law. But Jesus took on my
punishment in order to satisfy that law. A substitute was
accepted, and now I am free: free from punishment and
self-condemnation, free from pouting over what may seem
like God's unfair treatment of me, free from blaming Him
for my less-than-perfect body.

O God, forgive me for believing, however fleet-
ingly, that You are punishing me. Forgive me, too,
Lord, for punishing myself with deadly accusations.
Help me to carry with me today the assurance of
Your love for me.   ☙

JANUARY 21 ❧ *New Every Morning*

Because of the Lord's great love we are not consumed, for his compassions never fail. They are
new every morning; great is your faithfulness.
Lamentations 3:22–23

After God freed the Israelites from a life of slavery in
Egypt, He promised to lead them to something better, a
land flowing with milk and honey. Even so, they com-
plained that they had nothing to eat and would starve. So
God sent plentiful quail each evening and manna every
morning. The people were to gather enough of the wafer-
like manna to feed each family member for one day. Any
more than a day's supply spoiled, and any left on the
ground bred worms.

It can be tempting when living with a chronic illness to
try to stockpile the larder. With so much of my life out of
my control, it may seem the least I can do is take care of tomorrow's nourishment today. After all, what if tomorrow
comes and I don't feel well enough to gather spiritual food
for that day? But I can trust God's Word. Whatever I need
for tomorrow will be faithfully provided, fresh and new and
unfailing in love.

Today, Lord, I will look for Your compassions.
Keep me from complaining and from trying to
hoard for tomorrow or search for more than
I need today. ❧

Therefore, brothers, since we have confidence
to enter the Most Holy Place by the blood of
Jesus . . . let us draw near to God with a sincere
heart in full assurance of faith. *Hebrews 10:19, 22*

The rising cost and growing unavailability of health insurance is a source of continual concern for many people with chronic illnesses. Ongoing, often preexisting, diseases such as diabetes, epilepsy, and asthma are becoming harder to medically insure.

Many people live in fear of the financial horrors that may lie ahead. I may wonder, Will my insurance company abruptly cancel me? Will I lose my job and the medical coverage that goes along with it? Perhaps I find myself without any health insurance at all.

Of course, no one can foresee the future. I can plan and prepare with God's help, but the rest remains with Him.

There is one thing, though, for which I am eternally insured. The one-time premium has been paid in full. Christ's death and resurrection insures me against having to bear the continual cost for my sin. His Cross and His Shield cover me. It's one policy that can never be canceled or revoked.

Lord, if You have given me as a gift the most costly
and comprehensive insurance of all, how can I
question Your care of me in my illness? Today,
Lord, I will depend on You to melt my anxiety and
meet all my needs. ❧

I will not forget you! See, I have engraved you on the palms of my hands.   *Isaiah 49:15–16*

While roller skating one day as a child, I decided to rest on a thick, waist-high iron railing. I hopped up and grasped the railing tightly with both hands before swinging backward from my knees. Whack! My head hit the sidewalk. My intention had been to hang freely upside down, but now pain pounded between me and any feeling of freedom. So now I have a small, hard scar on my scalp. Sometimes I comb over it too brusquely and am reminded of that day so many years ago.

Chronic illness can make me wonder if God has forgotten me. But when God in Christ looks at His scarred hands, He is reminded of my name. Nails etched it on both His tender palms. Engraving is permanent; it's used to identify cherished possessions. God can never forget me. And when God's hands are outstretched to me, issuing an engraved invitation, neither can I forget Him.

Today, Lord, help me to hold onto Your strong, scarred hands as I make my way through the many hazards of living with illness.   *

He set my feet on a rock and gave me a firm place
to stand. *Psalm 40:2*

A few years ago I found myself seated on the cool, safe
bank of a bubbling stream. It was a welcome respite from
the heat of summer as well as from the stifling heat life itself had become.

My husband and children played their way to the other
side of the water. "C'mon, Mom!" they called, but I was
comfortable and didn't want to move, especially since picking my way through and across the moving water looked as
if it required more courage and effort than I had to give.
Those rocks looked wobbly and unstable. Would they hold
my weight?

Sensing my hesitation, my husband offered his hand
and pointed out just which ones were fixed and firm. Trusting his strength and wisdom, I arrived on the opposite ·
bank dry and unhurt, able to celebrate the day with my
family.

Illness may keep me sitting on the banks of life, afraid to
venture out into a new thing no matter how much joy it
may promise. Taking risks is a scary business. The offered
hand of God may not be something I am used to taking,
but think what I might miss!

Dear God, as I dare to risk living more deeply with
You, give me the courage I so desperately need.
Don't let this illness cheat me out of trusting You
today.

There remains, then, a Sabbath-rest for the people
of God; for anyone who enters God's rest also rests
from his own work, just as God did from his.
Hebrews 4:9–10

After God created the Earth and pronounced it good, He
rested. He took a break, ceased striving, and became re-
freshingly inactive. On a musical staff, a rest is a symbol
telling the musician not to play any notes for a certain
number of beats. The silence between tones creates con-
trast and deeper meaning in the music, and the melody is
sweeter. God's rest in the music of His creation is known
as the Sabbath, or seventh day.

But the peace of creation was shattered in Eden, and
God's Son left Heaven to come to earth and be my Sabbath-rest. His atoning work allows me to cease the constant worry about sin, illness, or any other issue in my life.

Having a chronic illness can mean always being vigi-
lant, having to be hyperalert to signals from my body and
coded messages from my brain. Day and night I'm on the
lookout for clues to solving my physical dilemma. But
God's provision in the sacrificial life and death of Jesus
Christ affords me a way to cease my striving and rest from
my watchfulness. Faith in Him is the door through which
I can enter the Sabbath-rest.

Dear God, I am weary from trying to figure everything out. Today I need strength and boldness to
enter into the open arms of Jesus, whose life and
death gives me rest.   ❧

Praise be to the . . . Father of compassion and the God
of all comfort, who comforts us in all our troubles, so
that we can comfort those in any trouble with the
comfort we ourselves have received from God.
2 Corinthians 1:3–4

Carol suffers from Ménière's disease, which affects the
inner ear, creating symptoms that range from mild ringing
to extreme vertigo and vomiting. Attacks are random, and
no one knows what triggers them. Although Ménière's is
chronic in that it will never get better or go away entirely,
it can go into remission for long periods of time.

During these remissions Carol wants no reminders that
at any moment she could be severely ill again. When
someone calls asking for information on Ménière's or advice or encouragement, Carol must fight the impulse to
beg off. She simply does not want to think about being
sick, much less talk about it.

Like Carol, I may sometimes want to forget I am ill.
When feeling well, I may even attempt to avoid others
who suffer. But God does not avoid me when I cry out. He
chose to leave a perfect existence and enter into suffering
with and for me. God comforts me in all my troubles in
order that I might not be alone.

Dear God, help me to pass on the comfort I have
received from You. Bring someone into my life
today with whom I can share Your love.   ✍

Then a great and powerful wind tore the mountains apart . . . but the Lord was not in the wind. After the wind there was an earthquake, but the Lord was not in the earthquake. After the earthquake came a fire, but the Lord was not in the fire. And after the fire came a gentle whisper.   *1 Kings 19:11–12*

In *The Problem of Pain*, C. S. Lewis wrote, "God whispers to us in our pleasure, speaks to us in our conscience, but shouts in our pains." If this is so, perhaps God shouts because I wouldn't hear Him otherwise. I may be bringing all manner of noise into my head to distract me from my suffering, until all I'm able to hear is a windstorm of my own making. I may be afraid to slow down long enough to listen to anything God might have to say. What if He's asking me to do something hard, such as continuing to put up with this illness or trusting Him even though I'm not getting any better or paying attention to my own questions and doubts?

But God is not in the windstorm of noise or earthquake of doubt inside me. If I silence the inner clamor, God won't have to shout. I'll hear His gentle whisper deep within, speaking the most thrilling words He ever has to say to me, "I love you."

Yes, Lord, sometimes I fear the solitude of being alone with You. Help me today to stop and listen for the loving heavenly whispers I know are there.   ❧

> When a woman who had lived a sinful life in that
> town learned that Jesus was eating at the Pharisee's
> house, she brought an alabaster jar of perfume, and as
> she stood behind him at his feet weeping, she began
> to wet his feet with her tears.   *Luke* 7:37–38

The woman on the radio call-in show wanted to discuss
her marriage. Raised by an alcoholic father, she was now
married to her third alcoholic husband. She'd held such
hope for this marriage, but now found herself with the
same problems and pain she had been taking to God for
so many years. Her voice breaking, she asked, "Is God tired
of my tears?"

The endlessness of living with chronic illness draws me
continually to God. I may fear that God responds to me as
I might to a whining child, by turning a deaf ear. My illness
is not going away. Is God? The woman who approached
Jesus didn't let these fears stop her. She came to Him out of
long-standing pain. As if she were a beggar, she knelt before Jesus and cried, her tears falling on and soothing His
hot, dirty feet. Ashamed, she tried to wipe them off with
her hair. But Jesus, though weary, was not annoyed. He
welcomed her and told her to go in peace.

God, thank You that although I may wear myself
out from crying, You never tire of drying my tears.
Today I will lay my life at Your feet.   *

> While he was in Bethany, reclining at the table . . . ,
> a woman came with an alabaster jar of . . . pure nard,
> . . . [and] she broke the jar and poured the perfume on
> his head. Some . . . were saying indignantly, . . . "Why
> this waste of perfume?"   *Mark 14:3–4*

In the first century, nard, which might cost a year's wages, was stored in a lidless, long-necked flask. To be opened, the neck had to be twisted and broken. The aromatic liquid then spilled out, its essence filling the room.

When the woman poured this perfume on Jesus, some of those present attacked her act of worship as a waste—of money, time, and costly perfume.

Being chronically ill can make me feel as if my life is a waste, that all my energies are used up in dealing with my illness. In being broken and poured out physically, I may have nothing left to give to others, nothing of what seems important to give the world.

But Jesus makes it clear that being emptied, pouring myself out on Him and wasting myself at His feet, is what is truly important. "Leave her alone," He said, "Why are you bothering her? She has done a beautiful thing to me" (Mark 14:6).

Lord, help me to remember that You have Your
own economy and in it nothing is ever wasted.
Make me aware today, Lord, how very precious
I am to You. Today I will worship You.   ☙

> You yourselves have seen what I did to Egypt, and
> how I carried you on eagles' wings and brought you
> to myself. *Exodus 19:4*

When a mother eagle decides it's time for her baby to leave
the soft nest, she begins to pluck the feathers and other
natural batting from between the twigs and sticks. The little bird's desire for comfort forces him to look beyond the
now-prickly nest. The only way out is to fly. But he is not
left on his own. The mother swoops under the young bird.
She is there not if but when he loses his strength and plum-
mets toward the hard ground. She glides quietly underneath him, her open wings providing a safe, sure landing
pad, and carries him back to the nest. The two continue
this ballet until the young bird learns to fly alone, however
long that takes.

Illness can cause me to feel as vulnerable and needy as
a little bird. Fatigue comes easily and often unexpectedly.
Throughout it all, though, God is with me—watching and
caring, protecting and providing.

Today, Lord, I need to hear the gentle flutter of
Your strong wings beneath me. It's so hard to hang
on sometimes and I fear falling. Thank You for the
assurance of Your constant, sustaining presence.   🕊

In your anger do not sin; when you are on your beds,
search your hearts and be silent. *Psalm 4:4*

Glenna's seizure came suddenly and without warning as she
prepared to help children cross at the elementary school
intersection. "It felt like God jumped me and then dropped
me in the street," is the way she describes that morning, a
violent first encounter with chronic illness.

As what happened to her began to sink in, her confusion turned to rage. "How dare You, God!" Glenna de-
manded. "I've been a good girl for a long time now, long
enough to earn some sort of protection. Am I still being
punished for past sins?" Although Glenna knew in her head
that a relationship based on grace didn't work this way, her
soul screamed its pain—and its anger.

God didn't "jump" Glenna again because of her anger.
And He doesn't tell me not to be angry, but just not to express it sinfully—not to drive myself into depression by
denying it or into jail by acting it out. He loves me enough
to listen to all my emotions, but too much to let them destroy me.

Living Lord, sometimes I get so angry and wonder
what I've done to deserve this illness. Today I will
be silent and search my heart for hidden anger,
offering it to You for healing. 📖

Since I myself have carefully investigated everything
from the beginning, it seemed good also to me to
write an orderly account for you . . . so that you may
know the certainty of the things you have been
taught.   *Luke 1:3–4*

What if it's all a joke? What if God never existed? Luke, a
careful historian—logical and detail-oriented and a scien-
tifically trained physician—set down a rational structure
of evidence that Jesus Christ is indeed the Savior of the
world. Luke's Gospel contains five miracles, fifteen para-
bles, and five narratives not contained in the other three
eyewitness accounts. Luke clearly meant what he said, that
he wished the reader to be certain, convinced of God's existence, power, and love.

Many diseases mask themselves. Asthma, once thought
to be psychosomatic, has been proven physiological. Many
autoimmune conditions, such as lupus, are believed to be
exacerbated by stress. With any illness, it's easy to fall into
thinking, "Am I crazy? Maybe I'm not really sick. Maybe it's
all in my head."

Or I may think, "Maybe God's all in my head." Discouragement and confusion can falsely persuade me there's
nothing to believe in except the reality of my illness. But
God assures me that His presence in my life is no joke.

Thank You, Lord Jesus, for writing it all down so
that I don't have to remain confused. Today I will
read some of Doctor Luke's investigation, allowing
You to strengthen my belief in Your loving concern
for my very real illness.   📌

> The anointing you received from him remains in
> you. . . . But as his anointing teaches you about all
> things and as that anointing is real, not counterfeit—
> just as it has taught you, remain in him.   *1 John 2:27*

Being a Christian who lives with a chronic illness and also believes that God can and does physically heal in many and varied ways can present a confusing dichotomy. Inwardly accepting that God is sovereign while at the same time outwardly working to get better may seem incompatible. This outlook may feel almost surreal, and I may wonder just what is valid and what is not. Two parts of me daily exist side by side under the umbrella of a God Who can, but chooses not to, heal my body. I may feel like a fraud, reading one thing in God's Word but experiencing something else.

That's why God asks me to do a reality check each day by spending time alone with Him in order to absorb the truth of who I am in Christ. I may not always *feel* anointed, or touched by God, but I never have to doubt that He or His love for me are very real.

When all is said and done and sick bodies fall away, the essential reality to remain will be the relentless compassion of God through His only Son, Jesus Christ.

Dear God, put my mind to rest. Stop the churning
of my mental gears and let me lean on the reality of
Your tender love for me. Today I will remain in
Jesus, Who daily waits for me to turn to Him.   ❖

He who began a good work in you will carry it
on to completion until the day of Christ Jesus.
Philippians 1:6

There are many universal experiences, incidents that are
commonly shared and understood. One of these is opening
an onion. If the onion is particularly pungent, my eyes may
burn and fill with tears. Making my way through the
onion's tough outer skin to its sweet and tender center, I encounter uncontrollable discomfort. In the process of
preparing the onion for use, tears are inevitable.

Life's suffering is another universal process in which I
feel the sting of pain and disappointment and its unavoid-
able tears. Just as the harshest onions often evoke the most
tears, so can the most passionately lived lives elicit the
most pain. And it's the onion that's been peeled and
chopped, setting its flavor free, that imbues an otherwise
bland dish with subtle, unmistakable tang.

The process, then, takes on more import than the
product. "What man calls the process," observes Oswald
Chambers, "God calls the end." The process itself is what
completes me.

God, having to go through a process that includes
chronic illness makes me doubt myself and Your
love for me. Today I will not forget that You're
the One Who started it, the One Who controls
it, and the One Who'll deliver me to flavorful
completion.   ❧

FEBRUARY 4 & *No Mistake*

For you created my inmost being; you knit me
together in my mother's womb. . . . My frame was
not hidden from you when I was made in the secret
place.   *Psalm 139:13, 15*

At age seven, the thing I wanted most was a Tiny Tears
doll. After "drinking" a bottle, she "wet" her diaper through
a hole in her rubber backside and "cried" through teensy
holes beside her eyes. Christmas morning that year
brought me my greatest desire. I soon discovered, though,
that my Tiny Tears was broken. Instead of wetting out of
the proper hole, she leaked where her legs were jointed.
And she didn't cry at all.

My mother told me we could take her back and get one
that worked, but I couldn't bring myself to do it. I identified
with that broken little doll. If anyone noticed my broken
spirit, would they try to return me, too?

Being ill can cause me to feel the same way now. Will
God abandon me because my body doesn't work the way
He designed it to? Did He make a mistake when creating
me, like someone on a doll factory assembly line?

Almost four decades later, I still have that doll.

Creator God, today I need to believe that You
knew just what You were doing when I was formed.
Help me to remember that You don't make
mistakes.   &

FEBRUARY 5   *Everlasting Love*

I have loved you with an everlasting love; I have
drawn you with loving-kindness.   *Jeremiah 31:3*

Before she developed asthma, Nancy and her husband
shared an active love of the outdoors. They hiked, camped,
biked, and boated together, things Nancy now felt the
asthma had stolen from them. Her husband never com-
plained though. On the contrary, his concern was getting
her to see things realistically, to take care of her health and
not overdo. But Nancy continued to condemn herself for
not being the consummate companion.

During one of their broken-record discussions on the
subject, he sat her down, looked her in the eye, and said,
"Look. I love you because you're you. Not because you go
hiking with me or not and not because of anything you can
or cannot do." Nancy knew this was true, but her heart
needed to hear the words just the same.

Because God made me, He knows I too need to hear
the words. That's why He had them written down, so that
I can read them over and over. God loves with a love that
always was and always will be, a love that is not limited by
time or dependent on my actions.

God of everlasting love, I confess that too often I
covet the affirmation of other people over Your
readily available Word to me. Thank You for the
continual reminder of Your eternal love. Today I
will bask in the light of that love.    

We know that the whole creation has been groaning
as in the pains of childbirth right up to the present
time. Not only so, but we ourselves . . . groan
inwardly as we wait eagerly for our adoption as
sons, the redemption of our bodies.   *Romans 8:22–23*

It's always darkest before the dawn, and this is never more
true than during the painful process of childbirth. My own
labor with a third child was fast and furious. And although
intravenous tubing, which I knew could be used to deliver
an anesthetic, dangled from my arm, the pain medication
was not forthcoming. I screamed at the nurses to knock me
out during the agony of what's known as the transition
stage of labor.

A friend was working the floor that morning, and she
told me calmly and firmly, "It's almost over. This is the
worst part and it won't last long. By the time the drug
would take affect, your baby will be born. Besides, I know
you don't want to put him at risk." She had heard me say
as much during my pregnancy.

Even so, I wanted to shoot her. But she was right. She
had said and done what I expected from a friend. The
worst physical torture of my life culminated in the birth of
a splendid new life.

Lord, it's such hard work being sick. I tend to forget
that I have the whole of creation keeping me company in today's efforts. Thank You for reminding
me that just when things look and feel the most
hopeless, a new beginning is most imminent.   ☿

FEBRUARY 7   *From Grief to Joy*

I tell you the truth, you will weep and mourn while
the world rejoices. You will grieve, but your grief will
turn to joy. A woman giving birth has pain . . . but
when her baby is born she forgets the anguish.
John 16:20–21

It only has to happen once. Too lazy, or feeling too
charmed, I fail to back up computer files. Class assign-
ments, personal letters, and a short story destined to win a
competition are all gone forever. I'm stunned, incredulous
that such a thing could happen to me. All my hard-won
creativity down an electronic drain. Surely somewhere,
somehow I can retrieve the thousands of words and sen-
tences. I beg God to return the missing documents as I
search my brain for new ideas and new thoughts. And I
grieve.

Grief is a desire to retrieve something that has been
lost, whether that something is a computer file or a healthy
body. No amount of technological knowledge will help me
retrieve computer data that no longer exists, just as pious
attempts at forcing God's hand will not get my old body
back.

What I can have, though, is something new and better.
God often gives me more exact information to replace
what's been erased. When I let Him, He'll provide a better
life as well.

Lord, I need You. Thank You for comforting me in
all my griefs. Give me the strength to quit trying to
retrieve yesterday. I need the joy that comes from
resting in You today.   ❧

FEBRUARY 8 ❧ *Blessed Mourning*

Blessed are those who mourn, for they will be
comforted. *Matthew 5:4*

Writer and television minister Robert Schuller calls them
the Be-attitudes, the outlook we need to be happy and full
of life. But what does mourning have to do with living? In
inhabiting a chronically ill body, I may feel some special
knowledge of what it is to mourn. After all, pain and small
deaths are daily companions.

But Jesus' word has to do with inner sorrow, the kind
that penetrates and shatters the soul when I recognize my
complete inability to please God. I can never do enough to
satisfy His perfect law. All He asks is that I be honest with
myself and with Him, that I allow what's at the core of my
being to surface so that I can accept the comfort that's always been there for me.

Happy am I when my heart aches over what my illness
has cost me and what I cannot do or be for God. Only then
can He enter into my world and bring me comfort. Surely,
then, there is joy in the mourning.

O just and eternal God, I exert so much energy
holding onto the burden of trying to be something
and someone for You that I cannot be. Today I will
mourn my losses and receive Your comforting
presence. ❧

Since the children have flesh and blood, he too
shared in their humanity . . . made like his brothers in
every way. . . . Because he himself suffered when he
was tempted, he is able to help those who are being
tempted.   *Hebrews 2:14, 17–18*

My mother, a registered nurse, had a wealth of human
interest stories to tell—some tragic, but most just plain
comical.

A local orthopedist (a bone specialist who operates on
and sets painful fractures) was notorious for never prescrib-
ing anything stronger than aspirin for his hospital patients.
The frustration of the nursing staff grew as they, armed
only with aspirin and soft words, were repeatedly left to
deal with people in very real pain.

One day, however, Dr. X himself appeared as a surgi-
cal patient. The staff seized the opportunity to demon-
strate the inadequacy of aspirin alone in relieving intense
pain. After having been put in his patients' place, the doctor began to approve stronger drugs.

Even though the Bible leaves out much of the first thirty
years of Jesus' life, one thing is for sure. Because Jesus put
Himself in my place and lived as a human being, He feels
the depth of my pain and knows just how best to treat me.

How can I thank You, Lord Jesus, for sharing in my
suffering today that I might have a share in Your
glory tomorrow? Today I am Yours.   ❦

❧ *Living Water*

Let us draw near to God with a sincere heart in full
assurance of faith, having our hearts sprinkled to
cleanse us from a guilty conscience and having our
bodies washed with pure water.   *Hebrews 10:22*

Hydrotherapy is an ancient art still enjoying worldwide
popularity. Healing pools like the one called Bethsaida
(John 7) were believed to cure all manner of diseases. Their
modern counterparts exist in health clubs and on backyard
decks in the form of hot tubs and spas. Arthritis sufferers
exercise in water, where the body is buoyant and movement easier.

Human life is surrounded by water before birth; it provides comfort and protection. After birth, the body's com-
position remains 97 percent water. Three quarters of the
earth's surface is covered by water. Water provides relax-
ation and refreshment; it falls from the sky and crops are
nourished and the land cleansed. It's possible for humans to
live for six weeks or more without food, but death by dehydration occurs in a matter of days.

Water also symbolizes death, burial, and resurrection in
the sacrament of baptism. Through the Living Water of
God's Spirit, I am healed, comforted, protected, sustained,
refreshed, fed, and purified.

Wash me, Lord. Shower me with Your healing love
and purifying power. Forgive me for the times I
convince myself that I can flourish without You.
Today I will listen for the sound of Your life-giving
raindrops on the roof of my soul.   ❧

I consider that our present sufferings are not worth comparing with the glory that will be revealed in us.
Romans 8:18

In *He Cares, He Comforts*, Corrie ten Boom recalls her most intense moment of suffering during her years spent in Nazi concentration camps. Surprisingly, it was not being beaten, going hungry, or forced into tortuous labor. "The greatest suffering," she wrote, ". . . was to be stripped of all my clothing and to have to stand naked. . . . This [was] worse than all the other cruelties [I] had to endure. Suddenly it was as if I saw Jesus on the cross, and I remembered that it says in the Bible, 'They took His garments.' Jesus hung there naked. By my own suffering, I understood a fraction of Jesus' suffering."

I can be comforted by the thought that Jesus enters into and understands my distress. But the empathy doesn't end there. Being ill, I have the distinct privilege and honor of experiencing a shadow of the torment He willingly bore in His life and on His cross for me. Mutual suffering leads to mutual understanding. The result of both will be a glorious future sharing in the grandeur of Christ Jesus Himself.

Lord, I hesitate to ask for deeper identification in Your suffering because it may require me to suffer more deeply. Be gentle with me. Today I will be glad and rejoice in the work You have completed on my behalf and the glorious tomorrow You promise. ❁

He came to that which was his own, but his own did
not receive him. Yet to all who received him, to those
who believed in his name, he gave the right to
become children of God.   *John 1:11–12*

Forced to allow other people to do things for her, Glenna
sank deeply into the depression brought on by a diagnosis
of seizure disorder. From her chaotic childhood, Glenna
had learned to be strong and in control. "I almost fanati-
cally shunned any assistance," she says. "I had a deep-seated
need not to be weak."

Then, suddenly, a chronic illness turned the tables. She
was no longer capable of all the busyness, of being over-
involved in serving others. Glenna felt weak when her
meals had to be brought to her because she couldn't cross a
room without getting dizzy. She felt powerless when she
couldn't keep track of her own medications without reminders. She felt vulnerable when her husband had to help
her into and out of bed and into the bathroom.

For many people, it's not only more blessed to give than
to receive, but easier, too. I may find receiving painful and
even embarrassing. But God asks me to receive, to open my
heart and accept His unearned favor. He wants to touch me
through the lives and hands and eyes and arms of others.

Father God, I need You. I come to You today
as Your child—open and vulnerable and willing
to receive. Teach me to give others the joy of
serving me.   🐦

In his great mercy he has given us new birth into a living hope through the resurrection of Jesus Christ from the dead . . . though now for a little while you may have had to suffer.   *1 Peter 1:3, 6*

Sociologists and others who track such things have identified a social trend dubbed "cocooning." It's the inclination to hole up in one's own home in the evening or over a weekend instead of engaging in activities with others. It's curling up with some goodies in front of the television, surrounded by the relative safety and warmth of home, while avoiding life with all its jarring realities.

Whatever my physical environment, God has given me a spiritual cocoon. Someday I will experience a physical new birth and the redemption of all my sickness. But for now I exist in a cocoon awaiting ultimate fulfillment. Just as a caterpillar changes into an exquisite butterfly inside its chrysalis, I am growing into a more beautiful and glorious someone inside a sanctuary of comfort that is mine. It's a blanket that no illness can penetrate, one that possesses a promise of divine fulfillment.

Most merciful God, not only have You made provision for my future, You have surrounded me with all I need to weather my present. Today I will picture the safety and warmth of Your enveloping arms, arms that gently deliver me into new birth through Jesus Christ.   🔊

Let him kiss me with the kisses of his mouth—
for your love is more delightful than wine.
Song of Songs 1:2

God uses the Biblical inclusion of Solomon's love song to portray the kind of daily relationship God desires with me. God is ever wooing me, longing for my companionship and our spiritual intimacy. God wants to be my one and only lover. To that end, the Bible is God's love letter, delivering the person of Jesus Christ, and sealed with God's kiss.

The modern symbol for kisses, the × × × with which lovers often affectionately sign letters, started in the early Christian era when a cross mark, or ×, carried the impact of a sworn oath. The cross not only symbolized the most profound of all loves, it was also the first letter of the Greek word for Christ. According to Charles Panati, the author of *Extraordinary Origins of Everyday Things*, "In the days when few people could write, a signature ' X ' was a legally valid mark. To emphasize their complete sincerity in an accord, they often kissed the mark, as a Bible was frequently kissed when an oath was sworn upon it."

When I cannot understand the world of ill health that surrounds me, I can comprehend the tenderness of an eternal kiss and the promise it holds.

My God and Lover of my soul, I come to You today, this day for love, and give myself to You out of a grateful heart. Help me to accept the gift of a holy kiss and the healing it can bring.   ❧

> However, I consider my life worth nothing to me, if
> only I may finish the race and complete the task the
> Lord Jesus has given me—the task of testifying to the
> gospel of God's grace. *Acts 20:24*

When the Tour du Pont bicycle race whooshed through the small town near my home, people filled porches and lined the streets to watch and cheer. Many held banners and signs encouraging their favorite rider. First aid and water stations had been set up, and the media were there to record the event. After so many months of preparation, the mounting anticipation of the crowd was finally rewarded with a forty-second flash of rainbow colors and an inspiring whirr of stainless steel.

It all looked stunning, but the true picture of bicycle racing includes flat tires, muddy skids, steep mountains, aching muscles and burning lungs, fog and humidity, and other near-irresistible temptations to quit. Quitting the race of life remains an option for those who deal with incessant illness. But just like those bicyclists' fans, all along my life's course people wait and watch and applaud my effort. The good news for the chronically ill racer is that finishing *is* testifying to the sufficiency of God's grace.

> God, I need all the support cyclists get and more
> to keep going in the race You have called me to.
> This illness slows me down, even though I know it's
> the task I've been given. Today may the gospel of
> Your grace be seen and heard through my
> perseverance. ❧

FEBRUARY 16   *Steadfast Love*

For the Lord is good and his love endures forever;
his faithfulness continues through all generations.
Psalm 100:5

The front of a greeting card attributed this comment to
Russian playwright Anton Chekhov: "Any idiot can face a
crisis—it's this day-to-day living that wears you out."

Day in and day out, night in and night out, my illness
continues. Can I continue along with it, or will it wear me
out? Will God continue along with me? After a while, I
may have misgivings about the dependability of anyone or
anything in life except the chronic predictability of illness.

Doctors and other health professionals are human.
They deal with many of the same life issues I do. They may
make mistakes or act uncaringly. The religious community,
though made up of warm and selfless individuals, is imperfect. Misunderstandings occur, and I may feel alone in my
distress. I may not always be able to rely on sensitive
friends and responsive family members.

Who can I count on to remain constant throughout illness, faithful in every minute of each lonely day and pain-
filled night? Only God can be that devoted and steady
supporter, unwavering in His companionship and loyalty.
His steadfast love and allegiance will continue into my
eternity.

With You as the most faithful of friends, Lord God,
I will continue through this day by Your side. Keep
me from forgetting how very near You continue
to be.   ☞

> May they. . . let the world know that you sent me
> and have loved them even as you have loved me. . . .
> I have made you known to them . . . in order that the
> love you have for me may be in them and that I
> myself may be in them.   *John 17:23, 26*

In *As Bread That Is Broken*, Jesuit priest Peter G. van Breemen says, "Self-acceptance is an act of faith. When God loves me, I must accept myself as well. I cannot be more demanding than God, can I?"

And yet I catch myself in self-denigration even in addressing the God who created me. The human birth, difficult life, excruciating death, and miraculous resurrection of God's Son, demonstrates that I meet with divine approval. Because of the sacrificial acts of Jesus Christ, I am approved of by God. I cannot be disapproved of because of my illness or any other circumstance in my life. God's love is not a response to any action on my part. Love is God's very being, His essential nature.

Van Breemen concludes that if God loves Jesus 100 percent, then He loves me the same 100 percent. God cannot love Jesus 100 percent and me 30 percent; it's not in His nature. And I'm not in a contest for God's love and approval. They are mine for the asking.

> Most Holy God, how I need 100 percent of Your
> love and approval today! Help me to open my
> mind and my heart that I might receive it all. Fill
> me to overflowing so I can water others with the
> love that spills out of me.   🐾

If our hearts do not condemn us, we have confidence
before God and receive from him anything we ask,
because we obey his commands and do what pleases
him. And this is his command: to believe in the name
of his Son, Jesus Christ, and to love one another.
1 John 3:21–23

"Maryland Welcomes You," the ten-foot sign declares,
"Please drive gently."

Heavy-footed, I am inclined to ignore the metal placard, and I have been, on occasion, ticketed for speeding.
What I tend to see as the unfairness of the situation always
gets under my skin. Didn't the trooper see those other cars?
Why was I singled out from at least a dozen other speeding
vehicles?

Of course, the simple facts are that I was breaking the
law and I got caught while the others didn't. Life itself is
unfair at the least and sin-ravaged at the worst. Some people get sick, while others don't. Some die young, and some
live long pain-filled lives.

In the midst of all this, God tells me to be gentle with
myself, not to practice self-condemnation or be anxious
about displeasing Him. "Accept the saving power of My
Son," He says, "accepting yourselves and one another.
That's what pleases me."

Life with illness welcomes you. Please proceed gently.

Lord, I know in my head that Your heart does not
condemn me for being ill. But in the pit of my soul
I sometimes feel the pinch of shame and self-
loathing. Heal my heart today, so that it does not
whisper condemnations, but shouts in faith.   *

And God placed all things under his feet and appointed him to be head over everything for the church, which is his body, the fullness of him who fills everything in every way.   *Ephesians 1:22–23*

Is the glass half full or half empty? It's a popular question used to peg people as either optimists or pessimists. The problem I may have as a chronically ill person is that although my glass may be 100 percent full, I may still feel empty.

"The sad truth is: There are dimensions of emptiness that by ourselves we cannot fill," writes psychologist Earl Henslin, "There is a certain dimension of emptiness that only God can fill. If we try to fill our emptiness with substitutes, the result is meaningless."

No amount of overperformance or achievement will fill my "God-shaped" vacuum. Medicines and sympathetic doctors won't do it. An abundance of material possessions or attempts to fill myself with food won't do it either. Religion won't do it and, not surprisingly, neither will the complete healing of my body.

Only Jesus Christ "fills everything in every way." There isn't a nook or cranny within me that He won't fill to overflowing.

Dear Jesus, You Who are the fullness of all things, sometimes I feel simultaneously full of illness and empty of meaning. Come satisfy my emptiness today and drain me of anything else I can survive without.   ❀

FEBRUARY 20 ❧ *Singing in the Prison*

About midnight Paul and Silas were praying and singing hymns to God, and the other prisoners were listening to them.   *Acts 16:25*

Recovery support groups have mushroomed in this country over the last several decades. People have found the combination of mutual understanding and the twelve-step programs of Adult Children of Alcoholics; Survivors of Incest; Emotions Anonymous; Overeaters Anonymous; and Shopaholics, Alcoholics, Narcotics, and Gamblers Anonymous to be enormously helpful, if not life-saving.

Carol, who must cope with the probability of no recovery from Ménière's disease, an incurable and chronic condition, sees this social trend embodied in the defiant philosophy, "We *will* recover. We *will* be released from our prison of pain." Although these groups do indeed provide strength and recovery to a great many people, this kind of relief goes only so far. "We desperately want to be able to soar above our problems," says Carol, "when what God may want is for me to learn how to live within them."

Paul and Silas were not intent on finding a way out of their prison. They had discovered what it was to prevail within it. And so can I.

Lord Jesus, I want to recover from this need to recover from every bit of suffering in my life. Flood me with the kind of love that makes trying to prove myself to You or anyone else unnecessary. Today I will sing, even in the prison of illness.   ❧

You, dear children, are from God and have overcome
them [your enemies], because the one who is in you
is greater than the one who is in the world.   *1 John 4:4*

Who or what are my enemies and how can I defend against
them? Most of the time my greatest enemy is myself. I may
erect barriers to my own spiritual progress and sabotage
healthy thoughts and feelings. I may make choices that
keep me stuck in a prison camp of fear and self-loathing.
Enemies I won't acknowledge can maintain power over me.

Pastoral counselor John Sanford writes, "Like the frog in
the fairy tale which was transformed into a handsome
prince when the princess accepted him as her partner in
bed, so the inner enemy is transformed into a useful part
of the personality *once it has been consciously recognized and
accepted as a legitimate and inevitable part of ourselves*" (Sanford's
italics).

The external circumstance of illness isn't my enemy. But
how I choose to respond to it can be. The ultimate enemy,
therefore, may not be evil itself, but the refusal to accept
my illness. "If there is no enemy within," goes an old
African proverb, "no enemy outside can do me harm."

Fill me so full of Yourself today, Spirit of God,
that there is room for nothing more—not fear,
not distorted self-image, not resistance to Your
love. May I never forget that You are mightier
than anything in this world or any enemy
within me.   ❧

He replied, "Whether he is a sinner or not, I don't
know. One thing I do know. I was blind but now I
see." *John 9:27*

After I had eased the car into the garage, my daughter and
I unloaded the few groceries and the mail and headed inside the house. To my surprise, my husband was sitting in
the den reading the paper. "You're home!" I exclaimed,
wide-eyed. It was only five o'clock, much earlier than his
usual arrival home from work.

"Didn't you see my car?" he replied. Of course, his car—
it was parked in the garage right next to mine. But I wasn't
expecting to see it, and what I didn't expect, I didn't see. As
far as his car was concerned, I might as well have been
blind. It didn't exist. Its presence just didn't register.

Because the people of Jesus' day didn't expect their
Messiah to be packaged as He was (and from Nazareth
yet), many did not see Him. To them He did not exist. Or
maybe He looked too familiar to catch their attention.

I may not be expecting Jesus to enter into this illness
with me or to bring about any healing in my life. If my relationship with Him has grown flat and familiar, I may miss
it when He does the unexpected.

I want to see, Lord, to really see. Purge me of any
blindness of spirit today, including the blind spot of
illness, that hinders me from getting a good look at
You. I want to know You, Jesus my Healer.   *

Let us throw off everything that hinders and the sin
that so easily entangles. . . . Let us fix our eyes on
Jesus, the author and perfecter of our faith, who
for the joy set before him endured the cross.
Hebrews 12:1–2

Homesteading Americans littered westward trails with
cherished belongings. As painful as it was, expensive furniture, heirloom china, a treasured piano or grandfather
clock, and anything else too heavy for their horse- or ox-
drawn Conestogas to haul through mud or up a mountain,
ended up abandoned along the way.

Not knowing what might be needed when they arrived
in an alien land, families had gathered up as much as would
fit in their wagons. As it turned out, many found lush
forests, prairies full of game, and streams and rivers teem-
ing with fish. There was land to farm and trees with which
to build. Towns had churches and schools and supplies of
goods for sale just like back East, perhaps making the loss
of possessions a little less bitter.

God asks me to shed everything—paralyzing guilt,
nagging doubt, deep-seated anger, just plain inattention—
that might be hindering our journey through life together.
And when illness itself gets too burdensome, He will carry
it for me.

I want to lighten the load for my trip through
illness today, Lord. I want to throw off anything
that comes between You and me, anything that
makes the journey to joy any harder than it has
to be.

Though he brings grief, he will show compassion, so
great is his unfailing love. For he does not willingly
bring affliction or grief to the children of men.
Lamentations 3:32–33

A certain man, after examining his life, concluded that God
had given him more suffering and hardship than he could
bear. "The cross You've given me to carry is much too
heavy," he protested to God, "I'm worn out from carrying
the weight of it around."

Sympathetic, God responded, "Give me your cross and
I'll put it back with all the other crosses that people bear
and let you choose any one you want."

The man was thrilled to get rid of his massive cross and
excitedly went about a selection process. But he found each
cross to be as or more burdensome than the one he'd already shed.

Finally, the man discovered one cross that seemed to
fit. "This one is much better," he told God with relief.

"Very well," God answered, "but I think you should
know—that is the same cross you had before."

God knows better than I what He and I can handle together and what we cannot. I was not arbitrarily handed
the cross of illness, and I am not left to shoulder it alone.

O God of unfailing love, help me to bow to Your
divinely compassionate perspective. Create in me
today the willingness to cooperate with Your Holy
Spirit and to look to You for help in carrying this
cross of illness, no matter how heavy it may get.   ❧

There was given me a thorn in my flesh, a messenger of Satan. . . . Three times I pleaded with the Lord to take it away from me. But he said to me, "My grace is sufficient for you, for my power is made perfect in weakness."   *2 Corinthians 12:7–9*

Some say it was his small stature and undistinguished speaking voice. Others have controversially suggested it was a struggle with homosexuality. But most New Testament scholars believe Paul had eyesight so poor that he considered it "a thorn in my flesh." Whatever the problem, it was physical and it was chronic. It did not go away no matter how much Paul pleaded with God to heal him. Paul's thorn, the scripture says, was from Satan, not from God, although God allowed it so that His perfect grace could be seen at work in Paul's painful physical weakness.

There may be many thorns in my life, not just the obvious one of chronic illness. But God's grace can always create something beautiful out of the worst situation. Consider the rose. If I start at the bottom of its stem and work my way up, I will encounter sharp, ugly, and painful thorns. But if I don't give up, I will eventually experience the velvety softness, heady perfume, and breathtaking beauty of a radiant rosebud.

O Maker of all things bright and beautiful, teach me to thank You for the thorns in my life today. Show me how to rely on the sufficiency of Your grace to meet all my needs.

> I sought the Lord, and he answered me; he delivered
> me from all my fears. Those who look to him are
> radiant; their faces are never covered with shame.
> *Psalm 34:4–5*

In the classic children's book, *Charlotte's Web*, E. B. White introduces Charlotte, an intellectual barnyard spider who befriends Wilbur, a runt pig. Charlotte wows the country folk by spinning words in her web describing Wilbur as "Some Pig," "Terrific," and "Humble," thereby saving him from the butcher's axe.

Having read about radiant action on a discarded detergent box, Charlotte next selects "Radiant" to describe Wilbur. "Run around " she orders the pig, "I want to see if you're radiant in action." Wilbur trusts Charlotte to save him from becoming tomorrow's bacon, a trust that proves well-placed. Charlotte ultimately gives her own life for Wilbur.

It's when I realize that my trust is well-placed in an all-loving and freeing God that I am filled with what pastor and author Lloyd Ogilvie calls "the radiance of the inner splendor." I am lit from within, knowing I am loved for who I am and that I can depend on Someone Who will lift me up and not put me down. Life becomes lighter and I can radiate the light of that indwelling power to others. Sick or well, I too can be radiant in action.

> Today I will seek Your radiance, Lord. Fill me
> with the light of Your love, and deliver me from
> dreading future suffering. Thank You for reminding
> me that with You there is no shame in illness.   🠖

The next day John saw Jesus coming toward him and said, "Look, the Lamb of God, who takes away the sin of the world!" *John 1:29*

"Why do we always have to do things according to the fact that you're sick?" When Jackie's husband finally spoke the words, oh, how they stung! She had often wondered if he was thinking it, and now it was out there. "Why, indeed!?" Jackie's spirit screamed back.

Bob was a paragon of patience, loving his wife and suffering with her through many years of undiagnosed symptoms. For the last two years they had withstood lupus together. She knew his only failing now was just being human. She experienced what therapists call "false guilt," taking the responsibility for an illness that was out of her control and its consequences.

The true guilt we all bear as imperfect, sinful humans was nailed to the cross with God Himself through Jesus Christ. God is long-suffering; He won't someday snap and blurt out unloving words. His love is more than enough to take care of all my guilt, true and false.

Thank You, dear Jesus, for bringing me to my knees when I need to confess sin and be forgiven. Thank You for reminding me when I fall into false guilt. Sustain my loved ones today and throughout the course of this illness. ☙

> Therefore, there is now no condemnation for those
> who are in Christ Jesus.   *Romans 8:1*

A friend once kidded me about some indiscretion or other,
and I shot back with Romans 8:1. "Oh," he said, winking.
"I didn't say God condemns you, just that I do."

Isn't that how many people tend to treat themselves? I
may know in my head the truth of no condemnation in
Christ, but living as if God really means it for me is another
story. When I come to God and confess specific acts of sin,
"He is faithful and just and will forgive" (1 John 1:9), and
then He promptly forgets. My guilt has been absolved. It's
my remembering and hanging onto what He's forgotten
that often gets me down.

"Failure to work through the real guilt and to accept forgiveness can lead to chronic . . . guilt, which manifests itself in a low-grade depressive lifestyle," contends Frank M.
Brown in a bulletin of the American Protestant Hospital
Association.

If Almighty God does not condemn me, I no longer
have to punish myself over real and imagined guilt. I can
accept His forgiveness and move on.

God, I've got enough chronic problems. I neither
need nor desire a load of chronic guilt. Please heal
me of the necessity to justify myself. Fill my heart
so full of Your love today that there'll be no room
left for anything but chronic praise to You.   ☿

No temptation has seized you except what is common to man. And God is faithful; he will not let you be tempted beyond what you can bear. But when you are tempted, he will also provide a way out so that you can stand up under it.   *1 Corinthians 10:13*

Looking at their flooded downstairs family room, Carol cried, "Why is God letting this happen to me?" Damaged furniture and ruined carpet faced her, as well as unknown amounts of money and effort. Carol's world of faith had been shattered by one dose of reality after another. Her failing health had not yet been diagnosed as Ménière's disease, and now a drowned basement qualified as the final straw. Her husband responded with characteristic wisdom, "Carol," he said, "just think of everything God protects you from."

It is true. Many are more surprised when things go wrong than the other way around. Yet, in a fallen world, I can expect problems and pain. My faith does not exempt me. Paul does not say *if* I face temptation and trouble, but *when*.

It may not take a flooded family room to remind me of life's realities. My illness smacks me in the face every day. I need a way to "stand up under it." But "God is faithful," and He will preserve me from being overcome by "what is common to man."

O God, creator and preserver of my life, forgive my ingratitude for the many times Your hand has intervened and I have failed to see it. Today I will open my eyes.   ☿

MARCH 2 ❧ *Facing Uncertainty*

For I am convinced that neither death nor life, neither angels nor demons, neither the present nor the future, nor any powers, neither height nor depth, nor anything else in all creation will be able to separate us from the love of God that is in Christ Jesus our Lord. *Romans 8:38–39*

Living with chronic illness can mean never being able to plan, being unable to confidently commit to a hair appointment or my daughter's weekend barbecue. When neighbors call inviting me to dinner, what do I say? What if Friday evening comes and I'm not up to it? I may go to bed feeling just peachy and wake up as sour and useless as a squeezed lemon.

Chronic illness travels with its own baggage of uncertainty and unpredictability. With God, though, there is one thing in my life of which I can always be certain: His consistent, abiding love for me. My illness may sometimes isolate me from family and friends, but it can never separate me from God. A connection made between me and God on a wooden cross two thousand years ago cannot be broken by my illness today.

God loves me. Of this I can be certain.

O Lord, how do I respond to Your kind of love?
Give me the certain knowledge today that You are never more than a whispered prayer away. ❧

But you are a shield around me, O Lord; you bestow
glory on me and lift up my head.   *Psalm 3:3*

When David cried these words to God, he was running
from his enemies, one of them his own son. "Many are rising against me," he wailed. "Many are saying, 'God will not
deliver you.'"

There may be those who mock me as well—those who
cannot understand why God does not heal me of this illness or those who, seeing my faith, ridicule God. "How can
you love a God," they may say, "who does this to you?"

Maybe those voices are my own. Voices that hammer
away at my belief in God's love for me. Voices that doubt
my own judgment. Voices that cause me to hang my head
in shame.

But God puts His hand under my chin and gently lifts
my head. He straightens my shoulders, smiles, and looks
me lovingly in the eye. Only then, beholding the eyes of
Almighty God, can I glimpse His glory, the same glory
that someday will be mine. His arms go around me like a
shield. But first I must look up.

Forgive me, Lord, for all the times my eyes are cast
down and my ears play the record of doubt. Today
I will look up into the certainty of Your love.   🐟

MARCH 4 ❧ *I Need People*

Two are better than one, because they have a good
return for their work: If one falls down, his friend can
help him up. But pity the man who falls and has no
one to help him up! Also, if two lie down together,
they will keep warm. But how can one keep warm
alone? *Ecclesiastes 4:9–11*

Coping with chronic illness tempts many to live in isola-
tion. "They just don't understand," I may think of those
around me. Others sometimes say or do things that imply
impatience with me or my illness. And though they don't
intend it, their words hurt. Self-protection takes over and I
learn to live alone.

But it is impossible to live the Christian life apart from a
community of faith. Life would become boring, more
painful, and very lonely.

It is also impossible to get a fire going with just one log.
Kindling and newspapers may start the process, but to sustain any warmth, at least two logs must be stacked together
so that they create a draft and feed the flame.

I am created by God to need people, to share their pain.
They also need me. They may never grasp what chronic
illness is like, but they'll learn about me and about themselves as well. And along the way we may both learn something about God.

Father God, thank You for friends. Forgive me
for the times I turn away from them out of fear
of being hurt. Help me to take a few risks today.
I don't really want to be alone. ❧

I the Lord do not change. So you, O descendants of
Jacob, are not destroyed.   *Malachi 3:6*

"Grandma, why do you hurt today and yesterday you
didn't?"

Trying to explain chronic illness to a child can be frustrating. He wants to know why Grandma can't pull him up
onto her lap and read a story, why some days they'll play in
the park and on others she's not even well enough to talk to
him on the phone, why she enjoyed his sister's dance re-
cital last month but today can't sit through his pre-school
play.

"Grandma, do you love me?"

My physical symptoms may go up and down, and my
spiritual health may ride the same seesaw. I may be filled
with gratitude to God one day and reproach Him the next.
Sometimes I may wonder how God can love a chameleon
like me, the colors of my heart changing with the onset of
each ache and pain.

But God's love for me does not waver. He is love, and
He is the same yesterday, today, and tomorrow. Just as my
illness is a constant companion, so is God's love an ever-
faithful friend.

Will I ever understand just how much You love me,
Lord? Thank You that Your love does not change
with my moods. Thank You that even today my
spirit is being changed by Your unchanging
Spirit.   ☞

Then the man and his wife heard the sound of the
Lord God as he was walking in the garden in the cool
of the day, and they hid from the Lord God among
the trees of the garden. But the Lord God called to
the man, "Where are you?" *Genesis* 3:8–9

When I was five I had scarlet fever. My mother, on doctor's orders, had to give me several shots of penicillin every
day. I remember screaming and trying to hide from the
needle by scooting under my parents' big bed.

Later on, I did the same thing when my parents' argu-
ments escalated to fist fights. Still later, I carried the pattern
into adulthood and retreated behind a closed bedroom
door every time my husband expressed anger or dissatis-
faction with me. "If I hide myself well enough," I thought,
"maybe I won't get hurt."

I can retreat into a dark room of self-pity and believe
that it keeps God away, too. I can imagine that God is
around only when I wish Him into existence, like some
magic genie. I can also use my illness as a barrier between
me and God, thinking that He can't or won't break through
my invisible restraints.

But God loves me too much to let emotionally locked
doors get in our way.

How thankful I am, Lord, that You continue to seek
when I hide. Today, I need You close beside me.
Give me the courage to open myself up and let
You in. ☙

> But for those who fear you, You have raised a banner
> to be unfurled against the bow.   *Psalm 60:4*

"Vaya con Dios," they say in Spanish. "Go with God."

Hearing that phrase in movies and TV westerns as a child, I thought it meant "May God go with you," with the emphasis on *you*. I saw myself marching forward, banner in hand, motioning over my shoulder. "C'mon, God!" I'd call, never pausing to make sure He was even there.

My immature understanding has since changed. I've learned the correct emphasis. God is the One out in front and I'm to follow Him.

Less-experienced golfers talk about allowing better, faster players to "play through." This means the novice steps aside, letting the veteran go ahead.

By letting God play through in my life, I give Him permission to be in control. I become secure in the knowledge that no matter what waits for me tomorrow, God is already there. He is in my future waiting to receive and care for me. His banner of love is raised, signaling His command and keeping me safe when the arrows of illness attack.

Today, Lord, I want to lower my banner of control, which signals fear and faithlessness. I invite You to raise Your banner of love and safety over me. Today I will go with God.   ❦

Blessed are the meek, for they will inherit the earth.
Matthew 5:5

The Hebrew word that is translated as *meek* means "to be molded," as clay is shaped by a potter. The Greek translation used here means "to be controlled"—to submit to a divine plan and give up the right to control one's own destiny.

"The word meek," writes Lloyd John Ogilvie, "is used to describe a person who, out of love and obedience, openly accepts the providence and guidance of God. He lives with the certainty of God's power and presence in all of life. The meek man or woman trusts that God knows what is best and will bring good out of evil."

That kind of trust finds its roots in God's promises, expectantly awaits their fulfillment every day, and cooperates with God by surrendering its own agenda. Coping successfully with the daily-ness of chronic illness demands that kind of relinquished will.

Happy am I when I let go of all my preconceived notions about life and about God and accept my limitations. Only then can I begin to discover God in me while I'm still on earth.

O God, here are my open, empty hands. Today they represent my heart as I give it all to You—the worry, the anger, the shame. Make me and mold me into Your will.   ₿

MARCH 9 🐦 *Prayer Support*

We always thank God for all of you, mentioning you
in our prayers. We continually remember before our
God and Father your work produced by faith, your
labor prompted by love, and your endurance inspired
by hope in our Lord Jesus Christ.   *1 Thessalonians 1:2–3*

When my grandmother died less than a year after my
mother's death, the double loss seemed too much. I expected the normal stages of grief, but I was stunned by the
near-total panic I felt one day. "Who will pray for me now?"
I suddenly thought. There wasn't anyone who had loved
me as unconditionally as those two, and I believed there
wasn't another who would pray for me as they had, either.

My apprehension was short-lived. I began to take note
of the prayer support I had already through my Bible study
group. An elderly great-aunt I rarely saw mentioned that
she prayed for me and my family at Mass every morning.
Over the years, unexpected notes of care, concern, and encouragement have come just when I needed them.

I began to understand that it was God Who initiated
all this support. He can be counted on to provide for all my
needs.

Thank You, Lord, for those who are praying for me
right now. I may not know each of them, but I do
know You. Today I will remember Your faithfulness
as I pray for someone else.   🐦

Do not grieve, for the joy of the Lord is your
strength.   *Nehemiah 8:10*

About six centuries before the time of Christ, God's chosen
people, the Hebrews, were taken as captives to Babylon.
Seventy years later, they were released to return to
Jerusalem. When the people had rebuilt their temple and
the city walls, the priests gathered them to hear the words
of God's law. In exile, they had neither been taught nor
practiced these laws. Now, on coming face-to-face with the
righteousness of a holy God, the people were overcome
with grief. Their lives had not met God's standards.

But the priests told them not to weep, that this was a
time to celebrate. In spite of their sinfulness, remembering
what the Lord had just delivered them from was a cause for
exultation.

God can deliver me from the bondage of this illness. He
has brought me a long way already, even though my behavior can never be good enough. Remembering this produces joy in me for today and strength for tomorrow.

Today I will take joy in You, O Lord, the One Who
promises me strength for the days ahead.   🐦

☙ *Thankful for Pain*

Give thanks in all circumstances, for this is God's will
for you in Christ Jesus.　　*1 Thessalonians 5:18*

My friend John visited his doctor complaining of abdomi-
nal pain. Diagnosed with diverticulitis, an inflammation of
the intestinal tract, John was sent home with medication.
When after two more weeks his pain had not subsided, X
rays revealed a cancerous tumor in John's colon. The tumor
itself was not causing John's pain; the diverticulitis was.
But it was this unrelated pain that prompted the doctors to
investigate further and uncover the malignancy in time to
completely excise it.

John and his family know what it's like to feel gratitude
for pain. It was pain that announced cancer before it could
become fatal. Pain is not always an enemy. God does not
rejoice when I suffer, but He did give me pain as an unignorable sign that something is wrong. Leprosy patients
yearn to be able to feel the pain that would keep them from
burning or injuring themselves.

My illness may not be God's will, but my thankfulness
in it is. Paul doesn't admonish me to give thanks *for* all circumstances, but *in* all circumstances.

Just for today, Creator God, I will thank You in the
presence of physical pain, if only for the reason
that it draws me closer to You.　　☙

I do not understand what I do. For what I want to
do I do not do, but what I hate I do. . . . For I have
the desire to do what is good, but I cannot carry
it out.   *Romans 7:15*

Jackie talks about feeling trapped inside her own body. She
enjoys making crafts but, because of lupus, some days her
hands won't follow directions from her brain. Her mind
instructs her fingers to pick up scissors and cut, but at a certain point they miss the mark. Maybe gluing will be easier.
No, nothing works there either. No matter how badly she
wants to cut or glue, Jackie's hands don't get the message.

For me, stuck in the mire of on-again, off-again depression, the struggle is with living in general. I may want a
clean bathroom or ironed clothes or lunch with my friend,
but many days I simply cannot muster up the energy, emotional or physical, to accomplish it. My brain says, "Do it,"
but there's another, stronger part of me that screams, "But I
can't!" It's as if I'm standing in wet cement. Will it harden
and trap me forever?

Paul knew what it was to feel trapped, both by a sin-
filled body and by a sinful nature. His, and my, desperate
question escapes: "Who will rescue me from this body of
death?" (Rom. 7:24).

Thanks be to You, Almighty God! For it is You who
rescues me through Your son Jesus Christ (Rom.
7:25). Thank You for the promise of a day when all
traps will be opened, bodies will be changed, and I
will be whole.   *

The Lord himself goes before you and will be with you; he will never leave you nor forsake you. Do not be afraid; do not be discouraged. *Deuteronomy 31:8*

As the Israelites prepared to enter the Promised Land, Moses told them he could not go, that Joshua would be their new leader. They had heard about the dangers that faced them, and they were afraid. Moses reminded them that the God Who delivered them from slavery in Egypt would prepare their way once again.

This ancient account is similar to modern warfare. Today's military enemy lays acres of buried bombs. Minesweepers must then clear the deadly ground to protect their own infantry.

Living with illness can feel like I'm picking my way through a mine field. But Jesus Christ goes before me. He has swept my future clean of hidden dangers. He knows just where I can safely step. Author and theologian Frederick Buechner says that faith is "stepping out into the unknown with nothing to guide us but a hand just beyond our grasp." Jesus' hand guides me daily through the emotional, spiritual, and physical mine fields of chronic illness.

Dear Jesus, help me to move out into my future with only Your open hand to show me the way. Today I will trust You.   *

MARCH 14 ❧ *Reflected Glory*

And we, who with unveiled faces all reflect the Lord's glory, are being transformed into his likeness with ever-increasing glory, which comes from the Lord, who is the Spirit.   *2 Corinthians 3:18*

Before her first seizure, Glenna had taken pride in appearing emotionally strong and physically healthy, the opposite of her own mother, whom she remembers as sick and complaining. The last thing Glenna ever wanted was for her children to perceive her that way.

Now, since the onset of seizure disorder complicated by serious allergies to medication, she has had to bear hearing words such as, "All you ever do is lie down, Mom." The words are not true; Glenna works and keeps a home. But regardless of the reality, this is the way her children see her. Consequently, Glenna's self-image became distorted, as if she were looking into a fun house mirror. By looking at her reflection in her children's eyes, Glenna did not see a true picture of herself.

Only one mirror matters, the mirror of God's love. It does not twist, warp, or deny who I really am. In the eyes of the One into Whose glory I am being transformed, my image is clear.

Lord, as I see myself mirrored in Your eyes of love today, I pray that others will find Your caring light reflected in mine.   ❧

We were harassed at every turn—conflicts on the outside, fears within. But God, who comforts the downcast, comforted us.   *2 Corinthians 7:5–6*

Two of the most exciting and hopeful words in the Bible are "but God." They act as a fulcrum, balancing the good and the bad. Any tragic thing can be happening on one end of the seesaw of my life, but God will always be found occupying the other seat, compensating for my weight. Sometimes His seat remains on the ground while I dangle precariously from mine. But God acts to provide stability and protection for me.

It can even seem as if I'm ready to fall off and death has won. But God reminds me of Christ's resurrection. I may be sick, but God provides a steady supply of comfort and hope. Fear may fill my days, but God promises relief. Pain may be with me every night, but God is awake and walks through it with me. Confusing physical symptoms may abound, but God is in charge. Illness and disease may cause me to behave in decidedly unloving ways, but God forgives.

Thank You, God, that with You there are always ifs, ands, and especially buts. Be with me today as I ride this seesaw called chronic illness.   🐦

I can do everything through him who gives me
strength.   *Philippians 4:13*

I don't for a minute believe that I can do every thing there
is to do. I can't draw a convincing picture of a horse. I can't
see in the dark or function well without sleep. And my illness prevents me from doing a great many things.

But God does call me to do some things, and He will
empower me to do all of those some things. A few years
ago I read these words by Lloyd John Ogilvie: "What He
desires, He inspires. What He guides, He provides."

God desires certain things from me in spite of my illness. But He promises to inspire me to their completion,
guide me in them, and provide whatever strength I need
to see them through.

God will also give me the strength of character to say
no to unnecessary tasks. He will furnish me with the physical strength to endure another day of pain and the spiritual
strength to live with doubt. I can do every thing God calls
and empowers me to do.

Lord, I'm looking to You to give me the exact
amount of strength I need today. Today I will rely
on Your strength, not my will. Today, Lord, You are
in charge.   🕊

I have come that they may have life, and have it to
the full.   *John 10:10*

I know people who percolate with enthusiasm. A hearty
laugh escapes from them, floats across a room, and fills
me with delight. Their eyes sparkle and shine with an in-
effable joy.

Jesus said He came to earth so that I could have that
kind of fullness, an enthusiasm that isn't dependent on the
condition of my physical self. The ancient Greeks believed
enthusiasm reflected the indwelling of the presence of
God. That's where the word comes from: *en* means *in*, and
theos means *God*. God in me.

"Instead of absorbing our spirits into His Spirit," writes
Jamie Buckingham, "[God] heightens our individuality by
placing His Spirit within each of us." Appropriating that
Spirit, I will experience all the best and highest of life, regardless of the state of my body, regardless of my long-
term prognosis. God Himself is here inside me, regardless
of any external circumstances to the contrary.

With Jesus, I am already living all the fullness life has
to offer.

Life-giving God, You bubble over with all the
enthusiasm I will ever need. Why am I so often
blind to Your presence within me? Sensitize me
today to that Presence in me as well as in others.
I want to be enthusiastic in spite of illness.   🐚

Man looks at the outward appearance, but the Lord
looks at the heart.   *1 Samuel 16:7*

"Gee, you don't look sick." Many chronically ill people
hear it all the time. External equipment like wheelchairs
and oxygen tanks aren't necessary for the majority of those
with multiple sclerosis, lupus, arthritis, and a variety of
other ongoing conditions and illnesses. The only indica-
tion might be at dinner when I mention my body's reaction
to certain foods or a sudden attack of fatigue that hits me in
the middle of a business meeting. Many simply do not, or
cannot, venture out on bad days, so others never see a display of symptoms.

The human mind tends to believe just what it sees. But
God takes the trouble to look beyond my unhealthy body.
He wants to know who I really am—my dreams and desires, my sorrow and shame, all my thoughts and feelings,
even those that have nothing to do with being ill.

Unlike many messages I receive from today's society,
God's word to me expresses His longing to know me, not
just to admire my body. Sick or well, it's me He wants.

Yes, Lord, appearances are deceiving. Please keep
me from ever trying to deceive You by not being
honest about what's in my heart. I wouldn't succeed
anyway. Today I will see myself as You do—
beautiful and treasured and needed. ☙

When pride comes, then comes disgrace, but with
humility comes wisdom.   *Proverbs 11:2*

Nancy, who has asthma, also has two young children. She
doesn't like to give in to her illness, doesn't want her children to remember her camped out on the sofa with a
breathing apparatus nearby and Daddy telling them not to
bother Mommy. She feels helpless and out of control.
When her breathing is threatened, Nancy cannot walk her
son to the school bus or read a picture book to her daughter or cook the meals her family is used to. She feels dis-
graced as a wife, as a mother, as a homemaker.

The proverb says that disgrace is a result of pride, of
placing too much weight on my own importance. When I
can see myself and my circumstances in the light of eternity, when I can accept today with humility of spirit, then I
can make wise choices.

Nancy's pride nudges her to fight her illness, but submitting to its demands gives her the wisdom to care for
herself today, ensuring that she's around to be someone's
wife and mother tomorrow.

O God, release me from the pride that stifles living
and keeps me from coming to You for help. Today
I will accept any help I am offered, especially
from You.   ✦

For God so loved the world that he gave his one and only Son, that whoever believes in him shall not perish but have eternal life.   *John 3:16*

During the Easter season in France, the same message can be seen on buses, in shop windows, on kiosks, literally spilling out of the churches and cathedrals. *"L'amour de Dieu est folie."* The love of God is folly. In other words, how foolish it seems to our human concept of God that He lavish love on anybody, on everybody, on whoever. Not whoever keeps His commandments or whoever goes to church or whoever never yells at her kids or whoever finds healing, but whoever believes. A whoever that includes fallen televangelists, addicts, Mother Teresa, hookers, Bob Hope, homosexuals, abortionists, and, among many others, those whose bodies remain chronically unhealed.

All these whoevers have at least one thing in common: The existence of sin has made an unignorable impact on their lives. But "God so loved . . ." "The more we find ourselves loved," writes author Sue Monk Kidd, "the more we are set free. Free to face what is before us, free to find joy, hope and meaning in spite of it."

O God of extravagant love, I want to experience
the loving acceptance that many consider folly.
I want to find joy, hope, and meaning in You.
Set me free to face illness today.   ❧

As the deer pants for streams of water, so my soul
pants for you, O God. My soul thirsts for God, for
the living God. When can I go and meet with
God? *Psalm 42:1–2*

I caught myself in an unexpected thought today. "I'm going
to have to spend more time with God," I mused. "This diet
just isn't working." I was imagining God to be a heavenly
vending machine: Put in the right amount of prayer time;
and pull that knob for will power, this one for answers, that
other one for healing. Instead of seeking just God, and
God alone, I was out to satisfy my prayer shopping list. Just
give me my daily dose of strength, perseverance, humility,
and so on, God, and I can get on with my day. I'm using
Him as just another resource in an increasingly informa-
tion-fueled society, to find answers in suffering, to demand
healing for my illness, to listen only for hints on how I can
escape my chronic condition.

God, on the other hand, never moves out of His loving
mode. He is always listening, always giving, always comforting, always answering.

Forgive me, God. I have missed Your voice even as
I enjoy Your blessings. Left on my own, I would
surely die from dehydration before I realized I was
thirsty. Resurrect in me today the longing to be
with You alone.   *☙*

Forget the former things; do not dwell on the past.
See, I am doing a new thing! Now it springs up; do
you not perceive it? I am making a way in the desert
and streams in the wasteland.   *Isaiah 43:18–19*

The Church refers to the forty days before Easter as Lent.
Many look back during Lent and recall the sorrows of Jesus
and the great sacrifice God made—remembering by temporarily denying themselves something important. But
maybe the true spirit of Lent is more one of preparation
than self-denial, a spirit of expectancy, not gloom. Lent,
after all, culminated in the most outrageously unexpected
act in history, the atoning death and resurrection of Jesus
Christ.

Even in the presence of daily, chronic illness, God is
"doing a new thing." He is recreating life, my life. In the
words of the Rev. Annie Perry-Daniel, "God makes a way
for us through our many trials and difficulties. [He is] always bringing alive that which seems dead, useless, and
hopeless."

In spite of earthly evidence to the contrary, God is making a way in the desert of my illness and bringing forth
streams in the wasteland of my despair.

God, forgive me when I fail to perceive the new
thing You're doing daily in my life. There's nothing
I want more, yet nothing I expect less. Give me a
heart today that remembers Your ability to restore
and recreate.   '

> All your sons will be taught by the Lord, and great
> will be your children's peace. *Isaiah 54:13*

Standing at my terminally ill mother's bedside, my grieving
grandmother whispered to her comatose daughter, "I wish
I could trade places with you."

"Why me?" is one thing, but "Why my child?" becomes
something entirely different. Many chronic illnesses are
hereditary. My parents or grandparents may have possessed a genetic predisposition to the very physical condition that confronts me now. The question of passing this
illness on to my own children may haunt me. Will the ones
most precious to me end up suffering as I do because of me?
Is there nothing I can do to head off the perpetuation of
this disease? Perhaps even now I am watching my child try
to manage her life while struggling with illness.

I have no real control over what health problems my
children will face. But I can teach them, by word and by
example, how best to find peace when their health and
their worlds are threatened. Instead of worrying about
passing on disease, I can think instead about passing on
Jesus.

Lord, You sustain me in pain and lead me through
uncertainty. You protect me and fill me with peace.
Help me today to pass on what You have given me.
Thank You for being the same God to my children
that You are to me. ❧

I delight greatly in the Lord; my soul rejoices in
my God. For he has clothed me with garments of
salvation and arrayed me in a robe of righteousness.
Isaiah 61:10

Easter brings back memories of new clothes. When I was a
girl, the holiday meant shopping for a frilly little hat, clean
white gloves, shiny patent leather shoes, and a real hand-
bag—all at a great sacrifice of time and money to my
mother. It was not enough to dress in the same old clothes
I had worn and torn all year long. Easter was a time to replace the used with the new. Snapshots show me and my
brother, well-scrubbed and smiling, in each year's new out-
fit—pictures that belie the crazy, ugly, real world of our
childhood.

Today, with Jesus, I still live in two different worlds:
the one inside my body where illness and pain create an atmosphere of chaos and suffering, and the other one, where
I am whole and well, outfitted in a disease-free, new body.
Easter, with its promise of resurrection, assures me once
again that this is indeed an accomplished fact. My body
has been made new. What I am now awaiting is that fact's
fulfillment.

O Father God, how I love new clothes! Thank
You for the garments of salvation that cost Jesus
everything. Help me to hang onto Your promise
as I anticipate the most glorious of attires.   &

For God is not a God of disorder but of peace.
1 Corinthians 14:33

In other Bible translations this verse reads, "God is not an author of confusion." *Confusion* in Greek translates literally as "negative downstanding" and denotes disturbance or tumult.

Certainly living with illness is disturbing, sometimes tumultuous, and often feels very negative. So much about so many illnesses confuses not only patients, but professionals as well. I may become confused if my symptoms are transient, appearing in one part of my body today and another tomorrow. This one thing alone can make diagnosis all the more confusing for my doctors, who may have been sure about my condition once, but must now change their expert opinions. Families, too, can be easily confused by illnesses they are not able to see or compete with.

Confusion runs amok among the unanswered questions about chronic illness. There often seems to be no rhyme or reason for any of this. Chronic illness simply makes no sense.

Despite the presence of confusion, though, God will override it with His peaceful presence.

God of order and peace, relieve my confusion over the most important question of all. Flood my soul today with the peace that comes from being sure that You love me and that You are making sense out of all the disorder in my life.   ☞

MARCH 26 ❧ *Dying to Self*

He himself bore our sins in his body on the tree,
so that we might die to sin and live for righteousness.   *1 Peter 2:24*

As unusual as it may sound, I've never been afraid to die,
not even as a child. I was taught that dying meant meeting
Jesus face to face. During a few rocky teenage years, I even
wanted to die. Having been instructed that my wicked behavior would keep me out of heaven, I thought just the
chance to look into Jesus' loving eyes when He came to
judge the earth would be worth going on to hell for.

I've since seen the holes in my immature theology, but
I'm still not afraid to die. What I am afraid of is the way I'll
die. Given the choice, I'd rather just not wake up some
morning. But I am not given that choice.

God does ask me to choose, though, how and if I will
die to myself and to my own earthly desires, so that I might
live on earth for His righteousness. Perhaps some unsur-
rendered attitudes are alive and thriving in me—the desire
to be physically healed or unconscious anger at God, false
guilt, or unreasonable expectations. Perhaps I need to die
to the unrelenting yearning to die. It is in this kind of death
that I truly come face to face with Jesus Christ.

Thank You, God, for with You even death is transformed and life with illness can be transcended.
Fill me with gratitude today for what my righteousness cost You. Quicken in me the unexpected last
words of Your story—The Beginning.   ❧

> Jesus answered, "I am the way and the truth and
> the life." *John 14:6*

To be chronically ill is to be perpetually exposed to un-ending advice from all kinds of people. "Take fish oil," some may say—or garlic or alfalfa or carrot juice or whatever's in vogue at the time, whatever people are convinced will cure them. "You've got to get out and exercise in the fresh air," others may tell me—or do aerobics or meditational yoga or stress-reducing techniques. Others may urge me to read the Bible more, pray more, confess more, seek forgiveness more, and do more good works as a way of gaining God's favor toward healing. I may even come up with a few solutions of my own in a vain attempt to force God's hand—eat right, keep busy, pretend, give up, get more sleep, reduce stress, anything that might just possibly fix what ails me.

Although some of this advice may relieve some of my symptoms, the only solution to the problem of suffering in life is Jesus Himself. He directs me in healthful ways. He always tells me the truth about His love for me. He will transform my unhealthy body and provide life's ultimate solution.

God, You are the only Way in life. Living, after all, is not a puzzle to be solved, but an opportunity to fall in love with You. Today I will follow You in love.   ☳

The blood of Jesus, his Son, purifies us from all sin.
1 John 1:7

Kidney dialysis patients know the importance of healthy blood. When kidneys are sick, they can't do their assigned job of filtering the blood and cleansing the body. Toxins then build up, poisoning the body and breeding disease that will ultimately bring on death. Through dialysis, a man-made device does the job a diseased body no longer can. Unhealthy blood is filtered mechanically and replaced clean and pure. Life is returned each day the patient enters into the dialysis process.

The spiritual analogy is clear. "Just as blood cleanses the body of harmful metabolites," writes Dr. Paul Brand, "forgiveness through Christ's blood cleanses away the waste products, sins, that impede true health."

Through Jesus Christ, my sin-poisoned life and body are presented to God clean and healthy again. But it's up to me to appropriate that life, just as kidney patients make a decision to accept dialysis or to allow someone to drive them to the clinic. The cleansing effect of God's purifying presence is as essential to life as clean, unpolluted blood.

Dear God, thank You for the blood of Your only Son, Who gives me fresh life and through it hope for a future. Today I will allow that unending supply of healing to flow through me and into the life of someone else.   ✍

For I desire mercy, not sacrifice, and acknowledgment
of God rather than burnt offerings.   *Hosea 6:6*

My mother was ill with cancer and overwhelmingly grateful that God had not turned away from her all the years she had ignored Him. She wanted to know if there was some sacrificial penance she should perform to thank Him.

I showed her this scripture. God wasn't looking for a certain behavior from her any more than I was. Before her illness, Mother spent a lot of time with my children and cared for them when my husband and I needed to get away. She was closest friend and confidante to both me and my grandmother, as well as being a nurse by profession. She found pleasure in giving, especially to those she loved. And now, she feared disappointing us and God because illness curtailed her ability to do things.

But all I ever wanted from her was the pleasure of her company. I loved and needed her for who she was, not for all the things she did for me. I wanted her to show herself some mercy.

God is not interested in the paralyzing guilt that only separates Him and me. He desires me, my yielded heart, not some tension-filled struggle to perform to his satisfaction.

Thank You, God, for loving me, for wanting me
just the way I am, illness and all. Today I yield my
heart to You, not only my actions. Today I will give
you the pleasure of my company.   🐦

Jesus called out with a loud voice, "Father, into Your hands I commit my spirit." When he had said this, he breathed his last.   *Luke 23:46*

In his classic daily devotional, *My Utmost For His Highest*, Oswald Chambers writes, "There are very few crises in life; the great crisis is the surrender of the will. . . . The whole of the life after surrender is an aspiration for unbroken communion with God."

Because Jesus' will was surrendered to God, He lived and died within that unbroken communion. He learned from intimate experience that He could trust His Father in any situation. He had confidence in God's loving participation in His life. So much so that when death came, Jesus could willingly give Himself over into trusted hands.

Living with a chronic illness can make confident trust in anything elusive. How can I trust God, I may think, when I can't even trust my own body, my own instincts, or my own feelings? There comes a time, though, when I must at last, or again for the hundredth time, have enough confidence in God's love for me to commit myself into those open, scarred hands.

Heavenly Father, into Your trustworthy hands I commit my spirit today. I commit to You this illness, my lack of trust, the mustard seed–sized confidence in You I do possess, and my heartfelt desire for consistent communion with You.   ❧

Because I live, you also will live.   *John 14:19*

Jesus yielded His will to the Father, committed His spirit into the Father's hands, and, according to Scripture, "breathed his last" on the cross. Jesus died. His body ceased functioning. But, just as a physical body could not contain the God of the universe, neither could sin and death maintain a hold on Him.

In nature, things happen much the same way. Seemingly dead seeds from a plant bury themselves in the ground, only to come alive again in new plants. The carcasses of animals decay, providing nutrients for the soil and feeding the forest, just as their bodily wastes once did. In God's scheme of things, that which dies does not remain dead. Death is not a futile end. It only provides opportunity for greater growth.

The death of my health means something; it has purpose in this world. Because Jesus was lifted from death, I am promised not only eternal life in heaven, but a resurrected quality of life on earth. Because He is alive and dynamic, I can face my losses, however large or small, and the guaranteed resurrections they will bring.

Most awesome God, You have put the universe together so precisely that even the illness of one person in billions contributes to life. Thank You for the obedience of Jesus Christ that made it so. Today I will celebrate life and not mourn death.   ♯

APRIL 1 ❧ *God Chooses the Weak*

But God chose the foolish things of the world to
shame the wise; God chose the weak things of the
world to shame the strong . . . so that no one may
boast before him.   *1 Corinthians 1:27, 29*

April Fool's Day. It may be too early in the day for you to
be made the brunt of some good-natured foolishness, but
where does this odd custom come from anyway?

Centuries ago, Church tradition included a lot of
clowning around. Death-white, clown-faced mimes were a
regular part of Christian worship. According to some
sources, they actually had their own special season, the
days following Easter. This was a time to pull light-hearted
tricks and to indulge laughter and the joy of new life after a
long, somber Lent.

These holy fools embodied the delightful surprise
inherent in Resurrection morning by personifying the
dancing heart of a child. The wisdom of silent clowns con-
founded the most pious, just as the existence of countless
numbers of devout, unhealed Christians today confounds
the most intellectual believers among us. I can rejoice that
God uses that which seems weak or foolish to carry out
His surprising purposes.

O God Who lived and died and lives again, thank
You for laughter and joy, silliness and surprises.
Help me to stop taking life so seriously. Today I
will allow my illness to witness to You. And maybe
I'll even have a little fun while You're at it.   ❧

APRIL 2   ☞   *The Lord Is Near*

The righteous cry out, and the Lord hears them. . . .
The Lord is close to the brokenhearted and saves
those who are crushed in spirit.   *Psalm 34:17, 18*

Finally, months after having been ambushed at work by a
seizure, Glenna was back on the job as a school crossing
guard. Images of that other day flashed through her mind,
carrying with them the dread of the same thing happening again this morning. She looked around the busy intersection, feeling utterly alone.

Up until her seizure she had daily invited God to come
along with her, asking Him to protect her and all the
young children she walked across the road. But now, staring at the same street and the same children, all she could
feel was a terror of being alone and without God. She had
been suppressing the feeling for weeks, but it wouldn't stay
buried any longer. She couldn't talk to God and so felt irrevocably separated from her best friend.

"It was overwhelming," Glenna says. "I couldn't get out
of the car. I had to reconcile with God in order to move."
She lowered her head and whimpered, "Please come back.
I need You." Her words were barely audible, but instantly
she knew that God had never left her.

> Most righteous God, thank You for reconciling me
> to Yourself through Jesus Christ. Forgive me for the
> times I pull away and forget how much I need You.
> Today I will cry out, remembering that You are
> ever nearby.   ☞

But if serving the Lord seems undesirable to you, then choose for yourselves this day whom you will serve, whether the gods your forefathers served beyond the River, or the gods of the Amorites, in whose land you are living. But as for me and my household, we will serve the Lord.　*Joshua 24:15*

Prioritizing isn't easy under the best of circumstances. People say, "First things first." But chronic illness can sometimes mean there's no first thing, only the one thing, the illness itself. Everything else gets pushed aside into a heap of et ceteras. Making choices and setting priorities becomes a game that many have come to believe they'll never win anyway. They think, So why even try?

This may be true if my first priority is my illness. But God makes it clear throughout the Bible that those who are called His children will have no other priorities before Him. He expects me to make a choice, just as Joshua and the Israelites (those whom God chose) were asked to make a choice. God wants me to choose Him first today and every day.

Then illness and all my et ceteras fall into line, making prioritizing the rest of my life that much easier.

Yes, Lord, serving the One Who chose me before the creation of the world seems very desirable to me. Forgive me for the many times I choose myself over You. Give me the wisdom I need to put my life in Your order today.　🐦

APRIL 4 ❧ *Hope and a Future*

"For I know the plans I have for you," declares the
Lord, "plans to prosper you and not to harm you,
plans to give you hope and a future." *Jeremiah 29:11*

A television panel of lupus patients was discussing living
with their disease one day at a time. An audience member,
the mother of a teenaged lupus patient, stood to caution
them about getting stuck in "today" kind of living. "In our
family," she said, "we plan some, so there are things to look
forward to."

It's a wise parent who gives a child things to look forward to. They discuss her birthday party next month or the
senior prom next year. They plan for a trip this summer or
college next fall. They might even be daring enough to
dream of special plans several years into the future. Yes,
illness might get in the way, but it might just as easily not
make a difference.

God is a good and wise parent. At times, He tells me
His plans for me; other times He'd rather surprise me. And
sometimes He waits for me to ask Him to reveal what He
has in store. One thing's for sure, though: His plans are
worth looking forward to.

O God of yesterday, today, and tomorrow, how
wonderful it is that You spend time planning things
for me. Today, Lord, I give You my gloomy feelings
and fears. Today I will look forward with
anticipation. ❧

APRIL 5 ❧ *God Hears*

Before they call I will answer; while they are still
speaking I will hear.   *Isaiah 65:24*

Communicating with doctors and other medical professionals can be difficult. Sometimes I may wonder if they
ever hear anything I say—or more important, what I'm not
saying. Sometimes the shoe is on the other foot and I can't
understand what it is they are trying to get through to me.

Just as frustrating can be communicating with family
and friends. They care so much, and yet they can't fully understand without actually crawling into my skin for a time.
I can explain and educate and express my feelings, but I
never really know for sure if I've been truly heard.

This is one worry, though, I need never have in my relationship with God. He says that even before I think to
ask, He will answer me. Before I even finish talking, He is
hearing me. God is ready and waiting for me twenty-four
hours a day. With Him, the line of communication is always open.

Thank You, God, that You and I don't need wise
words and flowery phrases to communicate. Thank
You that Your ear is always inclined toward me,
even hearing what I'm not saying. Today I will
speak to You, expecting answers and knowing
that I am heard.   ❧

So God created man in his own image, in the image
of God he created him; male and female he created
them. God blessed them and . . . saw all that he
had made, and it was very good.   *Genesis 1:27–28, 31*

What's normal? Being chronically ill can mean forgetting
what it's like to feel normal, to look normal, to be normal.
But again, what's normal? Does normal mean being just like
everyone else? Does it mean meeting some nebulous crite-
ria of physical or spiritual perfection? Or is normal anything that I'm not? And by whose yardstick am I making
this determination?

Webster's New World Dictionary defines normal as "corre-
sponding to the average of a large group" and "conforming
with or constituting an accepted standard." Although I may
be an average chronically ill person, I probably don't represent the average of a group that includes people who are
not chronically ill. Who wants to settle for average anyway? And what, or whose, "accepted standard" have I
adopted?

God made it clear from the very beginning: I am made
in His image and that is good. God sees me and I am good.
In Hebrew, good means pleasing and delightful to God.
Sick or well, I meet His standard.

Father God, in Whose image I have been
fashioned, forgive me for losing sight of that
wondrous fact. Help me to understand that normal
is whatever You design. Today I will look for the
family resemblance.   🠄

APRIL 7 ❧ *God Cannot Forget Me*

> Can a mother forget the baby at her breast and have
> no compassion on the child she has borne? Though
> she may forget, I will not forget you!   *Isaiah 49:15*

One of the biggest frustrations of some chronic illnesses
can be memory loss, and it's not always a physical symptom of ill health or a side effect of medication. This failure
to remember can be a manifestation of having overloaded
my brain's circuitry with more information than it can handle. Ongoing illness means ongoing education. Through
doctors, the media, and my own research, I am constantly
inundated with new scientific data pertinent to my illness.
This information can occupy larger and larger portions of
my brain until it seems to reduce the room I have left for
storing unrelated facts.

This is akin to what my mother labeled "young mothers'
syndrome." The mother of two or more preschoolers or
young children is awash in details. She must remember
when each one eats and sleeps, who's allergic to what,
whose stitches or teeth need checking, who's out of which
size diapers, who's afraid of dogs, who loves dogs, which
store's running a sale this week, and so on.

But God is far greater than even the most super of
moms among us. When it comes to one of His children,
God's memory never fails.

Thank You, God, for the assurance that You are big
enough to absorb and remember all things. I will
carry with me today the memory that You are
remembering me and thinking of me.   ❧

Blessed are those who hunger and thirst for
righteousness, for they will be filled.   *Matthew 5:6*

Very often the first symptom of diabetes is overwhelming
thirst. It is a signal, like pain, that something is wrong,
something in the body needs water. Eating disorders cause
a craving for food even though the real yearning is emotional.

God wants me to have this same kind of instinctual
drive for Him and Him alone. The word *righteousness* describes God's essence, His nature. He wants to fill me with
Himself, to satisfy my every longing with Himself. He
wants to fill the void created by my illness with His righteousness, not with my own self-righteousness.

The Greek meaning of *filled* is not just to satisfy, but to
fatten—to bring nourishment to a lean soul. It is important to remember that a container must first be empty before it can be filled.

Happy am I when my appetite for Jesus is all-consum-
ing. Then, and only then, will my emptiness be satisfied.

O righteous God, there are so many days that
illness drains me and I feel empty inside. Please fill
me today with all that You are. Satisfy my soul and
nourish it for the days ahead.   ɛ

Do you not know that your body is a temple of the
Holy Spirit, who is in you, whom you have received
from God? You are not your own; you were bought
at a price. Therefore honor God with your body.
1 Corinthians 6:19–20

When I'm not feeling well, I may do what I know is good
for my body. I may make healthy food choices and get
enough rest and obey my doctor's suggestions because my
illness is immediate and I want to feel better. But when I've
been feeling well for awhile, it's easy to slip away from all
the small daily decisions that led to that state of wellness. I
can be just like someone who's lost ten pounds through di-
eting and exercise, is tempted to slack off, and all too soon
finds five unwanted pounds registering on the scale.

Diet and exercise are particularly important considera-
tions for diabetics. They must keep track of all they eat and
drink and get regular exercise or risk what could be fatal
consequences. But it's hard to keep at something every day,
day after day. One young woman with diabetes says this
scripture is her impetus for daily physical discipline. Keeping in mind that a loving, caring God lives within her body,
she is motivated to care for Him—and herself in the
process.

Precious Holy Spirit, teach me today to honor God
with and in my body. I may not always be great to
look at, but I am where You choose to reside. May
I always make You feel right at home.   ❦

God has said, "Never will I leave you; never will I forsake you."   *Hebrews 13:5*

Jackie says there are too many "what ifs" in her life. Lupus is a roller coaster illness—she feels fine and fit one day and is unable to get out of bed the next. What ifs tumble around in her head like clothes in a dryer. What if the pain gets too much for me? What if I lose my medical insurance? What if I die—who will take care of my children?

What ifs often tend to be negative thoughts. But suppose my next what if sounded like "What if they discover a cure for my disease tomorrow?" "What if Jesus comes to take me to Heaven today?" "What if I wake up on Thursday totally healed?" "What if God really means just what He says?"

At least one thing in my life is not left hanging in the air. God will always take care of me. He will never forsake, desert, abandon, disown, renounce, or discard me. God will never leave me, not ever.

Lord God, today I take You at Your word. I am staking my life on it and on You. Today I hand over all my what ifs.   ♣

But now, this is what the Lord says . . . "Fear not. . . .
When you pass through the waters, I will be with
you; and when you pass through the rivers, they will
not sweep over you." *Isaiah 43:1–2*

It takes more than good intentions to keep a promise. No
matter how badly I may want to promise help to a friend or
time to a child, I know better than to speak too quickly. I
have to count the cost, understanding that promises can be
called on account of illness.

When God makes a promise, though, I know I can depend on His word. After destroying the earth with a six-
week downpour, God promised Noah and his family that
He would never again cut off life by the waters of a flood. I
used to think that wasn't such a big promise. After all, God
could still destroy the world through plague or pestilence,
fire or famine, or a host of other ways—not the least of
which is the prolonged affliction of chronic illness. But now
I see that God may have meant He would never again allow
His children to experience anything that would drown
them, whether by water, disease, or any circumstance.

God promises not to leave me alone in this illness and
not to allow it to overcome me.

Lord, I believe. Help me in my unbelief. My head
knows Your promises are true, but my heart often
doubts Your presence. Help me to hang onto the
promise today that Your arms are always there
keeping me afloat through the deep waters of
illness.   🐦

APRIL 12 ❦ *Healing Laughter*

A cheerful heart is good medicine, but a crushed
spirit dries up the bones.   *Proverbs 17:22*

There's a physician in Sweden who believes laughter truly
is the best medicine. Dr. Lars Jungdahl's medical bag has
become his own special bag of tricks. He keeps a red clown
nose between the tongue depressors and syringes and
makes his post-surgical hospital rounds pushing a fully
equipped LaffWagon, joking and juggling his way through
examinations.

Dr. Jungdahl has learned what Dr. Bernie Siegel writes
about in *Love, Medicine, and Miracles*: "We . . . find that rigid
persons who can't let themselves play are the ones who
have the hardest time healing or changing their lives to
deal with illness."

Scientists know that certain pain-inhibiting brain chemicals, the endorphins, are released when I exercise, when I
sing, and when I laugh. Given enough of it, laughter and
pain are mutually exclusive.

As Johan Weiss has said, "The laughter of man is the
contentment of God."

God of all contentment, it's so easy to lose my
sense of humor while dealing daily with the
seriousness of chronic illness. Restore in me today a
cheerful heart. Besides, I don't need dried up bones
on top of everything else.   ❦

But the worries of this life, the deceitfulness of wealth
and the desires for other things come in and choke
the word, making it unfruitful.   *Mark 4:19*

God speaks the promise of His love to me over and over,
but something keeps me from hearing it. Jesus says the
worries of this life are causing my deaf ears. What am I
worrying about? Eating and drinking and clothing myself.
Medicines and miracles. Questions and answers. Doctors
and decisions. Pain and pretending. I worry about the
whole gamut of living life with a chronic illness. And, to
top it all off, I'm not content with that. I may worry for
everyone else around me. What will *they* eat and drink and
wear?

Jackie's lupus counselor cautions her clients against such
thinking. "We tend to pile problems one on top of another," she advises, "making them spiral down. Instead, try
to imagine problems side by side." This way, rather than
sucking me down a drain already clogged with worry, my
problems can be viewed more evenly, thus exerting less
"worry weight" on me, and life will feel lighter.

Lord, I confess that I do desire other things, any
thing other than this illness. And then I worry
because I do not get what I desire. Forgive me,
omnipotent God. Today I will line up all my
worries and lift them up to You.   ❧

Therefore, do not worry about tomorrow, for
tomorrow will worry about itself.   *Matthew 6:34*

Reading Corrie ten Boom's books used to scare me. Ten
Boom was a Dutch woman whose family hid Jews during
World War II. They were all eventually arrested and sent to
concentration camps, where she told other prisoners of
God's love. "I could never do that!" I often thought in horror, borrowing trouble. "What if God brings such a frightening situation into my life?"

Recently I watched a TV movie about women in Army
boot camp. The rigors of basic training and the barracks violence that were portrayed terrified me. "I could never do
that!" I cried. My husband looked at me quizzically and
said simply, "But you don't have to." There I was relaxing
in a soft, warm bed and projecting groundless fears into my
future.

I may react much the same way when it comes to my illness, comparing myself to others who are sicker than I am.
"I could never endure her level of pain," my mind may tell
me, or "his lack of mobility," or "her loneliness." That's when
I need to stop and remind myself: "Today I don't have to."

Lord, help me face today with the assurance that
my future is held by You. Give me the strength I
need to allow You to do my worrying for me.   &#0;

As for you, you were dead in your transgressions
and sins. . . . But because of his great love for us,
God . . . made us alive with Christ . . . and raised
us up with Christ and seated us with him in the
heavenly realms.   *Ephesians 2:1–6*

After marrying young and above her social class, Roxanne
Pulitzer made headlines in the mid-1980s. She had enjoyed
the high life in ritzy Palm Beach, Florida, and, despite her
new-found social and financial significance, Pulitzer found
herself embroiled in a dirty divorce trial and nasty national
publicity. At the end, she was left with nothing, not even
the custody of her children. She summed up those years
with these words: "When you lose a sense of who you are
and where you've come from, you lose everything."

Chronic illness can strip me of everything that's ever
been important to me. I may be left feeling naked, insignificant, like a teenager again, wondering just how and where
I fit into life, wondering where I'm going and where I came
from.

Being physically sick now, I may not want to think of
myself as having been spiritually sick. But until I do, I'll
never be able to appreciate my present significance in
God's sight—forgiven, alive, raised up, and seated beside
Him and His Son.

God, Your word doesn't say that only well people are
seated with Jesus in heaven. And it doesn't say I'm
there today through my own significance, but rather
through Your great love for me. Thank You for giving me back everything I've ever lost and more.   🐾

I have told you these things, so that in me you may have peace. In this world you will have trouble. But take heart! I have overcome the world.   *John 16:33*

Years ago I stitched a needlepoint canvas of a large, green, dopey-looking toad wearing a golden crown. The sentiment on this pillow means as much to me today as it did then: "Before you meet the handsome prince, you have to kiss a lot of toads."

Then I was applying the philosophy to dating. Now I know it describes the Christian life as well. There is a handsome Prince to be met, and He has not promised anyone toad repellent. In fact, He states straightforwardly, "In this world you will have trouble."

There is a difference between Christians and non-Christians, but it is not an absence of hardship and suffering. As a Christian I can deal with chronic illness or whatever life throws at me. Non-believers will see it. "The greatest converting influence of all," wrote William Barclay, "is a life which clearly and obviously is possessed of a power which can cope with the human situation in all its problems, in all its tragedy, and in all its pain."

Thank You, Jesus, for always being honest with me. Thank You for never leaving me alone in my troubles. Thank You for the peace that Your presence brings me. Today I will take heart knowing that You are more powerful than any illness. ❧

We pray this so that the name of our Lord Jesus
may be glorified in you, and you in him, according
to the grace of our God and the Lord Jesus Christ.
2 Thessalonians 1:12

In *As Bread That Is Broken*, Dutch Jesuit Peter G. van Breemen
writes, "Once we know that suffering has a purpose, or at
least once we can believe that there is a meaning to it, we
can endure much more. . . . People can grow bitter through
suffering but they can also become beautiful. And the latter
serve as a grace to others. Their suffering has made them
transparent, more open, wise, and gentle. . . . Pain can glorify us, make us radiant and give a fruitfulness to our lives."

Maybe I don't want the radiance that can come from
pain because I don't want the pain to begin with. But that
choice is gone. Illness has invaded my body, and I can't go
back.

I'm now faced with the choice of whether or not to
allow Jesus into it with me. Of anyone, He understands my
agony. Jesus Himself was glorified, but not until after He
yielded His suffering to the transcendent power of God the
Father.

Jesus, most glorious Lord, shine from me today.
May others see You through me even in the
presence of my illness. Teach me how to accept
this mystery and, in the receiving, pass it on.   ❧

✍ *Riding It Out*

This is what the Lord says—your Redeemer, the
Holy One of Israel: "I am the Lord your God, who
teaches you what is best for you, who directs you in
the way you should go." *Isaiah 48:17*

Nancy enjoys white-water canoeing. Fresh air, warm sun-
shine, and the sound and smell of rippling water heighten
her attention to natural laws. Since Nancy is small, she sits
in the front of the canoe while a heavier person paddles
from the back.

When rapids are sighted, someone in the boat must de-
cide how and where to enter the churning water. To avoid
flipping over, it's best to hit the rapids dead center. Immediately, the front of the canoe drops, and it seems to Nancy
as if the whole river will come rushing in and drown her.
But just as suddenly, the boat is heading upwards again.
The canoe is under control, and Nancy must simply ride
out the rough water. For the occupants of the canoe, trying
to avoid the rapids or resist the current would only result in
their being tossed into the turbulent water.

Nancy has asthma, an illness that like a river is sometimes calm and sometimes crazy. Meeting my river of no
return head on and riding it out can be frightening. But
the One Who directs my way will not let me drown.

My God and my Redeemer, when I resist Your direction and refuse to go with the flow you have set in
motion in my life, I am only hurting myself and I
risk drowning. Today I will trust Your wisdom and
strength as You steer me through this river of
illness. ✍

"Lord, if it's you," Peter replied, "tell me to come to
you on the water." "Come," he said.   *Matthew 14:28–29*

I wonder if Peter couldn't see Jesus clearly. Was there a fog
or mist on the lake? Maybe he just couldn't bring himself to
believe that the man he knew was actually walking on the
same water Peter fished in every day. "If," he said. "*If* it's
you, Lord."

Peter got out of the boat and began to move toward
Jesus on the lake's surface, but when Peter took his eyes off
Jesus and noticed the winds, fear caused him to sink. "Immediately," the scripture says, "Jesus reached out his hand
and caught him" (Matt. 14:31).

God calls "Come," but doesn't let me drown when illness blurs my vision. He immediately steps in. God calls
me out of the confines of this illness. "Come," He says.
"Laugh. Sing. Pray. Crawl out of the safety of a floating
boat and let Me show you how to be alive in spite of the
frightening reality of chronic illness. I will see you and
catch you even when you can't see Me."

If it's really You, Lord Jesus, I will come, but I need
help. I don't always recognize You and I'm afraid
of the unknown winds. Teach me to trust what I
see. Teach me to reach for Your outstretched
hand today.   ➤

APRIL 20   *A Good Habit*

> Let us not give up meeting together, as some are
> in the habit of doing, but let us encourage one
> another—and all the more as you see the Day
> approaching. *Hebrews 10:25*

They say a habit, something done often and easily, takes three weeks, twenty-one days, to inculcate. If I can do any one thing for that long, by definition it will become a habit. Once I've formed this habit, good or bad, it will take at least the same amount of time to break myself from doing it.

The writer of Hebrews refers to the habit of people gathering for worship and fellowship in order to encourage one another with God's word and work in present-day life. But it's possible to see the scripture as meaning meeting together with God, just Him and me alone having a time of quiet communication, allowing Him to encourage me in illness so that I can in turn encourage others who are ill.

A habit is nothing more than a chronic condition. If I develop the habit of chronically communing with God now, it will come in handy when I don't feel well enough to cultivate the same habit later.

O God, may my chronic illness come to coexist
with the chronic health of daily meeting with You.
Today I will begin a new habit. With You, I can
do anything for twenty-one days.   *

He is before all things, and in him all things hold
together. And he is the head of the body, the church.
Colossians 1:17–18

God has made me "in his image," which is the title of a
book by Dr. Paul Brand. During his thirty years spent caring for leprosy patients and others, Dr. Brand was confronted with the dilemma of human pain and suffering. He
concluded that the existence of pain, not the lack of it, is
proof of God's love. Instead of asking why God allows people to suffer, Dr. Brand suggests wondering why God allows Himself to suffer.

God in Christ "has now ascended," writes Brand, "and in
the new role of Head He receives messages of pain report-
ing in from all over His Body. My brain does not feel pain
inflicted on its own cells—protected in a skull of bone, it
needs no such warning cells. Yet it desperately feels the
pain of other cells in the body. In that sense, Jesus has now
placed Himself at the receiving end of our pain, with actual
consciousness of the pain we endure."

Almighty God and Suffering Servant, what a
revelation! You do know what it feels like; You do
understand. How can I find words to tell You how
I feel about You? Today and forever, I love You,
Lord. ✿

Love the Lord your God with all your heart and with
all your strength and with all your mind; and, Love
your neighbor as yourself.   *Luke 10:27*

There are many rules for living, and being chronically ill
just throws another bushel's worth onto the heap. Often it
only takes one more medical direction or spiritual suggestion to make me want to turn my back on them all.

But Jesus reminds me of God's Golden Rule, to love the
Lord with my whole being and my neighbor as myself.
Sometimes I get so tired from doing so many things that
this rule seems like just more to do. Christian teacher, au-
thor, and psychologist Dr. Earl Henslin says that many
Christians have been taught the mistaken directive to put
"Jesus first, others second, and myself last."

Perhaps if I started at the end and worked backwards,
learning what it is to love myself, I wouldn't find God's
commandment quite so demanding. What if I allowed myself to accept God's lavishly bestowed love? Would gratitude then dictate a love for Him and others that flowed
effortlessly from me? Maybe the hardest work involved
with this rule is learning to let Someone else take care
of me.

O Lord my God, please help me to stretch my
understanding and acceptance of Your love for me
so that I can find delight in Your rules. I will love
You with as much of my heart and strength and
mind as I am capable of doing today.   ☞

Blessed is the nation whose God is the Lord, the
people he chose for his inheritance.   *Psalm 33:12*

Ménière's disease can steamroller Carol right out of com-
mission. She can feel an attack coming on, just as a steamroller can be seen approaching from down the street. But
Carol is helpless to do anything about it. She can't stop it
or get out of its way. She can't choose not to experience the
nausea and dizziness, and she can't choose when and where
the attacks will occur. Certainly, Carol never chose to have
Ménière's disease in the first place.

There are some choices, though, that still remain for
Carol. She can ask for help. It's been a long process, but
Carol now knows when she shouldn't be driving a car and
makes other arrangements for transportation. She now
knows better than to try to hide her condition, and cancels
appointments when necessary. She chooses to allow others
to lovingly serve her.

God has choices, too, and the psalmist says that God
chose me. He chose to create me, to love me, to take delight in me, and to give me everything He owns.

O grand and glorious God, how awesome You are!
Forgive me for the times I have chosen not to come
to You for help. Teach me today, Lord, the pleasure
of preferring You in sickness and in health.   ☙

A friend loves at all times, and a brother is born for adversity. *Proverbs 17:17*

A television network documentary on harmony in marriage reported that "study after study shows that the single most important factor in happiness is a good relationship. It ranks higher than a good job, plenty of money, and even good health."

It's impossible to be chronically ill and not have learned to appreciate the importance of good relationships. Having that supportive spouse, small group of close friends, or compassionate and helpful family can make a big difference in how I manage my illness and live my life. If my relationship with God Himself is not a good one, then certainly true happiness will elude me.

Jesus makes that relationship possible by being both my friend and my brother. He wants to be close to me, share things with me, tenderly care for me, and be both friend and family, in good times and bad, in prosperity and in pain. God through Jesus Christ is always at my side, calling me into an ever-deepening relationship with Him.

What a friend I have in You, Jesus! You bore all my sins and still bear my many griefs. Today I will look for one relationship I can make better by being to someone else the kind of friend You are to me.   ✍

> I pray that you, being rooted and established in love,
> may have power, together with all the saints, to grasp
> how wide and long and high and deep is the love of
> Christ, and to know this love that surpasses
> knowledge.   *Ephesians 3:17–19*

Due to strained finances, our large swimming pool had
been uncovered and unattended all winter. When a couple
of mallards winged over it on their way north that spring,
they saw what looked like an inviting pond. They visited
our backyard for a while, maybe too tired to search any farther, and then flew away—we thought.

About a month later, we awoke early one morning to
the sounds of gentle quacking. Sure enough, Mr. and Mrs.
Drake had expanded their family by nine, and Mama was
introducing her fuzzy brood to black, slimy pool water. In
spite of the overwhelming attraction of the scene, I felt sad.
The ducks believed this was the real thing. But we knew
they, and their children, wouldn't survive long in an artificial pond. In the process of nesting and settling in, they
had settled for less than the best.

God's best for me is to believe His unlimited and immeasurable love when, all too often, I may allow my illness to make me settle for less. All God asks of me is to
embrace His boundless love.

> When am I going to get it into my heart, O God,
> that You truly love me? For today, just for this
> day, teach me how to sit with You and feel Your
> pleasure. Today I will settle for nothing less.   ❧

The eternal God is your refuge, and underneath are
the everlasting arms.   *Deuteronomy 33:27*

Being diagnosed with a chronic illness can feel like I've
fallen into a bottomless nothingness. Waking up day after
unending day and finding that illness still with me may feel
as if I'm living in a place so deep and so dark that I'll never
again breathe the clear air or glimpse the light of pleasant
living again.

But God says no matter how far I may fall, His arms will
always be there to catch me, to protect me, and to lift me
up again. In the meantime, they provide a place of safety
for me to recuperate emotionally and spiritually. He will
never let me descend any further than His arms can reach.
Corrie ten Boom experienced that descent during her years
in Nazi concentration camps. With conviction, she later
wrote, "There is no pit so deep that God is not deeper still."

When compounded by the presence of chronic illness,
the normal lows of life may often seem that much lower.
But no circumstance is so low, no situation so hopeless, that
the everlasting arms of Almighty God will not provide
refuge.

O God, You are the One to Whom I run for safety,
the One in Whom I hide. When I'm afraid, when I
hurt, when I'm confused, You are my refuge. Lift me
and cradle me today in the strength and warmth of
Your arms.   🪶

> Who shall separate us from the love of Christ? Shall
> trouble or hardship or persecution or famine or
> nakedness or danger or sword?   *Romans 8:35*

Terry Anderson, America's last-released hostage in the
Middle East, speaks about the agony of watching the world
go on without him. He had been an Associated Press re-
porter and had enjoyed being an eyewitness to history. In
captivity, the occasional newspapers he was allowed to
read told of a revolution in the Philippines, the toppling of
the Berlin Wall, and tanks in Red Square—stories he
mourned not being able to cover. Anderson had been
forcibly separated from all that he valued—his job, his
country, his home, his family.

Being chronically ill is like being held hostage against
my will. I may be kept from doing the things I enjoy,
watching life go on while I sit on the sidelines. I can't always do what I want and be where I want. Illness has the
power to separate me at various levels from my career, my
family, and my friends—even from my own sense of self at
times.

But no matter how serious or severe my illness is at any
given moment, or how convincing my thoughts and emotions to the contrary are, God will not allow illness to dis-
connect me from Him.

> Nothing and no one has the power to separate me
> from Your love, O God. Lift me above fear and
> worry and doubt today, and carry me through the
> trouble and hardship of chronic suffering.

For since death came through a man, the resurrection of the dead comes also through a man. For as in Adam all die, so in Christ all will be made alive.
1 Corinthians 15:22

Some people are born with chronic conditions. For others, a diagnosis comes later, often well into adulthood, when a physician's words may feel like an ambush.

Terry Anderson was on his way to play tennis in Beirut when he was taken hostage. He had no more control over his kidnapping than he did over his eventual release. A situation existing between political factions caused his unjust imprisonment by others, and his freedom depended on the actions of others as well. Throughout the entire process, he was unable to control his physical circumstances, but Anderson could and did take control of his mind and spirit.

Through Adam's sin and disobedience illness entered my body, and because of the sacrifice of Jesus Christ, it will one day leave. I can control neither the fact that my illness began nor how and when it will end. But I can choose how I will respond to Christ's offered gift of eternal life—and whether or not I will accept the strength He provides me to survive and grow within illness.

How good and reassuring it is, O God, to know that You are in control of my life and my illness today. I'm beginning to see that illness isn't my fault, nor can I make it go away. Thank You for Jesus who ransomed me from eternal sickness and sin. ❧

> The Lord is good, a refuge in times of trouble. He
> cares for those who trust in Him. *Nahum 1:7*

As I watch my oldest child excitedly packing her things
and preparing to move three hundred miles away to college, I'm excited for her. She's as mature and capable as
they come at eighteen, and she has a bright, inviting future. But I'm having trouble letting her go. I'm not worried
about her studies or dating or how much I'll miss her. What
does bother me are the unknowns. Several times a year,
she'll be driving six hours alone on major highways. I read
the papers. I know about kidnapping, rape, and brutal murder. It's not easy watching her go off into a scary, sin-filled
world.

At times, it's equally hard to release control of my illness
to God. I can't dictate what will happen to me. Things may
get unpleasant. But just as I know that the time has come to
entrust my child more than ever to His care, I also know
that the time has come to let go of even more areas of my
illness. My daughter will never be alone, and neither will I.

Thank You for reminding me of Your goodness and
utter trustworthiness, O Lord. Help me to trust
You even more today, that I might experience the
peace that comes from knowing into Whose hands
I am letting myself go. 💀

APRIL 30 ❧ *A Future Hope*

There is surely a future hope for you, and your hope
will not be cut off.   *Proverbs 23:18*

People with a terminal disease lose their future. They know
what they're up against, and many are given some pretty
precise answers as to when and how they will die. They are
often quoted the odds for recovery, and there is a known
and expected end to their suffering.

For those with a chronic, interminable illness, however,
the future doesn't go away, it just becomes cloudy. The
many unknowns may cause my future to dim and lose its
meaning. Suddenly, life becomes a great, big question mark
and decision-making becomes more complicated. How
many more years will I live, and how much money will I
need? Should I or shouldn't I buy more life insurance? Will
the advancement of medical technology keep me healthier longer than I now anticipate?

There is, of course, no way to know any of this. What I
do know is that God will not leave me alone in the many
unknowns. It's been said that it's not what you know, but
who you know that matters. I am not left without hope.

O God, You Who are my hope, thank You for the
promise of a future that will always include Your
company. May I know today the pleasure of that
company in the unknowns of chronic illness.   ❧

Be perfect, therefore, as your heavenly Father is
perfect.   *Matthew 5:48*

In the Sermon on the Mount, Jesus counseled those listening with these words. But what in the world do they mean?
If Jesus knew He would die in my place because God
doesn't expect me to be perfect, then why would He say
this?

The Greek word translated here as *perfect* means something that has reached its end, its fulfillment. It is complete.
Today's psychological counselors might use the term *inte-
gration.* In this sense perfection means that I have learned to
accept all aspects of my personality and to allow them to
contribute to the creation of a whole, complete person. "Be
whole and complete," Jesus says, "just as Your Heavenly Father's love for you is total, complete, and perfect."

For someone with a chronic illness, that might mean accepting and integrating my illness into the rest of me, that
I might be made whole in Him.

Father in Heaven, perfect me today. Help me to a
new understanding of Your absolutely complete
acceptance of and love for me. Only then, no
matter what shape my body's in, will I be truly
whole.   ✒

But godliness with contentment is great gain. For we brought nothing into the world, and we can take nothing out of it.   *1 Timothy 6:6–7*

Pretend for a moment you are about to appear on a TV game show, one offering astronomical amounts of cash and goodies. You've qualified, been accepted, and are on the plane. Daydreaming about the new car you need or the money that could erase mounting debts, you might visualize yourself sweeping the competition.

Aside from these dreams and expectations, you are staking nothing on the game. You are playing for their prizes and their money, so you should have nothing to lose. Nothing, that is, except your increasing expectations. Contentment with what you now have begins to fade.

Isn't it easy to do the same thing with life? An unexpected chronic illness comes along and dashes my expectation that life owes me something, when in fact I have lost something that was never mine to begin with. Rev. Billy Graham is fond of saying he has never seen a hearse pulling a U-Haul behind it. Just as neither health nor wealth come into the world with me, I cannot expect to take health and wealth with me when I leave. Godly contentment is in knowing how to enjoy what I have in Christ right now.

Loving Lord, I know I will not be disappointed in expecting too much caring and consolation from You or in anticipating too much compassionate concern. Create in me today a cushion of Godly contentment, on which I can rest when illness presses in.   😀

> Therefore, if anyone is in Christ he is a new creation;
> the old is gone, the new has come!   *2 Corinthians 5:17*

The sun shines and the weather warms. Birds sing in blossoming trees as the sky clears. Grass grows, weeds appear, and windows display winter's grime. Springtime and an undeniable urge to tidy the nest arrive. This can be a frustrating time of year for someone with an illness that doesn't change with the seasons. Chronic disease doesn't hibernate during the winter and then recharge me with new life in the spring.

On the contrary, just when life is bursting out all over, I may feel dead and useless. I may even slip into a springtime depression because illness prevents me from enjoying the feel and smell of rich soil or causes me to neglect the upkeep of my yard.

But, according to Paul, like bright new tulips, precious baby lambs, and sparkling clean window glass, I myself am a fresh, new creation. Striving to do things doesn't keep me spiritually young and vigorous. Neither does fighting wrinkles or middle-aged spread. Only professing the substitutionary life, death, and resurrection of Jesus Christ guarantees me a daily spring cleaning.

Creator God, thank You for constantly recreating me, for doing away with the old and bringing refreshing newness of life to me today and every day. 🐦

> I have set my rainbow in the clouds, and it will be
> the sign of the covenant between me and the earth.
> Whenever I bring clouds over the earth and the
> rainbow appears in the clouds, I will remember my
> covenant between me and you.   *Genesis 9:14–15*

"Look, a rainbow!" Sometimes my kids will announce it, but now that they're older, I'm usually the one appointed to experience the thrill for all of us. With my eyes toward heaven, it's like some secret God and I share. After a summer downpour, I know if even one ray of sunlight manages to sneak through the clouds, my heart will leap at the sight of such splendor.

God set the rainbow, a symbol of His remembered promise that nothing could ever overwhelm me enough to separate us, *in* the clouds. When clouds overshadow my life—clouds of disappointment and fear, clouds of illness—I can know for sure that there's a rainbow somewhere inside them. After all, God has taken up residence within a cloud at other times as well.

All it takes is the radiant love of His Son as a reminder to bring out the brilliant expression of God's unforgettable passion for me. But to fully appreciate the beauty I have to look up. . . into the clouds.

> Lord, when life is cloudy, everything just looks
> dark. Thank You for the cleansing rain of Your
> Holy Spirit and the promise of a rainbow. Today I
> will look into my clouds and see that I am safe in
> the shadow of Your Son.   😟

MAY 5 ❧ *God's Guarantee*

> At once I was in the Spirit, and there before me was a
> throne in heaven with someone sitting on it. And the
> one who sat there had the appearance of jasper and
> carnelian. A rainbow, resembling an emerald,
> encircled the throne.   *Revelation 4:2–3*

With chronic illness, there are no guarantees—except, of
course, the one that promises I can always count on more
of the same. With God, though, I have a covenant, a
promise, on which I can rely.

God paints a symbol of that promise across the sky for
all to see. The rainbow is first mentioned in Genesis, at the
beginning of the Bible. In Revelation, near the end of the
Bible, God reveals that a rainbow encircles His heavenly
throne. Although it is incomprehensible to the human
mind, a covenant broken on earth is still honored in
heaven.

Here on earth the half of the rainbow I can see repre-
sents the half of the covenant I think I am able to keep. In
heaven, the circle is unbroken, complete. God more than
makes up for my lack. From His throne, in any direction
God looks, He is reminded of His promise to love me in all
circumstances, for richer, for poorer, in sickness and in
health. God is as good as His Word. "Peace, my child," He
whispers. "You are loved. I guarantee it."

O majestic God, how I look forward to setting my
eyes on that unbroken heavenly rainbow. Thank You
for the unbroken promise I can already see in Jesus.
Today Your guarantee will be enough for me.   ❧

O great and powerful God, whose name is the Lord
Almighty, great are your purposes and mighty are
your deeds.   *Jeremiah 32:18–19*

"I was a nut case for a reason," Glenna says about the
months following her seizure. "I was compulsive about
finding a physical explanation. Doctors could tell me *what*
had happened, but not *why* my brain decided to short-
circuit when I was thirty-five years old. I couldn't take the
maybes and the many possibilities.

"Finally, a doctor told me there was one sure way to find
out—an autopsy!"

And so Glenna began letting go of her quest for reasons, and with it her longing for a way to fix herself. If a
cause could be pinpointed, she had thought, then medicine
could take corrective measures. But she slowly began to understand that there was no way to ever get the answers she
sought.

The explanation Glenna often gave her children
echoed in her head: "Who said life would be fair?" Even
so, with the onset of any new medical problem since then,
Glenna still wonders, "Could this be the reason for my
seizure?" But by her own admission Glenna is inching ever
closer to recognizing a God Who owes her no reason except "Because I love you."

O great and powerful God, save me from the self-
destructive quest for answers and quick solutions.
May I come to accept deeds and purposes my finite
reasoning would never comprehend. Today I will let
it all go into Your exalted and loving purpose.   ❧

> I have learned to be content whatever the
> circumstances. . . . I have learned the secret of being
> content in any and every situation.   *Philippians 4:11–12*

An African-American store owner in the inner city of Los
Angeles surveyed what was left of his business after it had
been looted and burned out for the second time in twenty-
five years. The rampaging, random violence all seemed so
pointless, especially since his enterprise existed to fight
poverty. He expressed a desire to rebuild and get back to
normal. "Why do we have hope?" he responded to a television newsman, "Because this is the only community
we've got."

The bad news for a chronic sufferer, just as for someone
trapped in the despair of urban America, is in not having
the luxury of choice, whether it involves another address
or a different body. This is the only one I get. The good
news is that my God is the only God I've got, but He's also
the only One I'll ever need. He is more than adequate to
meet my needs and fill my only body with hope and contentment.

Paul learned to be content through adversity and suffering. He learned, no matter what the circumstance, that
God is enough.

> I want to learn the secret Paul did, O God, but I
> really don't want to suffer to do it. Please be gentle
> as You teach me the meaning of Your sufficiency in
> my life. I'm grateful You're all I need for today.   ✣

Blessed are the merciful, for they will be shown
mercy. *Matthew 5:7*

Blessedness, as described by author Max Lucado, is "sacred
delight . . . what you'd always dreamed of but never expected." God blesses me with mercy; He is mercy itself.

People, on the other hand, can be unmerciful in many
ways. One of the most popular methods seems to be silence. That is, by withdrawing my company from another
person, by not talking to him, I can punish him for hurting
me. Egocentric, certainly, but we all do it nonetheless.

Because of my illness, I may find myself in this situation with God: avoiding Him, not talking to Him, maybe
talking plenty about Him, but not being direct with Him.
Because of that, I can't get past my own pain in order to
reach out to others who despair. Many chronic sufferers
may need to forgive God, to show God mercy.

Happy and delighted am I when I can let go of resentment and bitterness over my illness. Then I will have made
room to receive what I've always dreamed of but never expected.

Today, Lord, my hands and heart are open,
releasing anything I may be holding against You,
even unknowingly. Forgive me as I forgive You.
Help me to practice mercy in all my relationships. ❧

MAY 9   *Change*

Listen, I tell you a mystery: We will not all sleep, but
we will all be changed—in a flash, in the twinkling
of an eye, at the last trumpet. For the trumpet will
sound, the dead will be raised imperishable, and
we will be changed.   *1 Corinthians 15:51–52*

My husband calls it "the dreaded 'C' word"—*change*. Because it meant facing the dark areas of himself, change was the last thing he ever wanted to do. But he did want a long, successful marriage, a happy wife, and a more contented self, so change he did. He became more open to and expressive about his own feelings and more emotionally available to me.

Therapist Earnie Larsen says, "In my experience, we do not change until we have some kind of awakening to the fact that we are going to lose something we are not prepared to live without if we do not change."

Just like any marriage, chronic illness involves a great deal of change—physical, mental, and emotional. I must change in order to accept my altered body or I will lose something of who I am.

For some it is easier or less painful to deny the need to change. Some who are ill choose not to change, and they forfeit a piece of themselves in the process. For some others, change comes in the growing awareness of God's love. I may have to change in order to accommodate a God Who, in illness, is turning out to be much more than I ever imagined.

Thank You, Lord, for a positive change that I can count on. For I am not prepared to live today or an eternity without You.   ☙

A man of many companions may come to ruin, but there is a friend who sticks closer than a brother.
Proverbs 18:24

In a television drama, the young doctor Doogie Howser says, "If you have to let go of a dream, it helps to have something else to hold on to . . . a friend." A make-believe doctor like Doogie may not be able to dispense much of anything I need for my illness, but the wisdom of his words can be healing.

With the onset of many chronic conditions, there comes the necessity to let go of, or at the least to alter, some tightly held, perhaps cherished, dreams. I may even have to experience the sadness of releasing friends—those who can't accept the fact that I'm ill or the effect that my illness is having on their own lives.

Even so, I need never be without a Friend. If I lose a wonderful red balloon at the fair, somehow it's not quite as disappointing if I have someone else's hand to hold as we watch it float out of sight together. Jesus is always that someone, close by my side, closer than any human brother.

Jesus, my Friend and my Brother, only You know how painful it's been for me to release my hopes and dreams to You. Please give me the courage to dream new dreams today. ❧

> Joseph named his firstborn Manasseh and . . . the
> second son he named Ephraim and said, "It is because
> God has made me fruitful in the land of my suffering."
> Genesis 41:51–52

Joseph's brothers first plotted to kill him and then ended up selling him into slavery. After working hard and distinguishing himself, Joseph achieved a position of prestige, only to then be falsely accused of seducing the boss's wife. He spent two long years in jail. Finally, Joseph came face to face with the very brothers who hated him enough to declare him dead. And yet, Joseph was able to see so much good resulting from all his pain that he named a son Ephraim, meaning "twice fruitful."

Raising fruitful trees can be a frustrating business. Unexpected frost, winds, drought, blight, disease, and hungry birds all conspire against the orchardist, who must invest hundreds of hours of worry and sweat for a healthy harvest.

For me, though, as for Joseph, it doesn't take physical health or special ability to reap the fruit of God's unfailing love. It's always there, whether in the darkness of a pit of suffering, in the slavery of dependence on drugs, or in the lonely exile of illness.

> Lord, I am nourished and sustained by the fruit of
> Your love which You cultivate for me, in me, and
> through me. Today may this same nourishment
> feed others, making "me fruitful in the land of
> my suffering." ❦

I am the true vine, and my Father is the gardener. He
cuts off every branch in me that bears no fruit, while
every branch that does bear fruit he prunes so that
it will be even more fruitful.   *John 15:1–2*

My grandparents raised prize-winning roses. They spent
their summers feeding, watering, spraying, and de-bugging
each of their seventy-odd colorful bushes. Soaker hoses
provided a steady supply of water, and fertilizing was a
dirty business that burned my nose and eyes. Dusting and
spraying afforded protection from bugs and disease, and
constant pruning produced ever more beautiful rosebuds.
After cutting off diseased and nonflowering branches, my
grandfather would seal the cut surface to protect it from
pests and disease and to promote healing.

Elisabeth Elliot, whose young husband was murdered
while he was a missionary in Ecuador, continued his ministry to the same people who made her a widow. Elliot believes we thrive and bear fruit, not *in spite* of suffering, but
because of it.

If I were a rose bush, I wouldn't much care for bug spray,
smelly fertilizer, and frequent pruning. But I certainly
would enjoy the exquisite flowers that resulted.

Lord Jesus, I need the Gardener's touch. Keep me
from complaining about my illness today, and help
me to see that God's pruning is creating in me the
fruit of a rare and lovely character.

Have mercy on me, O God, have mercy on me, for in you my soul takes refuge. I will take refuge in the shadow of your wings until the disaster has passed.
Psalm 57:1

Carol, who suffers from the nausea and noisy vertigo of Ménière's disease, says, "When I'm in the middle of an attack, I feel like a person just hanging on, desperate. I'm convinced I'll never get any better. I worry that I'll find myself in my bedroom under the bed for the rest of my life—like I could just melt into the wall."

The only place Carol can find any escape "until the disaster has passed" is under God's sheltering wings. "That's the place I have to be," she says. "During those times when things are spinning out of control, the only place I have is in the Lord."

Begging for mercy comes easily when pain pushes me to my knees or under my bed or up against a wall. The trouble is I often crawl out from under a bed of pain and His wings at the same time. Once my disaster has passed, I may no longer feel the need for a protective shadow. But though my disasters will pass, His refuge will never disappear.

O most merciful God, You are my refuge and the strength of my soul. Restore me today in the shadow and safety of Your broad wings.   ☙

> As they pass through the Valley of Baca, they make
> it a place of springs; the autumn rains also cover it
> with pools.   *Psalm 84:6*

The Valley of Baca was a desert much traveled by Hebrew pilgrims making their way to the annual feasts in Jerusalem. Its name means "valley of weeping."

Weeping is one of a human being's first acts. The tear ducts mature at three weeks—long before a baby can roll over or even smile responsively. As people mature, though, tears are often suppressed—especially in situations where adults fear ridicule or derision for their vulnerability.

But crying serves a useful purpose. The Tear Research Center (yes, there is such a place) found that tears provide natural stress relief. Stress chemicals that build up are eliminated through the mechanism of tears. Tears not only provide emotional release, they literally cleanse the system.

Thus, tears are God's gift, watering the desert of my suffering and showering it with pools of blessings. I, in turn, can do the same for others by being honest about my pain and the hope I find in God in spite of it. My tears can water someone else's, and my own, growing faith, making it "a place of springs."

O Living Water, God of this desert of illness, thank You for the tears You have wept over me, tears of love that restore me today. May my tears ever be a sacrifice to You and a source of refreshment to others.

MAY 15 ✿ A Mother's Comfort

As a mother comforts her child, so will I comfort you.
Isaiah 66:13

Being sick is never any fun. It can be even worse when the patient is a child. Sore throats and fevers, headaches and broken bones, all are miserable enough without the ultimate punishment of not being able to play with friends. Having had insult added to misery, a child can end up isolated in his or her room or relegated to the sofa in front of the TV.

Often, a sick child's only salvation is a mother's company. She takes the child's temperature, fluffs pillows, crushes ice to suck on, and plays games with the child. She devises ways to make the medicine go down more easily. Her gentle words and tender presence assure the child that this sickness will end and they will travel through it together.

So it is with God. I am not left alone, quarantined to a life without joy and fulfillment. God is here in this illness with me—nurturing me, keeping me company, taking my spiritual temperature, and administering comforting treatment as needed.

Today, Lord, I can almost feel Your cool hand on my brow. May I begin to sense the healing that inhabits Your touch. Thank You for Your tender concern for me. ✿

But the Counselor, the Holy Spirit, whom the Father
will send in my name, will teach you all things and
will remind you of everything I have said to you.
John 14:26

When my children are scheduled for exams at school, I
often ask God to help them relax, concentrate, and remember what they have studied. During one of those
prayer times, it occurred to me that I could not ask God to
bring facts to their minds that they had not already spent
time learning. I could not expect God to miraculously in-
tervene when the groundwork had not been laid.

At the same time, I was struck with the parallel in my
own spiritual life. When tests of faith are put before me,
how do I react? Am I cramming frantically, asking God for
answers at the last minute without having put in much
study time on my own? Or do scriptures I have read, taken
in, and consumed either yesterday or twenty years ago
come back to me when I most need the comfort and joy
today?

Whether I live forever in Heaven does not depend on
how much time I spend learning about God from the Bible.
But my ability to cope with chronic illness increases as I
allow the Holy Spirit to teach me through God's Word.

Spirit of God, my mind doesn't always work well,
and memory is often elusive. Today I will rely on
You to remind me of what I already know. Today
I will remember that Jesus takes all the fear out
of God's final exam. ❧

"Martha, Martha," the Lord answered, "you are worried and upset about many things, but only one thing is needed." *Luke 10:41–42*

Anxiety can be so much a part of living with chronic illness that I may not even realize the extent of its reach. Jackie was "worried and upset about many things" and woke from a sound sleep one night. Because of lupus, Jackie has very little control over her own life and body. That night, she suffered a "control attack." She was trying to figure out ways to govern what was happening in other people's lives: her husband's health, their financial situation, her children's futures, even problems in the lives of her friends' children.

Before long, Jackie realized what was happening. She took control of her worries instead of allowing them to control her. She chose to go back to sleep, and, in fine Scarlett O'Hara fashion, simply decided to think about her troubles tomorrow. Jackie needed rest, so she made a 9:00 A.M. appointment with her anxiety.

Jesus knows my greatest need is to be filled with His love for me, something that will not happen while I'm busy filling myself with anxiety or anything else. He calls me by name to relax in that love.

Dear Jesus, I confess that my worries create distance and lack of intimacy between You and me. Teach me how I can empty myself of these concerns and sit patiently at Your feet. Fill me today, Lord, with all that You are. ❧

> You will keep in perfect peace him whose mind is
> steadfast, because he trusts in you.   *Isaiah 26:3*

Sometimes thinking about taking one's life is normal and
human, even for a Christian. Especially for the Christian,
it's easy to desire life after death without all the problems
and pain of today.

For the Christian with a chronic illness, this fantasy
may become compounded. Certain drugs and medications
can have unwanted psychological side effects. And then
there's the fear of not being able to cope, of knuckling
under to the pressure of illness and losing my grip on reality. Suicide is nothing more than a control issue, hence the
title of the popular stage play and film, *Whose Life Is It Anyway?* Is my life mine to do with as I please? Or do I belong
to God, bought with a price?

Perhaps the better question would be whether I trust
God to care for me through pain and doubt. When I am
trusting God, I hand over control of my life to Him. When
I am trusting that God knows best, my mind is healthy.
When I am trusting that God loves me unconditionally, I
am kept in perfect peace.

> O God, I want that perfect peace, that total and
> complete trust in You and Your love for me. I trust
> You, Lord; help me in my distrust. I know You love
> me; help me in my not knowing today.   *&*

I give them eternal life, and they shall never perish;
no one can snatch them out of my hand. My Father,
who has given them to me, is greater than all; no one
can snatch them out of my Father's hand. I and the
Father are one.   *John* 10:28–30

Consider a woman in childbirth. If labor is prolonged, she
may strike out at her husband for "causing" her to undergo
such torture. But he understands where the irritation and
impatience come from. He is aware of the circumstances
and knows that this isn't her true personality. He doesn't
take her attack seriously, throw up his hands, and file for divorce.

God is like that, too. He understands that I'm ill and
confused. He comforts me by reassuring me that it will all
be over soon. He doesn't withdraw His love, His many
gifts, and His desire to be with me just because of a few
words uttered in pain or some acting out under extreme
stress.

Because I can't earn, win, or buy God's love, I can't lose
it either. No one, and no amount of pain and suffering, can
tear me away from my Father's hand. The saying "It's too
good to be true" doesn't apply here. It is too good, and it
is true.

Almighty God and heavenly Father, today I am
secure in You. There is nothing I can do or say or
be that would make You turn away from me. Please
hold me tight during those times I think I might
want to get away from You.   ☙

Abraham looked up and there in a thicket he saw a ram caught by its horns. He went over and took the ram and sacrificed it as a burnt offering instead of his son. So Abraham called that place The Lord Will Provide. *Genesis 22:13–14*

The story of Abraham, in which he was prepared to give up Isaac, the son of his old age who remained obedient and did not rebel, is a foreshadowing of the sacrificial work of God through Jesus thousands of years later.

And this work didn't end at the cross; God still provides. He provides a way out of my sins today, just as He substituted a ram to get Isaac out of his predicament then. He equips me daily to deal with whatever illness may throw at me.

Abraham didn't know to ask God for a ram, just as I don't often know what to ask Him for. The cry of Abraham's heart was for the life of his son, just as my heart's cry is for a simple, pain-free existence. God knows what's in my heart. He knows what I need better than and before I do. In fact, there may be times when He provides for me and I miss it entirely. Whether I acknowledge Him or not, whether I see His provisions or not, God still provides.

O God, my Provider, I admit I am often unwilling to step down off this altar of ill health. It's easier to play the martyr than accept so free and lavish a provision. Today I will open my eyes and ears to the sights and sounds of Your provisions around me. ❧

  Cured and Preserved

When Ephraim saw his sickness, and Judah his sores,
then Ephraim turned to Assyria, and sent to the great
king for help. But he is not able to cure you, not
able to heal your sores.　*Hosea 5:13*

An old Russian proverb says, "Those who have the disease
called Jesus will never be cured." Cure can mean very dis-
similar things at once. The cures scientists and patients
search for can restore someone to a former condition, relieve pain, repair what's broken, and recover what's been
lost. They can be antidotes or remedies to a distressing situation and deliver healing. I may even spend a great deal of
my own time and energy exploring this type of cure.

Curing is also a process by which a thing is preserved,
conserved, or reserved. Hams and other foods are cured.
They are sustained and maintained through curing—saved,
spared, sheltered, safeguarded, and shielded. This is the
kind of cure God dispenses throughout the Bible.

I may be chronically ill, but God has cured me. I am
preserved *in* illness, not necessarily *from* it. Through Jesus,
I have been restored to my former sinless condition, and
He will continue to sustain me.

Lord, I don't want to be cured of You. I want to
find curing in You. Pickle me, smoke me, salt me
today. Whatever it takes to maintain this "disease"
called Jesus.

MAY 22   *Simple Living*

Let your "Yes" be yes, and your "No," no.   *James 5:12*

Life really is quite simple. A chronic illness, which insists I live simply, can unignorably hammer that fact home. The religious community known as the Shakers believed that it is a gift to be simple, to take life as it comes, day by day, hour by hour.

By necessity, some things that once seemed critical before the onset of illness may now appear trivial. The everyday problems of living—budgeting, relationships, scheduling, career—take on a lower level of intensity within the confines of chronic illness. If I focus too much on one problem or one expectation, then I might miss out on some simple pleasures. In the words of crusty Gus Mc-Crae in the screenplay of Larry McMurtry's *Lonesome Dove*, "If you want only one thing too much, it's likely to turn out a disappointment. Now, the only healthy way to live, as I see it, is to learn to like all the little everyday things . . . like a soft bed . . . [and] a glass of buttermilk."

Yes, Lord, I see the value in simplicity. No, Lord, I don't know how to appropriate the gift, except to ask in simple faith, with simple faith, "Please show me how to simplify my life today."   *

Be still, and know that I am God.   *Psalm 46:10*

In Scripture, to know is to experience, to perceive, to have intimate knowledge through the senses. Those who are ill can develop ultrasensitivity to things like the temperature or noise level in a room or to pain, easily recognizing its impending onset. I may have an advantage then in experiencing, or feeling, the presence of God over some who are not ill. Illness can make me more practiced in that regard. "Be still," God tells me. "Simplify your life, simplify this day, and concentrate on seeing Me and feeling My love."

Knowing God is a relationship that thrills someone's heart. It is not an intellectual assent to the words of His book or to the Church, but a living, pulsing, risk-taking alliance with a heavenly Father, a glorious Bridegroom, an approachable King, an understanding Shepherd. To know God is to hear Him in the words of the Bible, to see Him in the face of Jesus, and to feel His comforting touch in the torment of illness.

I want to know You, God. I need to know You.
Still my soul and come to me today that I might
recognize You. Open my heart, my eyes, my ears,
my hands. Saturate me with the experience of
Your love.   ☙

How great is the love the Father has lavished on us,
that we should be called children of God! And that is
what we are!   *1 John 3:1*

Equally as profound as the question "Who are You, God?" is
the corollary, "Who am I, God?" In the current American
scene, I can identify myself in many ways and look for
identity in many things: material wealth, the success of my
children, my job title or academic degree, the attractive-
ness of my body. Conversely, the lack of any or all of these
may lead to a loss of identity, a firm sense of who I am.

It is also possible to define myself as an illness. "Hello,
I'm the colostomy." "Hi, my name is Arthritis." Or "Just call
me Cripple." Jackie, who has lupus, says it's all too easy, and
often very tempting, to "hang your hat on that chronic illness, to become the illness itself."

But if I follow this line of reasoning, then who I am is
dependent on some external circumstance and not on an irrevocable relationship with God, my Heavenly Father. But
in reality, the only identity worth having is " Child of
God," and the only vital question then becomes not "Who
am I?" but "Whose am I?"

Father God, give me the childlike faith today to
see myself belonging to You, one of Your family,
adored and special. Whatever the circumstance,
I want to be known as my Father's child.   s

For everyone who exalts himself will be humbled, and
he who humbles himself will be exalted.   *Luke 18:14*

Nancy, who has asthma, had been listening to another
friend talk about a painful financial burden before I joined
them. Because I had experienced almost identical problems
and could identify with her feelings, I was able to encourage our friend. She was comforted by my understanding
and the fact that our family managed to survive the same
pain.

Later Nancy confided to me that before I arrived she
had felt helpless to reassure our friend in any way. "I've
been physically humbled," Nancy said, "while God has
humbled you financially."

What did she mean? "Everybody has a burden to bear,"
Nancy went on. "That experience makes you more empathic, specifically and generally, and humility is total release. You have to let go of your disease or your house or
whatever it is. It's been removed from your hands. You have
to wait and accept."

In the process of waiting on God and accepting His
humbling, all are promised a place of honor with Him.

Here it is, Lord, all of it. Here's my illness, here's
my money, here's my heart, here's my will. Here I
am. Today I will exalt You and take my proper
place in Your presence.   🐚

MAY 26 ❧ *Lasting Victory*

Thanks be to God! He gives us the victory through our Lord Jesus Christ.   *1 Corinthians 15:57*

I can be subtly led to believe that victory in Jesus allows no imperfections. If I am in financial need, have a weight problem, feel unable to pray, or am faced with an ongoing, unhealed physical condition, then I am not a "victorious" Christian. If my illness exposes me to pain and doubt so intense and recurring as to be almost unbearable, then I am failing to gain "the victory."

Many believers are still in search of a rose garden that was never promised them in the first place. If I am not perpetually happy, hopeful, and spiritually satisfied, I may feel I have somehow let God down, that I am a loser, I have failed to find victory.

But Paul says that I don't have to find victory, or earn it or feel it or even believe it. The victory of life over death, hope over despair, is an accomplished act that has been given to me. Victory is portrayed in Jesus hanging on a cross. Christ's victory while suffering for me now belongs to me.

O victorious Lord, through You my spirit can prevail over illness and discouragement. Today I will continually thank You for the gifts of strength, courage, and hope I find in the mystery of a lasting victory that is Jesus Christ Himself.   ❧

You are precious and honored in my sight, and . . .
I love you. . . . Do not be afraid, for I am with you.
Isaiah 43:4–5

One evening my husband left a greeting card on my pillow.
"I just wish you could see yourself through my eyes," it
read, "because you'd see someone wonderful." He knows
that when I look in a mirror, I see a not-so-perfect body
and behavior that misses God's mark. I see someone who
is ill and struggling, someone God couldn't possibly love
with abandon. Precious and honored in His sight? Me?

If all of God's ways are truly beyond human understanding, then why shouldn't the depth of His love be beyond me as well? It's almost impossible for me to absorb the
truth that the great and awesome God has a passion for me.
I might as well just accept it as I do other aspects of God
that I can't explain.

According to writer Brennan Manning, "Christianity is
not an ethical code. It is a love affair." Viewed that way,
verses in the Bible like this one are God's love notes to me.
I am someone wonderful—precious and honored in God's
sight.

Lord God, lover of my soul, teach me what it is to
be seen through Your eyes and to get lost in that
love. Today I will not fear, for You are with me.   ❖

MAY 28   *Charity for All*

The King will reply, "I tell you the truth, whatever you did for one of the least of these brothers of mine, you did for me." *Matthew 25:40*

Brennan Manning has written, "Before I am asked to show compassion toward my brothers and sisters in their suffering I am asked to accept the compassion of Jesus in my own life, to be transformed by it, and to become caring and compassionate toward myself in my own failure and hurt, in my own suffering and need."

Jesus tells me to consider myself the least of all (Mark 9:35). Therefore, my charity must begin at home with me, with someone to whom I may often be the least charitable. So often other people get the benefit of my approving glances, complimentary words, and listening ear. When I encounter someone else experiencing the physical pain and emotional distress of chronic illness, I respond with a caring heart.

Jesus wants me to treat myself the way I would treat Him were He here in the flesh. Why can I not see Jesus, the Creator God, in my flesh? If I can't be accepting and kind to Jesus in me, how will I do the same for Jesus in others?

O God, Your Word continually discloses how very dear I am to You. Refusing to care about myself in a balanced way is putting myself above You. Today I will think about Jesus' words in a different light and practice charity toward all—including myself.

But God demonstrates his own love for us in this:
While we were still sinners, Christ died for us.
Romans 5:8

I don't have to do or be anything to get God to love me. He doesn't expect me to be other than I am and He loves me just this way. But He loves me too much to let me stay this way.

Even so, God doesn't go around shaking a heavenly lightning bolt in my face saying, "You should be doing thus-and-so," "You should be acting this way or that," or "You should be praying or fasting or loving more." God's love is a pure gift. He loves me just as I am, not as I think I should be. He loves me when I am angry and rail at Him over my illness. He loves me when pain causes me to curse His name. He even loves me when I turn from Him and ignore Him for months.

Why then do I make more demands of myself than God does? A poster carries this caption: "Thou shalt not should on thyself." Faith does not begin by telling me what I should do, but by proclaiming what God has already done.

Today, with Your help, God, I will not carry around a load of "shoulds." You have already taken the burden of sin off my shoulders and buried it forever. May my life be a perpetual thank-you note for that purest of all gifts.

Look to the Lord and his strength; seek his face
always. Remember the wonders he has done, his
miracles, and the judgments he pronounced.
1 Chronicles 16:11–12

The day I took my children to Washington, D.C., to visit
the Vietnam Veterans Memorial was warm and sunny. As
we walked, I tried to explain the meaning of this long gran-
ite wall to them. Silently, we read the names of dead soldiers, while all around we saw faces in pain and tearful
embraces. People remembered a lost son, a faithful friend,
a father never known, a war that ripped a country apart.

When we stepped back to view the black wall as a
whole, our images were superimposed over the names. I
had never met any of the soldiers identified there, so I was
not remembering any one in particular. But the memory of
their collective sacrifice on our behalf was undeniable.

In the same way, I can remember God and His won-
drously loving acts on my behalf, the miracles He has performed in my life. Remembering God's sacrifice by looking
into the face of Jesus at Calvary, I can gain strength, hope,
and joy in the midst of ongoing illness.

Lord Jesus, it is good to remember. Today I will
remember Your sacrifice on my behalf—one that
ensures me freedom from the sentence of sin, joy in
the presence of suffering, and the promise of a
glorified, healthy body yet to come. ☙

Wait for the Lord; be strong and take heart and wait
for the Lord.   *Psalm 27:14*

Over a decade ago I yearned to attend seminary. The Bible
fascinated me and I wanted to learn all there was to learn—
fast. "Surely," I thought, "God wouldn't stand in the way
of anyone desiring to learn more of Him and His Word."

We had some money from my mother's estate, but three
very young children as well. By the time they were older
and I felt more comfortable about leaving them, the money
was gone. Even the small amount from my grandmother's
will was needed to keep us afloat during hard times.

I never went to seminary, but now I realize that my
longing to learn the Bible has been satisfied. For ten years,
I participated in the structured and comprehensive Community Bible Study. Over those years, I felt disappointment, thinking God had either ignored my prayer for
seminary or had answered no. Until I looked back I didn't
understand that God had been in the process of answering
my prayer all along. What seemed like either a deaf ear or
a no at the time, had actually been "Wait."

I don't like to wait, God. But You tell me to wait
and watch: "Wait on Me and watch what I will do."
Today I will be strong in Your strength. I will
remember the many times You have granted my
petitions. Today I will take heart and wait.   🜜

June 1   *Grace Increasing*

> Where sin increased, grace increased all the more, so that, just as sin reigned in death, so also grace might reign through righteousness to bring eternal life through Jesus Christ our Lord.   *Romans 5:20–21*

It's been said that *grace* is the acronym of God's Riches At Christ's Expense. I have been given all the riches of God as a gift. I don't have to qualify by buying an expensive sweepstakes ticket or entering a physical or spiritual beauty contest I am sure to lose. God declares me a winner before the competition even gets started. He opens His arms to me not just in spite of sin and illness, but with it.

As hard as it may be to understand or accept, even my illness can be seen as a gift—a gift of grace—inasmuch as it allows God's merciful presence not merely to increase, but to superabound. Illness can also be a gift in that since I probably don't have enough mental energy to analyze grace anyway, I can only accept it.

The wise rabbi Joshua Abraham Heschel grasped this. "I do not ask," he wrote, "to see the reason for it all; I ask only to share the wonder of it all."

Almighty God, how I marvel at all Your glorious riches. Help me to allow the graciousness of Your presence to permeate my weary soul. Today I will consider the possibility that this illness is indeed part of Your plan of increasing grace.   ❦

Finally, brothers, whatever is true, whatever is noble,
whatever is right, whatever is pure, whatever is lovely,
whatever is admirable—if anything is excellent or
praiseworthy—think about such things. . . . And the
God of peace will be with you.   *Philippians 4:8–9*

Jackie won't go so far as to say she's a Pollyanna. Nor does
she bring every life circumstance under the power of positive thinking. What she does believe, though, is that her
mind, her thought and attitude pattern, affects how she
feels physically. On days when lupus is causing physical
pain or mental confusion, Jackie finds it's easy to give in to
self-pity and resignation. On the days when her mind is
able to turn against this thinking, Jackie discovers her body
responding in kind.

Psychologists encourage us to act "as if." If I act lovingly
toward my kids when I don't feel loving, soon the feelings
will follow. When I focus on the good things today will
hold, no matter how minor, soon I start to feel good, too.
God's Word tells me that if I fill my mind with helpful
thoughts, I will experience God's peace.

God of peace, I need You to reprogram my mind
today. Help me to choose true, pure, and excellent
thoughts. I want the peace of mind and body that
comes from focusing on You.   ❧

Come to me, all you who are weary and burdened,
and I will give you rest.   *Matthew* 11:28

Illness, especially any chronic illness, can be an onerously
heavy burden. It's physically, emotionally, mentally, and
spiritually draining to have to deal with all the ins and outs,
decisions and disappointments, and highs and lows of constant illness added to all the other demands in life.

But Jesus makes it clear that He expects me to become
worn down by living, to get frazzled at the edges. He is not
surprised when I react to a consistent diet of pain and uncertainty with occasional bouts of despair, discouragement,
depression, and downright anger. Jesus truly loves me, and
He really does know what I'm going through. He wants me
to talk to Him about my feelings and to accept the comfort
He offers. He wants to carry my burden for me much like a
love struck ten-year-old boy who thinks carrying his girl-
friend's book bag after a long day in school is a privilege.
And she, once the burden of heavy books is gone, can run,
skip, and swing, freely expressing herself.

O God, You Who are my companion and my
comforter, I come to You today and hand over the
burden of this illness. I am tired. I'm weary from
pain and from worry, and I need Your rest.   ❖

JUNE 4   *Resting in God*

> Trust in the Lord with all your heart and lean not
> on your own understanding; in all your ways
> acknowledge him, and he will make your paths
> straight.   *Proverbs 3:5–6*

I stared at the poster in the bookstore. It was as if someone
had sketched a picture right out of my life. A smiling
young girl in a frilly dress and double-buckle shoes was
swinging, her hair flowing as her legs pumped the old-
fashioned wooden seat. Way above her, the thumb and
forefinger of a huge hand held the swing's ropes lightly yet
securely.

Stunned, my mind returned to my girlhood, when
swinging meant escape, freedom. I would swing high and
sing, "With Jesus in the family, happy, happy home!" My
home was not a happy one, but for a little while I could
pretend it was.

At the top of the poster I read, "Will you trust me?" God
had a firm grip on the ropes of my life in the chaos of my
childhood, just as He does now that I confront the chaos of
chronic illness. He will not let me go flying off into an uncontrollable orbit or drop me into nothingness. Knowing
that He holds the ropes can be liberating, freeing me to
swing higher and higher, resting in His strength.

Lord God, thank You for having a hold on my life
even when I don't acknowledge Your presence.
Thank You for allowing me to rest in Your capable
hands even when I don't realize I'm doing it. I want
to trust You today and find freedom in resting
in You.   ✍

> Now we know that if the earthly tent we live in is
> destroyed, we have a building from God, an eternal
> house in heaven, not built by human hands.
> Meanwhile, we groan, longing to be clothed with our
> heavenly dwelling.   *2 Corinthians 5:1–2*

When my mother was undergoing months of cancer treatment, I called her regularly. One day I asked, "How are you
today?"

"Rose is great!" she replied in an upbeat tone. "Her
house is falling down around her, but she's doing great."

Somewhere in the process of learning to cope with her
condition, Mother had discovered an important truth: The
body that is my dwelling now is nothing but a tent. It lets
in rain, heat, and cold, and it restricts my movement. It is
fragile and easily damaged, or is blown away entirely, by
the hurricane that is chronic illness. The real me lives between houses, now in a continually dilapidated one but
looking forward to moving to a permanent eternal
dwelling that cannot be destroyed.

I may not be able to control my body's physical deteri-
oration, but I can choose how I will live within it.

Lord, thank You for the promise of a nice new
house in heaven. In the meantime, invade my
tattered tent today. I'm only happy here when You
live in it with me.   ℞

JUNE 6   ✒   *A Safe Dwelling*

Lord, you have been our dwelling place throughout
all generations.   *Psalm 90:1*

Overstressed businessmen have been known to run away
from their pressure-cooker careers. Unjustly treated children often run away from homes that are not safe. And a
chronic sufferer might wish to run away from a mutinous
body, even if just for a time. I may know someone who
seems a perfect specimen of physical health and fancy myself running away to live inside her body. I may even wish
to escape from what may seem like my home away from
home—the world of clinics, hospitals, and doctors' offices.

Running from something, though, is only half a solution. I can escape from or take a vacation from, but I am left
with finding a place to run to. What was true five thousand years ago remains true today. The very presence of a
smiling, open-armed Heavenly Father is a place I can always escape to. Nothing stands between us, not even my
illness. When I can't bear one more minute inside this
body, I can escape for awhile and dwell safely in God.

God, You have been, are now, and will be my
dwelling place, the only place I can truly call home
and find rest. Today I will not be so timid about
running to You and asking myself in.   ✒

Dear friends, do not be surprised at the painful trial you are suffering, as though something strange were happening to you. But rejoice that you participate in the sufferings of Christ, so that you may be overjoyed when his glory is revealed.   *1 Peter 4:12*

I was a young mother and a young Christian struggling through many unanswered questions when I heard another woman sincerely pray these words: "Thank You, God, for pain."

I was astounded. Never had I considered the thought. Grateful for pain? Never! I had spent the better part of my life trying to avoid pain, running from it in all ways possible. You mean, God, following You might mean I need to stop running and face my pain? I thought.

There was a part of me that believed God would just love all the pain away and somehow protect me from any further suffering. I had even struck a bargain with God: "You know I have a very low pain tolerance, Lord. Give me all the mental stress You want, but please keep me from physical pain."

God answered my prayer by giving me what I needed, not what I wanted. A new way of seeing has grown within me, bringing me to agree with Simone Weil that the greatness of Christianity is not that it supplies salve for suffering, but that it provides perspective on pain.

Dear God, I don't even know if I really mean the words yet, but thank You for pain, thank You for this illness. Today I will consider Jesus' suffering and the eventual release it promises me.   ☿

Blessed are the pure in heart, for they will see God.
Matthew 5:8

The Beatitudes, in one way or another, all speak of seeing God. This one mentions seeing Him with the eyes of my heart. Spiritual perception can become muddied, just as physical eyesight can be clouded by cataracts. My heart can become encased in the pain and fear that accompanies chronic illness.

I may pray for God to heal my body when my real need is for cleansed vision and a healed heart. God waits for me to ask for that which I truly need, and then He is quick to provide. He wants me to see Him, really see Him.

My life and my attitude toward my illness can be changed if I allow God to change my heart. Purity of heart means being single-hearted, having singleness of motive, wanting God and God alone—wanting and seeing Him beyond what He does or doesn't do for me.

Happy am I when I grant God permission to remove any cataract-like growths clouding my heart's vision. Then I will truly behold the eternal, unchanging God of love.

O pure and holy God, whether today finds me sick or finds me well, I want to see You. Remove anything that gets in the way of my recognition of Your loving smile. ☙

The Lord God said, "It is not good for the man to be alone." *Genesis* 2:18

God created a world and beings to inhabit it. He saw that it was not pleasant, sufficient, satisfactory, or delightful (all synonyms for *good* in Hebrew) for the one human to be without another human, to be isolated from people. Even with all the beautiful and interesting animals living in the garden, God knew that Adam could not relate to them in the same way he could to another person.

Likewise, a chronically ill person cannot always find understanding in other people who are not chronically ill. To this end, support groups are formed, and like gravitates to like. God knows it is not good for me to avoid other people out of my fear, pain, or fatigue. I was created to need people, just as I was created to need God.

Hand-in-hand, in mutual understanding with others, I can find and give strength and encouragement. Heart-in-heart with God, there exists pleasure, delight, satisfaction, and sufficiency.

Thank You, Creator God, that I am never truly cut off, isolated, or alone, for You are always with me, looking out for my good. No matter how much I've allowed illness to separate me from others, today I will make some small effort to reestablish contact. 🐦

> As a bridegroom rejoices over his bride, so will your
> God rejoice over you.   *Isaiah 62:5*

Flowers, candlelight, and champagne are things not always
compatible with chronic illness. Indeed, for many who are
ill, romance becomes a thing of the past. At the very least,
romantic relationships are forever changed.

If my illness makes sleeping difficult, my spouse and I
may no longer share a bed or even a bedroom. I may awake
in the morning determined to prepare a special dinner and
set aside time for intimate sharing, but when evening
comes the unpredictability of illness may prevent me from
following through. My body may not need or remember
romantic encounters, but my mind and my soul have not
forgotten what it's like to be wooed and wanted.

When illness gets in the way of satisfying intimacy with
another person, it also colors the quality of my intimacy
with God. But, unlike human relationships, intimacy with
God does not depend on how I feel. God woos me continually, always seeking my best, never putting pressure on
me, ever rejoicing over me.

O eternal God and everlasting Bridegroom of
the Church, how I long to hear Your tender
expressions of delight in me today. Remove from
my ears the discords of life that keep me from
experiencing deeper intimacy with You.

> Do not be anxious about anything, but in everything,
> by prayer and petition, with thanksgiving, present
> your requests to God. And the peace of God, which
> transcends all understanding, will guard your hearts
> and your minds in Christ Jesus.   *Philippians 4:6–7*

God never tires of hearing prayers. He is so eager to receive my petitions that He commands me to pray. Prayer is
nothing more than a conversation with God. It is, in the
words of teacher and writer Dr. Maxie Dunnam, a "sorting
out of our feelings as we bring them to God who cares and
understands. It is the clarifying of our wishes and our needs
and getting perspective in the light of his love and will."

It's like a mother and child sitting at the kitchen table
talking over a cup of cocoa. A wise parent allows herself
to be a sounding board, so that the child can figure things
out independently. The parent knows that more important
than answers and specifics is the relationship they are
building. God is always available for one of these chats,
and there is nothing I cannot ask or tell Him. In fact, Paul
says that as I come away from time spent with Him, peace
will guard my heart and mind.

It's often said that prayer changes things. Perhaps even
truer, prayer changes me.

> Lord God, free me from the belief that prayer is
> a duty, not a privilege. Heal me of praying only
> when I'm ill. Instead, instill in me such hunger for
> You today that I can't wait to talk everything
> over with You.   ❧

JUNE 12   *Secure to Risk*

> Let the beloved of the Lord rest secure in him, for he shields him all day long, and the one the Lord loves rests between his shoulders.   *Deuteronomy 33:12*

Throughout the Bible, God is wooing His people. In the Song of Songs, He even compares our relationship to a couple of newlyweds. In life, though, the first blush of marriage eventually fades, and the husband and wife may lose some of that honeymoon fervor. On some occasions, for any number of reasons, one or the other may not be in the mood for physical intimacy. There are times, however, when acting "as if" and taking a risk, enables the real thing to follow. A mate can only take this risk, though, when secure in the love of a faithful spouse.

The same is true in my relationship with God. When I trust in God's tender, abiding care, I can make choices involving my illness that I might not otherwise make. Should I take a chance and moderate that meeting when I'm not feeling quite well? What are my options? If I go, then get sicker and have to leave in the middle, God's not going to stop loving and wanting me. If I go and don't get sicker, I'll be glad I did and even more grateful to Him for His care.

So what if my whole life seems like a failure to me, God? Nothing I could ever do or not do will make You agree with Your beloved on that point. That's the security that frees me to risk another "failure" or two today. I love You, Lord.   ☞

> Jesus answered them, "It is not the healthy who need a doctor, but the sick. I have not come to call the righteous, but sinners to repentance."   *Luke 5:31–32*

A dull scalpel would tear the flesh and leave an unsightly scar, but a skilled surgeon uses instruments so sharp and finely honed their physical penetration may not be immediately felt. However, not even the best of surgeons can treat me unless I admit I'm sick and give permission to operate. I must first go to the doctor's office, say what my problem is, and be honest about the intensity of my pain. If I allow it, the surgeon may save my life by diagnosing a cancer or other life-threatening condition and cutting it out of my system.

Recognizing the true state of my spiritual health may not be as easy. Perhaps I need some divine surgery that I've been avoiding. God can use my illness to bring attention to diseased areas of our relationship. He will then carefully and skillfully cut away any malignancy and tenderly stitch my ragged edges back together. While I'm busy asking for physical health, I just might be neglecting the most authentic health of all.

Lord, teach me the meaning of true health. Show me how I need to change in order to attain it. Today I will be honest with You about the depth of my pain and how much I need You in every area of my life.   ❤

"Rabbi, who sinned, this man or his parents, that he
was born blind?" "Neither this man nor his parents
sinned," said Jesus "but this happened so that the
work of God might be displayed in his life."
John 9:2–4

Thousands of years after Job, people are still stuck in the
belief that financial calamity or physical infirmity points
to sin in a person's life. Jesus, Who is God Himself, replied,
in effect, "Life happens." And in a sinful world pain and per-
plexity are facts of that life.

Jesus did not discuss the situation. Instead, He evidenced the power and mercy of God by restoring the man's
sight. Neither did Jesus attempt to explain, except to pro-
claim that the power and glory of God are as much present
in suffering as they are in health. Something, after all, had
sustained this man up until then. When he was healed, profound gratitude revealed his spiritually open heart. And
through this man's healing, other hearts and eyes were
opened to God in their midst.

It is possible to let go of the need for explanations, the
desire to place blame—either on myself, others, or God—
for my illness. In her book *After Great Pain*, Diane Cole
writes, "The world bears you no grudge; it is the nature of
life to leave us vulnerable."

Most glorious God, blame is something I cannot
afford today. All it does is separate me from You.
Give me the strength to accept Your loving
authority in my life and in the world.

> Store up for yourselves treasures in heaven where
> moth and rust do not destroy, and where thieves do
> not break in and steal. For where your treasure is,
> there your heart will be also.   *Matthew 6:20–21*

Treasures are often hidden, they must be sought after and
searched for. Weekend treasure hunters, metal detectors
in hand, can be spotted in farmers' fields or on resort
beaches scanning the ground for buried booty. Seafaring
adventurers, pursuing the joy of discovery, explore the
oceans and investigate sunken ships for the presence of
mythical treasures. And once so much effort has been ex-
pended and the treasure found, it is carefully protected so
as not to be destroyed or lost again.

Jesus says the safest place to keep what's most valuable
is in heaven, entrusted to Him. He labored tirelessly and
sacrificed everything to provide me with the riches of eternal security. Trusting my emotional, spiritual, and physical
health to the circumstances of this world invites the dam-
aging forces of such as moths and rust and thieves. In Jesus'
hands, however, nothing can eat away at, corrode, or steal
my heart from God, and illness has no power to nullify or
destroy my trust in Him.

Thank You, Lord, for drawing me a treasure map
and directing my path toward You. I want my heart
in Your safe, comforting hands, so today I put the
issue of my health there, too. Today I will trust
in You.   🐾

And you and the Levites and the aliens among you
shall rejoice in all the good things the Lord your
God has given to you and your household.
Deuteronomy 26:11

The Israelites were camped on the verge of their promised
land, and Moses had some specific commands for them,
commands to protect them and enrich their lives. Commands can be thought of as threatening decrees or punish-
ment-laden laws. But pastor and prolific Christian author
Eugene Peterson puts it this way: "A command is a word
that calls us to live beyond what we presently understand
or feel or want." The commandments of a loving Lord create a climate in which freedom abounds and growth is encouraged, and rejoicing celebrates this liberty.

With a chronic illness, it may sometimes seem as if
there isn't much to celebrate. It's nearly impossible to smile
through constant pain or a foggy future. But I am commanded to rejoice in the good God gives, because embrac-
ing only the bad would eventually overwhelm me.

Throughout the Bible, God commands remembrance.
"Remember how I saved you, how I've loved you, how I've
kept my promises," God says. "Especially now in illness, remember I am good."

O Lord my God, Your commands are easy and
Your burden is light. Keep me from whining about
their weight today. Teach me to remember Your
goodness and rejoice, even when I don't feel
like it.   *

> But Ruth replied, "Don't urge me to leave you or to turn back from you. Where you go I will go, and where you stay I will stay."   *Ruth 1:16*

Relationships between people are difficult enough under the best of circumstances. In marriage, two very separate and distinct individuals with the highest of intentions unite to form a whole. They each have their own foibles and ways of doing things. Each has a uniquely different perspective on the relationship that is garnered from a vision of their own parents' marriages.

Time passes and people grow and change. Doubts may begin to surface about the survivability of the relationship. Perseverance, commitment, and the belief in the value of honoring a contract are essential in any relationship, if it is to survive. Toss a chronic illness into this emotional and mental potpourri, and watch life really get complicated.

In other scriptures, God likens His connection with me to a human marriage. What will my response to Him be when illness tempts me to walk away from the loving and committed relationship He and I once had? God has not changed. Will I? Or will I choose to trust His written assurance of ongoing, continual loving care?

My loving Lord, don't let me draw away from You. Wherever You take me today, whatever the situation, the emotion, the dilemma, I will go with You and there I will stay.   €

JUNE 18 🐦 *God's Family*

In him and through faith in him we may approach
God with freedom and confidence. . . . For this
reason I kneel before the Father, from whom his
whole family in heaven and on earth derives
its name.   *Ephesians 3:12, 14*

Nancy and her husband had planned to take a bicycle ride
in the country later that evening, but asthma was causing
Nancy to feel increasingly weak. When he called during
the day to see how she was doing, her husband offered to
stay home with her. But even though Nancy felt worse, she
resisted admitting that she was scared and wanted him
there.

"I try to accommodate other people, to my detriment,"
Nancy recognizes. "I'm guilty of saying 'No, go ahead—I'm
fine' because I don't want to admit that I'm afraid." Nancy is
afraid not only of being alone with asthma, but also of
falling into the trap of using her illness to control others.
"But we must help each other," she continues. "By not letting my family help me when I need them, I'm only weak-
ening the family itself."

I don't have to fear admitting my need or seeking and
accepting my heavenly Father's loving aid. His arms are
open, waiting for me to come to Him in freedom and in
faith.

Dear Jesus, thank You for providing access to Your
Father, the One Who delights in taking care of me
today. Help me to accept the blessings that come
from being part of God's great family.   🐦

JUNE 19 ❧ *The Spirit Is Given*

> But I tell you the truth: It is for your good that I am going away. Unless I go away, the Counselor will not come to you; but if I go, I will send him to you. *John 16:7*

The fiftieth day after Passover is known as Pentecost, the Jewish festival of first fruits, a time to recognize God as the giver of all things and to return to Him a portion of one's labor. On the first Pentecost of the infant Christian Church, God gave it all back. His Spirit appeared as a "violent wind" and "tongues of fire" binding people together and proclaiming His presence on earth (Acts 2).

Since His ascension to heaven, Jesus' disciples had been waiting. They felt alone and powerless without Him, and they wondered if all He had told them was true. In illness, it may often seem as if Jesus has left me. But His Spirit is present with me every day, every hour, every minute, everywhere. Just because I can't feel it doesn't mean He's not here.

Jesus left his friends on earth because He was limited in the form of a human. His presence everywhere at the same time could only be realized through a Spirit. Jesus never leaves me alone or without hope. He has already provided for any situation I may face.

Triune God, You have left nothing to chance. Everything in my life is planned and provided for by You. Today I will rest in that knowledge and return, not a portion, but all of my life to You. ❧

> If we are thrown into the blazing furnace, the God we serve is able to save us from it. . . . But even if he does not, we will not serve your gods or worship the image of gold you have set up.   *Daniel 3:17–18*

God was often found in fire—in a burning bush, guiding His people through the desert, at Pentecost. In the natural world, fire can be an agent of rebirth. Giant redwood forests, for example, are prone to lightning strikes that ignite small, smoldering blazes on the forest floor. The heat coaxes Sequoia seedlings from the tall trees and buries them in the rich undergrowth. The trees themselves are not destroyed, and without fire, regeneration would never occur. Foresters use deliberately set, controlled fire to restore and to cleanse. What may look like disaster to an untrained eye may actually be growth.

Three young men in Nebuchadnezzar's court were not afraid of fire. They were so confident of the care of their God that they uttered the most astounding words: "but even if he does not." Once again, God chose to enter a fire and He walked in it with them. He saved them from destruction, but it was their faith that convinced a king.

Most holy God, the fire of chronic illness gets way too hot for me sometimes, and I can't see You in it with me. I'm afraid to say, "But even if You do not. . . ." Today I will remember Who inhabits and controls the fires that cleanse and recreate.

When he cries out to me, I will hear, for I am
compassionate.   *Exodus 22:27*

Ever hear of the good patient syndrome? "No, I'm fine,
Doctor," the good patient says, smiling. "No, the pain isn't
too bad," the good patient tells friends cheerfully. "So many
others are worse off than I am."

This syndrome can also carry over into one's spiritual life. "No, I'm not afraid, God," I may pray between
clenched teeth. "I'll be all right on my own," as if it's an
admittance of failure to be sick or in pain or afraid or as if
I'm a better Christian if I just grin and bear it.

A paraplegic for twenty-five years, Joni Eareckson Tada
has this perspective on suffering: "An irksome housefly can
momentarily rob a person of joy every bit as much as a
broken leg in a cast," she writes. "God's grace is just as sufficient for a paralytic as it is for a boy who doesn't make the
baseball team."

God knows what I'm feeling and gives me permission to
feel it, to give up minimizing my pain and pretending I
don't hurt. Why not just be honest with Him, myself, and
others in the first place?

I'm afraid You won't love me, God, if I cry out.
Help me to see that You don't hear whining, only
a sick, scared little child. I hurt and I need Your
compassion today.   ❧

And we know that in all things God works for the good of those who love him, who have been called according to his purpose.   *Romans* 8:28

In his book *To Kiss the Joy*, Robert Raines writes, "So often we're blind and deaf to God's presence in our difficulties because of our own pain or anger, resentment, self-pity. We indulge in what may be called the 'if only' syndrome." If only I could change jobs or win the lottery. . . . If only I had a different spouse or obedient children. . . . If only I was healthy and didn't have to put up with this illness. . . .

If God is working in all things, then He's right here in this illness with me. The Greek words equivalent to *purpose* mean literally "to place before"—the same words used when the offering of shewbread was placed on the altar in the temple. Thus, God calls me to be an offering to Him, a sacrifice. I am called according to His purpose, called to place myself before Him, surrendering "all things," my illness included. "Growths begins," Raines continues, "when we stop saying 'if only' and start to recognize that difficulties are opportunities to grow." And God is growing good in me.

Lord, sometimes this can be a hard scripture to hear, because some people use it glibly to explain away pain and suffering. Today I will meditate on Your words, asking for new insight and comfort through them.   ❧

> You intended to harm me, but God intended it for
> good to accomplish what is now being done, the
> saving of many lives. So then, don't be afraid. I will
> provide for you and your children.   *Genesis 50:20–21*

Young, handsome, and bright, Joseph was his father's favorite, so much so that Jacob gave him a multicolored coat,
setting Joseph apart from his brothers. When the opportunity presented itself, their jealousy took over, and they
trapped Joseph in a pit and sold him into slavery, telling
their father he was dead. But God had other plans for
Joseph and he became influential in his new home. Years
later, during a famine, those same brothers came to Joseph
begging him for food. Joseph didn't blame his brothers for
all that had happened to him. He was able to see that God
had orchestrated his life events. Joseph's past suffering was
now being used to save his family from starvation.

Living with chronic illness can feel like being trapped in
a pit of pain and uncertainty. I can't see what good things
God has in store for me, only today's pain. But Joseph's
story assures me that what now seems "intended to harm
me," God intends to use for ultimate good—in both my life
and others'.

Lord, it's so easy to look only at the evil of illness.
I forget You are always at work for good in my life.
Today I will look for the good that may already
have come from being ill.   ☙

JUNE 24 ❧ *A Thankful Heart*

> Sacrifice thank offerings to God, fulfill your vows
> to the Most High, and call upon me in the day
> of trouble; I will deliver you, and you will honor
> me. *Psalm 50:14–15*

A sacrifice is nothing more than a gift—of time, of money,
of self. If I put aside a little money each week in anticipation of a friend's birthday, I am sacrificing not only money,
but the time I'll spend in taking my friend to lunch that day.
I may also be sacrificing the part of me that wanted to keep
the money. By spending time and money, I am saying I am
thankful for and pleased by my friend's presence in my life.

God wants me to have that same attitude with Him, to
give Him the gift of my sacrifice of thankfulness. He wants
me to give up something, to surrender my right to health,
and accept His supremacy in my life, all the while thanking
Him for His loving, saving presence.

God's promises have always been sealed by blood sacrifice. But God is saying here that He no longer requires
the blood of bulls and goats. Jesus' blood was substituted
instead. I have been delivered, and God's only requirement
now is a grateful heart.

Most High God, teach me to be truly thankful.
Teach me the meaning of sincere sacrifice. You are
always there for me, delivering me in the days of
my trouble. Today I will honor You. ❧

> Therefore, I urge you brothers, in view of God's
> mercy, to offer your bodies as living sacrifices, holy
> and pleasing to God—this is your spiritual act of
> worship. *Romans 12:1*

As we approached my grandfather's coffin for the first time, my mother said, almost inaudibly, "That's not my father. That's just the house he lived in."

If, indeed, my body is the structure that my soul, or the real me, inhabits, then it ought to be easier to dedicate that structure to God, especially when I remember God's overwhelming love and mercy. Because He has given me every thing, how can I hold any thing back from God?

All this may seem easy enough for someone with a healthy structure, but chronic structural instability may make for grudging sacrifice, which, of course, is not sacrifice at all. I don't possess this rundown body. God bought it with a sacrifice of His own. He and I have a landlord-tenant relationship, and He is entitled to do anything He wants to the property and to take it back at any time. He owns my body, but doesn't need it. I don't own it, but I do need to give it.

> Today, with Your help, Lord God, I offer my body
> to You as an act of worship. I give You the pain:
> each confusing symptom, all the unfulfilled desires,
> and my so-called rights to total health. Today my
> body and my soul are Yours. ❧

He took Peter and the two sons of Zebedee along
with him . . . and . . . said to them, "My soul is
overwhelmed with sorrow to the point of death. Stay
here and keep watch with me." *Matthew 26:37–38*

Even Jesus Christ needed people. He chose to surround
Himself with a group of intimate friends now commonly
known as the Twelve Apostles. There were others, too, including many women, who journeyed with Jesus. He
needed the closeness of others as much as He needed intimacy with God. In Gethsemane, at His lowest emotional
point, Jesus wanted His confidants with Him, supporting
Him and praying for and with Him.

Humans are created by God to need each other. Even
in the Garden of Eden, when Adam talked and walked with
the Creator Himself, God saw that Adam's spirit required
another human.

I am no different from Adam or from Jesus in that regard. But in my lowest moments of emotional and physical pain I may be tempted to withdraw from others rather
than reach out for their love, support, and prayers. God has
given me family and friends to be "Jesus with skin on," as
the phrase goes. In their comforting words and open arms,
I can experience the words and arms of Jesus Himself.

Dear God, I know You understand when my friends
let me down. Yours did, too. Keep me from using
this as an excuse to withdraw from all people and
especially from You. Today I will look for You in
the eyes and hands of others. ❧

JUNE 27 *Obedience*

Through him and for his name's sake, we received grace and apostleship to call people from among all the Gentiles to the obedience that comes from faith. *Romans 1:5*

For the most part, Ménière's disease doesn't get in the way of Carol's enjoyment of league softball or even her recent opportunity to play fast-pitch softball, which more closely resembles baseball. Carol watched each batter step out of the batter's box and look to the coach for instructions before every pitch. After a few weeks of doing the same thing and feeling more confident in her own ability to play the game, Carol found herself forgetting the coach. The more experienced players, though, continued to seek the coach's call before each pitch.

What a picture this was to Carol of how she tends to react in illness. During and right after a Ménière's attack, when her suffering is fresh and remembered, she continually looks to God for guidance. But as time passes she begins to forget the pain and her need of divine direction. Carol knows that those who deal successfully with a chronic condition accept heavenly supervision based on faith in the decisions of a wise and loving God.

O God, forgive me for forgetting to look Your way, for forgetting that You know better than I do. Teach me to obey Your subtle signals today. Coach me, Lord, in what it is to have faith in Your leading. 🐦

As the Scripture says, "Anyone who trusts in him will never be put to shame." *Romans 10:11*

In his book *The Way Out of the Wilderness*, psychologist Dr. Earl Henslin writes about shame. Healthy shame, he says, is a "natural result of being in the presence of a holy God." Unhealthy shame, on the other hand, is "a deep feeling of worthlessness, inadequacy, and failure." A sense of shame, then, can be as chronic as any illness. It can define who I am by changing from an emotion to a state of being.

My chronic illness, in fact, can trigger varying degrees of shame and disappointment. I may be feeling disappointed because God does not seem to come through for me in the form of specifically answered prayer. Or I may feel that I have disappointed my family, friends, doctors, God, or even myself by being sick, by being less than whole.

God wants his people to know that He does not shame them or put them down. He is eager to lift me up. Anyone who trusts in God will never be disappointed in Him. And God is never ashamed of anyone who trusts in Him.

God, I hang my head and admit that, among other things, I am ashamed of being sick and ashamed of feeling the shame. I want to trust Your Son enough to raise my arms so that He can lift me out of it. Heal my unhealthy shame and fill me with confidence in You today.

I no longer call you servants, because a servant does not know his master's business. Instead, I have called you friends, for everything that I have learned from my Father I have made known to You. You did not choose me, but I chose you.   *John 15:15–16*

Almost everyone has at one time or another been part of choosing up sides for a playground game of baseball, hopscotch, or Red Rover. Selection is based on size, strength, and ability, since naturally both sides want to win. It can also be blatantly apparent that nothing more than a popularity contest is going on. The last to be chosen often feels humiliated and friendless, their personhood in shreds.

In my relationship with Him, however, God has jumped in and prevented rejection from ever happening. Before I even knew I wanted to be on His side, God chose me. There exists no condition, whether clumsiness, unattractiveness, nerdiness, or chronic illness, that hinders me from either claiming His friendship or being chosen to play on His team. Esteem for myself, for the person God calls His friend, emanates from God Himself and from belief in His great love for me.

Friend Jesus, how could I not respond in love to Someone like You? Thank You for befriending me. Thank You for choosing me. Today I will remember that You are on my side.   ☞

Are not two sparrows sold for a penny? Yet not one of them will fall to the ground apart from the will of your Father. And even the very hairs of your head are all numbered. So don't be afraid; you are worth more than many sparrows.   *Matthew 10:29–31*

"They took my license." Glenna kept repeating the words and shaking her head. She was returning home from the hospital after more than a week of testing and recovering from the concussion her seizure caused. "They took my license," she would tell people with a vacant look in her eyes. Somehow Glenna's dignity, her sense of her own worth, was tied up in the possession of a driver's license. With it, she had permission to transport her kids safely to school, to drive herself to work, to shop for food and otherwise care for her household. Without it, she felt weak, unimportant, and trapped. "They" had taken her freedom, and with it her dignity.

My innate worth cannot be snatched away—not by any illness or condition, including the chronic condition of sin. As my Creator, God knows how vital it is for me to feel important. So His Word continually assures me of my value and reminds me that His divine dignity has been imputed to me.

Dear Jesus, You have declared me important enough to die for, and there can be no greater dignity than that. Today the circumstances of my illness will not dictate my worth. Thank You for loving me.   ❧

JULY 1   *Affirmed by God*

How beautiful you are, my darling! Oh, how beautiful! Your eyes . . . your hair . . . your teeth . . . your lips . . . your temples . . . your neck. . . . All beautiful you are, my darling; there is no flaw in you.
Song of Songs 4:1–7

Magazines are full of it. Television talk shows glorify it. Even Christian media confront the issue. Sex sells and sex is everywhere. Except, perhaps, in my own life. One of the first casualties of chronic illness may be sex, or sex as I once knew it. Since illness changes the body, every physical function, including sex, changes and becomes different. Pain or fatigue may be brand new issues or my spouse and I may sleep separately.

How I'm able to adjust and compensate may depend on whether I have a positive or negative body image. Illness may have taken its toll in drying or blemished skin or in excess or diminished weight. I may be bloated and puffy from steroid medications. The list of imperfections could go on ad infinitum. But God agrees with psychologist Anna Freud who said, "Sex is something we do. Sexuality is something we are."

When God looks at me, He doesn't see a sick, sin-ravaged, repulsive body. He sees the person He loved so much that He was compelled to create me just so we could be together.

My Lover and my Friend, how I thrill in the delight You take in me! Today I give myself over to You and exult in Your love.   •

JULY 2 ❧ *Favorite Child*

The Lord your God is with you, he is mighty to save.
He will take great delight in you, he will quiet you
with his love, he will rejoice over you with singing.
Zephaniah 3:17

When asked if they have a favorite child, most parents
would probably say no, that they love all their children
equally. Chances are, though, if pressed (and honest), a
large percentage would mention a child by name. Perhaps
it's the teenaged daughter desperately unhappy over young
love and struggling with a delicate self-image or the married daughter fearing for the fragile life of her unborn child.
Maybe it's the son who's been out of work for months or his
baby brother learning to deal with peer pressure. Or the
prodigal whose spiritual and moral fiber is hanging by a
thread. More than likely, my favorite child is the one who
needs me the most right now.

So it is with God. Whenever I need Him, I'm His favorite child. I'm the one on whom He focuses and lavishes
His love. The one with whom He spends time and in
whom He delights, the one over whom He rejoices, the
one whose pain and fear He quiets with His love.

I need never worry about where I stand with You,
heavenly Father. Sick or well, working or idle, I am
always Your best-loved and favored child. Today I
will remember that You are with me, ready to
comfort me in my need. ❧

Cast all your anxiety on him because he cares for you.
1 Peter 5:7

It's been four years since Glenna's last noticeable seizure, but she still lives in fear of having another one. "Even when I think I've put it away, the fear is always there," she says. "If I'm feeling even slightly dizzy from a normal, average cold, I have to reassure myself out loud that this is just a cold." Even though the possibility of another seizure is unlikely as long as she's on medication, Glenna still thinks about where one might happen: while driving a car, or at a party or the movies where other people would see her?

This kind of chronic fear can be described as dread, always being on the lookout for a calamity, having a continual sense that something bad is waiting to happen just around the corner.

Chronic illness is a fertile breeding ground for chronic fear. But God invites me to cast my fears on him, to throw them off and hurl them at Him. God will catch and carry my persistent dread because "He cares for you affectionately *and* cares about you watchfully" (1 Pet. 5:7, AMPLIFIED BIBLE).

Heavenly Father, hauling around a mass of fears drains me of much-needed energy. I even dread the unknown of giving up my anxieties. Teach me how to throw off my worries and escape the trap of dread. Just for today, I will practice tossing a few Your way. ✿

JULY 4   *The Spirit's Freedom*

> Now the Lord is the Spirit, and where the Spirit of
> the Lord is, there is freedom.   *2 Corinthians 3:17*

Wendy Roth is a video and television producer who is confined to a wheelchair with multiple sclerosis. Within the last few years, she has traveled over 32,000 miles doing research for a book for the handicapped, *Easy Access to the National Parks*. There are many things Roth cannot do for herself, and she must depend on loved ones and attendants to assist her. This kind of service was continual while she researched and wrote the book and made its companion video.

In spite of so much dependence in her life, Roth maintains that people can "always be independent, regardless of how much others help you." She has learned that independence and freedom are matters of one's spirit, not of one's physical condition.

For the Christian, independence is a matter of Spirit as well, the Spirit of God Who assures me that in the face of the dependence of illness God grants independence. His unending, unfailing, unconditional embrace sets my heart free.

O God, You Who are totally and completely
independent, how grateful I am that You want to
be with me. Thank You for Your Spirit who
breathes freedom into my spirit today.   ❧

It is for freedom that Christ has set us free. Stand firm, then, and do not let yourselves be burdened again by a yoke of slavery.   *Galatians 5:1*

In his letter to the church at Galatia, Paul refers to those who are slaves to the yoke of the law instead of free people in Christ. But there are many ways I can fall into slavery. I can make a yoke of my illness, allowing it to dictate my thoughts, my feelings, my dreams, my interaction with others, even my relationship with God.

Although I may be physically enslaved to an uncooperative body, my spirit, the authentic me, can be and do anything I want, and through it, I can mentally wander anywhere I want. Most of all, I am free to experience even greater intimacy with Jesus Christ, the One Who set me free.

In 1864, abolitionist Senator Charles Sumner declared, "Where Slavery is, there Liberty cannot be; and where Liberty is, there Slavery cannot be." Experiencing a growing spiritual freedom in Christ and remaining an emotional slave to anything is a contradiction in terms. Jesus has provided me freedom from spiritual slavery to anything, including this illness. Spiritually, I'm free. Physically, the process continues.

O greatest of all Emancipators, chronic illness is a hard taskmaster, and it often feels impossible to get out from under its thumb. Today I will not go on my feelings, but rather on the reliability of Your Word, the freedom You guarantee in Christ.   ❧

JULY 6   🐦 *Why?*

As the heavens are higher than the earth, so are my
ways higher than your ways and my thoughts than
your thoughts.   *Isaiah 55:9*

The time had come for my five-year-old's booster shot, and
I knew there was going to be trouble. She was terrified of
needles. It took three of us to hold her down in order to in-
ject the vaccine. When it was over, she glared at me. How
I wished I hadn't had to put her through this. But neither
did I want to sit by her bedside later, watching her painfully succumb to what could have been a preventable disease.

All my cleverest reasoning would not have helped her
understand why I insisted on this experience. All she knew
was that needles hurt and I had let a nurse stick her with
one. My child felt betrayed.

If God could explain to me why I must endure this illness, I wouldn't understand His reasoning any more than I
do now. All I know is that I hurt. Because my intellect is so
much smaller than God's, He sent Jesus Christ as a living,
three-dimensional picture of His love for me so that I could
believe He loves me even when I suffer.

Most holy God, I am reminded that even Jesus
asked why as He suffered on the cross. Thank You
for hearing my questions and enduring my doubt.
Today I will take Your hand and be content in the
knowledge that You are with me.   🐦

> There is a time for everything, and a season for every activity under heaven:. . . a time to be silent and a time to speak.   *Ecclesiastes 3:1, 7*

"Please," I said to my friend over the phone, "I don't want any advice, just someone to talk to."

Sometimes well-intentioned comments can be crushing. What I needed right then was a listener. When I need a sounding board or am too emotionally fragile to deal with others' opinions or suggestions, I've learned to say so. Otherwise, I don't get what my soul requires—someone who cares enough about me to communicate it through silence.

Certainly there are times in the life of anyone dealing with chronic illness when this is true. Deep thoughts, intense feelings, and nebulous questions can build up. I need to express them and I need someone to hear them. Perhaps the times I am filled with the most emotional and intellectual turmoil are some of the same times God seems maddeningly silent. I may find it frustrating, not understanding that God knows better than I what I need right then. He is being the Listener my soul so desires.

God, You are always listening. Even when I can't feel Your presence, You are close enough to hear my whispered cries. Today I will enter into that place of silence with You and speak my need.   ☙

JULY 8   *Shalom*

Blessed are the peacemakers, for they will be called
sons of God.   *Matthew 5:9*

"The opposite of peace is conflict and the reason we do not
have peace of mind and soul is that we are at war within
ourselves," declared pastor and author Charles L. Allen.

In Hebrew, *shalom* means peace, absence of strife. It can
also signify the inner peace that wholeness brings.

For an ill person, the ability to integrate the sick and
well parts of myself into a whole human being can be like
going to war within myself. I can also be at war with God
without even realizing it—wanting my will and not His,
anxious because I can't do what I want to do today, worrying about what's going to happen next instead of remembering God is not the enemy.

The only way to deal with this inner clamor is to es-
tablish an active, two-way communication between me and
a God Who is also an approachable Father. I can express
my conflicting feelings and appropriate His *shalom.*

Happy am I when I can make peace with God and
within myself. Then I shall know how it feels to be His
child.

Father God, help me to live in peaceful coexistence
with my self, with my illness, and with You. Today
I will listen as You speak the word I need most to
hear, *shalom.*   &

> The Lord God formed the man from the dust of the
> ground and breathed into his nostrils the breath of
> life, and the man became a living being.   *Genesis 2:7*

Drawings and diagrams of the human body may seem to reduce flesh, blood, and spirit to an easily explainable and controllable mechanism. Some sciences and philosophies declare that the world is mechanical and can be comprehended and manipulated through human reasoning alone. Even some religious teachers present a mechanical view of man's relationship to God: Present your problem to God invoking the "correct" scriptural references while possessing enough "faith," and God is bound by His own spiritual laws to grant your request. There's a mechanistic medical view, too, that forgets that the practice of medicine is as much an art as it is a science.

None of these mechanistic beliefs do justice to the mystery of life. Human beings are not machines, and my doctor is not a mechanic. My living body, however ill, is more than a druggable, cuttable entity. I am the personification of the Creator God Himself, and just as much a mystery.

Dear Lord, how precious I must be to You and how
it must hurt You when I suffer. I am part of You.
You are my lifeline, and we are inseparably linked.
Help me get in touch with that wondrous
connection today.   ☙

Taste and see that the Lord is good; blessed is the
man who takes refuge in him.   *Psalm 34:8*

"Do I have to eat that?" Somewhere between the compliant
preschool years and the maturing-into-politeness older
teen years, my children have whined these words, and
often. "What's this?" one will demand on one of the infrequent occasions I've been able to spend hours shopping for,
planning, and cooking a well-balanced, healthful meal at
which we can spend some "quality time" together. I have
only my family's long-term physical health and best inter-
ests at heart, yet the tasty new casserole and I are met with
suspicion and derision. They don't even want to taste it to
find out for themselves whether it's "yucky" or not.

   It's hard to admit that I can act the same way with God
at times. "Do I have to eat this, Lord? Can't I have anything
more appealing than this illness? Maybe some other difficulty today?" But often all it takes is my willingness to give
God a chance, openness to tasting His goodness for myself, and I am lifted out of useless resistance.

   Help me curb my whining and complaining about
   this illness, Lord. I know complaining is human
   and You're not surprised or hurt by it, but I'd just
   rather not be doing it. Today I will try some new
   delight from Your hand. Today I will take refuge
   in You.   🐦

Like clay in the hand of the potter, so are you in my
hand, O house of Israel.   *Jeremiah 18:6*

Jackie called this morning to say lupus was getting in her
way again. She overexerted herself yesterday and couldn't
make our meeting today. I sensed her frustration at not
being able to follow through on plans and some false guilt
at what she perceived as letting me down.

When chronic illness flares up once again, seeming to
come out of nowhere, it can feel as if I'm living on the far
edge of a furiously spinning potter's wheel. The potter controls the speed of his wheel, and sometimes it feels as if I'll
topple right off.

But my Potter is merciful, and He has an eye for beauty.
As His wheel turns, His hands are always surrounding me,
shaping me, protecting me, providing security. I can never
disappoint Him, no matter how misshapen my body is. As
author Patsy Clairmont puts it, "God uses cracked pots."
What may look and feel like chaos to me is an Artist's plan
at work.

You are the Master Potter, O God. I can feel the
warm strength of Your hands dissolving the chaos
within. Help me to remember today that falling off
Your wheel is impossible with Your hands there to
contain me.   ☞

He came to a broom tree, sat under it and prayed
that he might die. "I have had enough, Lord," he said.
"Take my life."   *1 Kings 19:4*

God's prophet Elijah is known for many things. He was
taken directly to heaven without experiencing death. The
wine goblet on a Passover table is called Elijah's cup, as
Jews today still await his return.

Once, the famed Elijah was so discouraged that he
wanted to die. This is perhaps the incident for which he is
most remembered. Running for his life, fed up with the Israelites' stiff-necked resistance to God's direction and their
violent hostility toward God's prophets, Elijah collapsed
and gave up.

Did God rebuke Elijah or strike him dead? On the contrary, God sent an angel to see that he was rested and
nourished before spending time with Elijah Himself, encouraging him and sending him back into the world refreshed and strengthened.

When the never-ending problems and continual per-
plexities of illness get to me, God does not nag me about
how faithless I am. He accepts my discouragement and
patiently tends to my needs.

Lord God, You know that every now and then I
can't take being sick one more second. I get so tired
of it all that I want to lie down and never wake up
again. Today, though, I will rest in Your shadow
and let You feed my needy spirit and fill my empty
soul.   ☙

The people who live there are powerful, and the cities are fortified and very large. . . . We can't attack those people; they are stronger than we are.
Numbers 13:28, 31

On an easel near my desk sits a special oil painting. It's not the artist's primitive style, talent, or use of color that impresses me: it's the artist herself, Sophie Gotoin. When her hands became severely crippled by arthritis, Sophie had to retire from fashion millinery, dressmaking, and crocheting—things she loved doing. But, at age sixty-eight, Sophie placed her bent fingers around a paintbrush and started a new career. Though painting is painful for Sophie, unlike fashion art, it is possible.

The Israelites had been just about to take possession of the rich and fertile land that God promised, when scouts reported that giants lived in the land. With that, all their courage disappeared. Sophie Gotoin did not allow the giants of fear, pain, disappointment, and lack of training to dis-*courage* her. Courage is not the absence of fear, but action in the presence of fear. And, it is Sophie's courage that gives her the ability to surmount her pain so that she might possess a land of personal fulfillment.

Lord God, my illness and its symptoms often seem like giants to me, and I feel so small and weak. Your presence sustained the Israelites and provided them with a future. Fill me today with that same divine en-*courage*-ment.   ☿

He got up, rebuked the wind and said to the waves,
"Quiet! Be still!" Then the wind died down and it was
completely calm. He said to his disciples, "Why are
you so afraid?"   *Mark 4:39–40*

I love thunderstorms. If God is trying to impress me, He
more than succeeds. I feel like a spectator inside a giant
planetarium, a silent witness to unlimited power, grandeur,
and strength.

Once, though, a neighbor's house was struck by lightning and the resulting fire destroyed their attic and all their
son's wedding gifts that had been stored there. I began to
understand why my grandmother would run anxiously
through our house during a storm, unplugging the TV and
turning off the lights. When all was secure, she would invite me up into her soft, safe lap to watch the remarkable
light show together. She never failed to be awed by nature's
majesty, and her awe was contagious.

Today storms of different kinds come into my life. I
don't have to be afraid of them either. I can enter into God's
lap of protection and enjoy the thrill of His power. I don't
have to fear the wind of illness or the lightning flashes of
pain. I know Who controls the storms.

Awesome God, no matter how healthy or calm
I may appear on the outside, You know there's
always a storm of fear brewing just beneath my
surface. Today I look to You as the Source of all
peace.   ❧

A bruised reed he will not break, and a smoldering
wick he will not snuff out.   *Matthew 12:20*

"Look, dear, isn't the ocean splendid!" Hearing voices, I
opened my eyes. An elderly man was pushing an adult-
sized stroller through the sand to an umbrella several yards
away from mine. His wife, also gray-haired, had spread out
some blankets there. The man continued talking to a
young woman seated in the stroller, even though she was
unresponsive. This pencil-thin, severely palsied adult, who
appeared blind and retarded as well, was the couple's
daughter.

The father placed both his strong arms under her frail
body and gently lifted her out of the stroller and onto a
blanket, all the while tenderly describing their grand surroundings. The mother checked her daughter's clothing,
placed a pillow under her head, and leisurely stroked her
arm. Then the couple, whose faces shone when they talked
to or about their child, carried on a typical day at the
beach.

All of a sudden, my day was anything but typical.

O heavenly Father, the tenderness of Your love
staggers my comprehension. For You are not a God
Who strikes me when I am down, but One Who
carries me and binds up my wounds with infinite
patience. Today I will rest in love that knows no
bounds.   ǀ

JULY 16 🕊 *Winds of Illness*

The rain came down, the streams rose, and the winds
blew and beat against that house; yet it did not fall,
because it had its foundation on the rock.
Matthew 7:25

Years ago, Hurricane Hazel roared into the town where I
lived. Winds howled as heavy rain washed swirling leaves
and tree limbs down the street. Thunder boomed and small
streams spilled over to flood area roads.

But the memory that remains most vivid is the clanging
of my backyard swing set. It was a place of peace and
security in a childhood otherwise ruled by chaos, a metal
A-frame anchored in cement so that I could swing as high
and free as my legs were strong. Now a storm threatened
to rip it apart, sending chains, seats, and my place of refuge
flying. Responding to my fears with rope and wire, my
grandfather fought against the powerful wind and pelting
rain until the swings were safely tethered to the side and
my harbor of solitude restored.

Living in the middle of the storm of chronic illness can
wear away at me and can threaten my faith in God. But
God continues to remind me that I am grounded in the
Rock, Jesus Christ His Son. Together we can weather anything.

The winds of illness may blow, and I may falter,
Lord, but today with You, I will not fall. 🕊

> The Lord is the everlasting God,. . . he will not grow
> tired or weary, and his understanding no one can
> fathom. He gives strength to the weary and increases
> the power of the weak.   *Isaiah 40:28–29*

After natural disasters such as earthquakes or man-made
ones like war, stories are told about the bravery people
show under extreme duress. Many find the strength and
courage to endure and sacrifice in the most distressing conditions, as long as the calamity is short-lived.

But when a negative situation drags on, as it has in
Beirut and Belfast, or when one tornado turns into a string
of natural emergencies, good-natured chin-upsmanship can
dissolve into fear, panic, selfishness, and plain old fatigue.

The same can be said for living with a chronic illness.
Persisting makes me weary. It's one thing to accept and find
the emotional energy to deal with a new physical diagnosis, but it's clearly another to continue that kind of upbeat
tolerance.

Emotional and physical weariness is natural, normal,
and expected. God, though, never gets tired of offering me
His shoulder and His ear. He never wearies of my chronic
need for Him.

Lord Jesus, You experienced what it is like to be
weary. Thank You for Your infinite understanding.
I need Your strength and Your power yet again
today. Thank You that I can rely on You to chronically provide it.   €

I will lead her into the desert and speak tenderly to
her. There I will give her back her vineyards, and will
make the Valley of Achor a door of hope.
Hosea 2:14—15

Charles Spurgeon, a noted nineteenth-century London
preacher, heard of a poor widow in need of rent. When he
knocked on her door with the funds in hand, she wouldn't
answer for fear it was her landlord coming to collect the
money she didn't have. The woman's fear of an unknown
on the other side of a closed door kept her from receiving
the very thing that promised to calm her fear and solve
her problem.

Having to face illness day after unending day makes it
all the easier to close a door that I may label Fear than to
open the same door, which God identifies as Hope. I may
be afraid He has more misery waiting there for me, so I
hide from God, thinking that if I don't open the door, if I
refuse to let Him in, I won't have to face whatever is on the
other side.

But what if splendid things—like tender consolation,
answered prayer, unfathomable love, and hope for my future—are waiting there? Best of all, God Himself is always
on the other side.

> Lord, sometimes I hide from You the same way I
> often hide from people. This illness looks like a
> door closed to Your hope on the other side. Today I
> will not let any doors remain closed between us.   ❧

Do not be terrified; do not be discouraged, for the Lord your God will be with you wherever you go.
Joshua 1:9

The fear of suddenly losing her balance and vomiting in a roomful of strangers follows Carol wherever she goes. "Sometimes I have to measure my days," Carol says, referring to Ménière's disease. "If I feel an attack coming on, I weigh the risks. It could be several more days before the actual vertigo and vomiting strike, or it may not happen at all, so I consider my chances. If I measure my condition as no more than a five or six on a scale of one to ten, then I'll go ahead with my plans. But seven to ten means I get someone else to drive. But I keep on going, thankful that I can."

The only time Carol alters this approach to her illness is when a trip with her husband is in the offing. "It's not that I stop paying attention to my body's signals," Carol says, "but when I'm with Jim, I don't get as worried. He can always help me out of a room in a hurry. I feel more free to take risks."

And as long as I have Jesus with me, I have nothing to fear either. I can take a few more chances.

I have my terror-filled days, Lord, and I do get discouraged at times. Thank You that Your faithful presence with me is never by chance. Today I will keep going in the knowledge that You are with me. ❧

> Find rest, O my soul, in God alone; my hope comes
> from Him. . . . My salvation and my honor depend on
> God; he is my mighty rock, my refuge.   *Psalm 62:5, 7*

Mood swings are not uncommon in people with physical ailments. The body's chemistry affects the brain and vice versa. Emotional ups and downs are common even in people of accomplishment. Christian leaders through the ages, including Martin Luther, Charles Spurgeon, and J. B. Phillips, have written about their times of depression. Robert Schumann, Virginia Woolf, F. Scott Fitzgerald, and Ernest Hemingway, among many others, lived on the fine line between creative genius and mental instability. Long before the advent of antidepressant medications, Lincoln and Churchill both felt helpless to do anything about their spells of severe despair.

Many people, especially Christians, may feel judged or perceived of as bad for not being able to choose their feelings and maintain an even spiritual outlook. But "my salvation and my honor" don't depend on the judgments of others or on my shifting emotional sands. They rest on the Mighty Rock. God may not choose to keep me even, but He will keep me.

My Fortress and my Rock, today I will rely not on what my emotions are saying, but on what You say—that I can hope in You and find rest in You. Thank You for holding me steady with Your reliability.   ﹆

JULY 21   *False Hope*

> Do not listen to what the prophets are prophesying
> to you; they fill you with false hopes. They speak
> visions from their own minds, not from the mouth of
> the Lord.   *Jeremiah 23:16*

"If not God, then Mrs. God," was the way a pastor friend described me. He was referring to my need to control things until they conform to my personal view. "I can see you sitting next to God in heaven," he continued with a twinkle in his eye, "surveying His creation and commenting, 'See that cloud over there, God? Maybe if You'd move it just a tad to the left.' "

So many things determine the way I respond to the world around me, and some of them can cause me to set myself up as God, thereby crossing the fine line from faith to presumption, from worshiping God to supposing myself to be God. This view of life makes it easy to believe those who preach the false notion that I can control God into healing me by possessing the "right" quantity and quality of faith.

In *Holding God Hostage*, Tom Watson writes, "Too often we mold God to our own design, naming and claiming what *we* want instead of recognizing the transcending importance of what *He* wants. . . . We dare not forget that in His activity among men, God seeks *His* glory, not ours."

I want to believe anyone who promises healing
now, Lord. Forgive me for presuming on You and
listening to voices not from Your mouth. Heal my
ears today, that they may discern the words of the
One True Prophet and the true hope He offers.

Do not reject me or forsake me, O God my Savior.
Though my father and mother forsake me, the Lord
will receive me.   *Psalm 27:9–10*

The essence of any chronic condition is that it never goes
away. Illness will be a part of my life until I die, which will
not necessarily be from this illness.

At the initial diagnosis, those closest to me may have
offered all kinds of loving support, encouragement, and advice. But the paradox is that just as I may be integrating a
chronic condition into my life, my family and friends may
be deciding they are unable to deal with it. They love me,
so it hurts them to witness my continual suffering. When
the same things drag on day after day, when it becomes ev-
ident that nothing they can do will make my illness disappear, will they grow weary and choose to disappear
themselves?

I, of course, have no such choice. My illness stubbornly
refuses to leave even while my support may be fading
away. God understands the pain of this kind of subtle rejection, and He vows to welcome me no matter who or
what may disappear from my life.

Thank You, O God, for the assurance of Your
constant company. Sometimes I feel so very alone.
Instill in me today a new realization of just how
continually close You are.   🪶

Why is my pain unending and my wound grievous
and incurable? Will you be to me like a deceptive
brook, like a spring that fails?   *Jeremiah 15:18*

"I'm not angry, I'm hurt" used to be my stock reply during
an argument with my husband, as if anger were unpardon-
able and hurt more acceptable. Being hurt meant someone
else was at fault, something had been done to me. Whereas
being angry meant I had to take responsibility for my own
feelings and reactions.

Can one relate to God in the same way? Maybe I'll
admit to being hurt about this illness, but certainly not to
being angry. But isn't my God mighty enough to take my
anger? "Our anger can be a measure of our faith," writes Eugene Peterson. "Believers argue with God; skeptics argue
with each other."

Biblical heroes got plenty angry, David and the prophet
Jeremiah among them. What did they do with their anger:
pretend it wasn't there or commit murder to vent their frustration? No, they prayed their anger, going down on their
knees before Almighty God.

God hears and accepts my outrage and then asks me to
leave it with Him and not indulge in ongoing bitterness.

Lord, because I believe You exist and are in control,
my anger about what is happening to my body gets
directed at You. Thank You that You are filled with
enough love to take it. Today, instead of denying it,
I will pray my anger and let You keep it.   🐦

Blessed are those whose strength is in you, who have
set their hearts on pilgrimage.   *Psalm 84:5*

The state of Maryland appointed a task force to study self-
esteem. After eighteen months, the panel reported that it
had identified 1,050 things that residents were doing to
make each other feel better about themselves. But, they announced, there was no money to disseminate this information. The group then asked the governor's office to support
a campaign to persuade businesses to fund a self-esteem
data bank.

What inanity humans will chase in order to quantify,
and thereby secure, happiness. Unhappiness is seen as
some sort of unnatural state of being, something to be
dodged at all costs.

I don't need government to define my happiness. True
happiness, or blessedness, is found in discovering God's
strength and making a decision to head toward it in order
to find mine. Setting my heart on a perpetual pilgrimage
in God's direction is what carries me through a life of persistent illness.

Mighty God, You Who are my strength, because of
You I am stronger than I know. I may even be much
less unhappy than I realize, too. Today I will keep
my heart set on pilgrimage toward You, not on
searching for an avenue out of this illness.   *&*

I tell you the truth, unless a kernel of wheat falls to
the ground and dies, it remains only a single seed. But
if it dies, it produces many seeds.   *John 12:24*

When we planted our first vegetable garden, I wondered if
my husband knew what he was doing. Would those tiny
seeds actually become pickles in jars or green beans on our
plates?

I made frequent trips to inspect our carefully tended
dirt. For weeks, it looked as if nothing was happening.
Then . . . what fun it was (and still is) to pluck a cucumber
off its vine, cross my own backyard, and slice fresh food for
dinner!

When seed is buried in the ground, it appears dead,
having no useful purpose for the moment. But if a small
seed, one that contains all it needs for regeneration, is
nourished and sustained, exciting things result. A single cucumber is full of seeds, hundreds in fact. And each one has
the capacity for manifold multiplication.

Like the dirt enveloping a seed, illness surrounds me,
and I may not be able to perceive the new life and growth
that's taking place beneath my surface.

O Jesus, when I can't feel life within me, help me
to believe it is there. Sustain me as surely as the
ground holds and feeds a tiny, fragile seed. Today I
will picture not only life after death, but life within
what appears to be death.   *

JULY 26 ❦ *Finding the Balance*

The Lord abhors dishonest scales, but accurate
weights are his delight. *Proverbs 11:1*

"Sometimes asthma wins," says Nancy, "and sometimes I
win. When I resist steroids, then I win. I've beaten it this
time."

Nancy's doctor has determined that the next step in her
treatment will be a side effect–producing drug that Nancy
would rather not take. Her husband cannot understand her
reluctance to use something they both know will restore
healthy breathing immediately. He watches as his wife is
robbed of days and nights at a time, loses weight, and
struggles for breath because of asthma. And Nancy herself
asks, "At what point does winning do more damage in the
long run?" With each attack she wonders, "Have I pushed
myself too far this time?"

Finding the balance between prudent health choices
and fear-induced reactions can be as chronic a dilemma as
my illness itself. So is the balance between asking and relinquishing in prayer. But God balanced all the scales by
providing the life and death of Jesus. With a God like that,
either way I win.

Lord God, Your scales are always balanced in my
favor. Today I will prayerfully present all my
predicaments to You and trust the stability of Your
answers. ❦

You will fill me with joy in your presence, with
eternal pleasures at your right hand.   *Proverbs 16:11*

After a period of illness and restricted physical activity, I
may be tempted to overdo it. Guilt or boredom can be the
catalyst. Or maybe it just plain feels good to flex my mind
or body once again. Whatever the reason, the temptation
to fix up the yard after three days in bed, for example, can
be intense. But if I give in to that temptation I may spend
twice as much time recovering from the short-lived pleasure.

"Moderation in all things" is good advice, but it's even
better advice for the chronically ill, who must ration out
their strength. Sometimes though, as gardening columnist
Henry Mitchell notes, "a little imbalance helps the general
equilibrium." In other words, it's possible to become so balanced as to stop living altogether, to cease being raucously
colorful and sweet-smelling in the garden of life.

God assures me there's plenty to enjoy about today and
that I will have eternity to savor all those things I wish I
could be doing more of now. One day, everything will balance out perfectly.

Until then, Lord God, fill me with the joy of being
in Your presence. Teach me how to appreciate the
subtle imbalances in my life today. I know I can
never overdo finding pleasure in You.   🐦

For whoever wants to save his life will lose it, but
whoever loses his life for me will find it.
Matthew 16:25

"You are not alone," the brochure for a local support group
announced. "If you are dealing with a life-threatening illness, there is help for you."

Life-threatening? It seemed an odd word, not applicable
to asthma or lupus or seizure disorder, conditions that most
likely won't end life. But the more I pondered the concept,
the more I was able to view chronic illness as indeed life-
threatening, a threat to life as I now know or once knew it.

My life as a healthy person is over. Trying to hang on to
the illusion of physical well-being only generates a kind of
death of spirit. But, according to Christ Himself, facing the
reality of illness and relinquishing my "right" to health *to*
Him will result in the discovery of an even deeper life *in*
Him. But to find that deeper life, I must first be on the lookout for it.

Lord Jesus, I want that life *in* You. So today I once
again give this illness *to* You. Show me how to leave
it behind *with* You. I want to move out into today
without having to carry the weight of my old life
with me.   *

The Lord is faithful to all his promises and loving
toward all he has made. The Lord upholds all those
who fall and lifts up all who are bowed down.
Psalm 145:13–14

Babies are born with just two fears: of falling and of loud
noises. A roller coaster ride involves both. Why then
would I subject myself to the climbing *click, click, click,*
knowing that the prolonged ascent will joltingly turn into
a roaring descent? But a great many people find this activity enjoyably thrilling. At peak season, large amusement
parks boast two-hour or longer waits for the privilege of
facing one of life's most basic fears.

Living with a chronic illness can be just like traveling
uncontrollably up and down, in and out, over and around
those metal hills—with two major differences: I didn't
choose to take the trip, but at the same time I'm not left
alone in my fear. No matter how hard or fast it may seem
I'm falling, God is there to stop the plunge and lift me up
again.

All the changes that illness brings are scary, Lord.
Some come slowly and with warning. Others
suddenly roar into my life and drop me full steam
ahead. Thank You for being there to catch me.
Today I will let You hold me.   *※*

JULY 30 ❧ *Something out of Nothing*

Now the earth was formless and empty, darkness was over the surface of the deep, and the Spirit of God was hovering over the waters.   *Genesis 1:2*

God didn't construct or assemble or build a world; He created it. He made something out of nothing, a world that had never before existed.

An artist may sit and stare at an empty canvas before creating a pleasing image, but that image is not entirely original. Likewise, a writer may stare at a blank piece of paper or vacant computer screen before setting down thoughts and ideas, characters and settings, but these are not entirely original either. Both the painting and the story are products of created beings.

Ernest Hemingway once said that the creative process of writing is easy: You just sit down and open a vein. God did just that. The earth and humankind are intimately entwined with the Creator God. He poured Himself out into the creation, knowing it would one day involve the painful opening of His own vein.

Being ill can feel like living in a vast, dark nothingness. But God recreates. At His own expense, God is forever bringing something out of nothing, even out of illness.

Precious Spirit of God, thank You for always hovering over me, preparing me for new creations in the midst of illness. Today I will remember that nothing about this illness is a waste, that there is life within the darkness.   ❧

Therefore, since we are surrounded by such a great
cloud of witnesses, let us throw off everything that
hinders and the sin that so easily entangles, and let us
run with perseverance the race marked out for us. Let
us fix our eyes on Jesus. *Hebrews 12:1–2*

Track-and-field events known as the Special Olympics take
place around the country each year, providing opportunities for mentally and physically challenged kids to exercise their bodies while stretching their self-concepts.

Although activities are varied, no child is in competition with another. Each is encouraged to be the best he or
she can be, and every participant who finishes a contest is
hailed a winner. Each has faced a test and given as much effort as he or she is capable of. Nothing more can be asked
of anyone. Individual volunteers are recruited for the heart-
warming job of hugging each child as he or she finishes the
event. Huggers provide someone to share the joy, someone
to verbalize outstanding effort, someone with whom to
make physical and emotional contact, someone to run to.

Similarly, life's race is not a competition. Everyone who
finishes in Christ, even those hindered by chronic illness, is
a winner.

Thank You, God, that I don't have to worry about
being in competition with anyone or putting forth
more effort than I am able. Today I will fix my eyes
on Your open arms waiting for me at the end of the
race and Your smile that keeps me going. &

AUGUST 1 ❧ *God's Design*

In him we were also chosen, having been predestined according to the plan of him who works out everything in conformity with the purpose of his will.
Ephesians 1:11

Stitchery has always been a popular and relaxing pastime. Needlepoint involves using colored wool yarns to fill in a design painted on a mesh canvas. Cross-stitch is similar, but uses cotton threads on a plain, open-weave fabric canvas. The design is copied, or counted, square by square from a charted pattern.

If I wish to stitch a specific design onto a fabric with a natural grid that is too small, a material known as waste canvas must be attached to it. Waste canvas provides the squares over which the design can be worked. Without it, following the pattern and transferring it properly would be impossible.

The process looks uneven and unappealing. The first time I tried it, I doubted the waste canvas would fall away as promised, after being sewn over so thoroughly. But it did, and I was left with a splendid picture of two cherubs resting on a cloud.

Illness may be the waste canvas of my life. When God finishes His work in me and pulls away the suffering, only a beautifully detailed pattern will be left. In God's design, nothing is wasted or without purpose, not even chronic illness.

It's so comforting to know, O Lord, that everything in my life fits into Your loving and carefully crafted design. Whatever today may bring, I will be aware that the work of Your hands goes on. ❧

I have set the Lord always before me. Because he is at my right hand, I will not be shaken. Therefore my heart is glad and my tongue rejoices; my body also will rest secure. *Psalm 16:8–9*

Glenna uses a notepad to keep track of the seizure medication she takes. Just a bit too much can build up to toxic levels over time and threaten her overall health. Too little could mean a compromised seizure threshold, risking the onset of another attack. Timing is important, too. If she takes it too early in the evening, she conks out before bedtime; too late, and she's sleepy the next day. Glenna must also remind each doctor and pharmacist of possible drug interactions. And the seizure disorder has left Glenna's memory somewhat less dependable. So she writes it all down—every day.

Glenna must also think about what she eats and drinks on a daily basis. She wonders which foods (caffeine? salt?) may have a bearing on her chronic condition. And every time she picks up her car keys, she is reminded that another seizure would mean the loss of her license once again. "There's a constant awareness," she says. "A daily-ness that begins to wear away at you."

No matter how oppressive chronic illness can be, God clings to me just as persistently. He is always before me.

Lord God, You are as constant a companion as my illness. Open my eyes to see You here with me and my mouth to express thanks for Your daily-ness in my life. Today my body and my mind will rest secure in You. 🐝

In his heart a man plans his course, but the Lord
determines his steps.   *Proverbs 16:9*

Nothing in the excitement of getting a new car equaled the
thrill of cruise control. Just a push of a button and I'm off
at a uniform, uninterrupted speed. What a feeling of control as I cruise past all those other cars. "Get out of my
way," I silently command. "Don't slow me down with your
penchant for a leisurely ride along the scenic route." And
never mind the roadside placard that suggests an interesting side trip or the passenger who is hungry or needs a
bathroom break.

More often than not, whether I always realize it or not,
I run my life the same way. I set my own course and take
off. God Himself had better not try to slow me down with
relevant facts or painful circumstances.

Illness can be viewed as a side trip on life's journey—a
side trip that might include friends I wouldn't have made
except for my illness or the opportunity to branch out into
new and challenging directions or a chance to share my life
with others in a way I never before would have imagined.

Lord, You alone are God. Today I will turn off
my life control and let You determine my steps.
Thank You for redirecting my course and showing
me the detours that make the trip worth taking.
Help me to see the value in this side trip of
chronic illness.

AUGUST 4 ❧ *God's Measurements*

Do not have two differing measures in your house—
one large, one small. You must have accurate and
honest weights and measures so that you may live
long in the land the Lord your God is giving you.
Deuteronomy 25:14–15

The ten-year-old had just been thrown out at first base
when his father arrived late to watch the rest of the Little
League game. Excited and grinning as he headed for the
dugout, the boy shouted, "I batted in a run, Dad!"

"Did you get any hits?" was the man's only reply.

A little boy had just been measured, and according to
those calculations he came up short. He had hit the ball,
but not far enough to get him on base, which to his father
was the only measurement of his worth in the game—
never mind that baseball is a team sport in which sacrifice
can mean the difference between winning and losing. A
boy was growing up absorbing his father's system of measurement.

What system of personal assessment have I taken on?
Do I keep two sets of measures in my heart, man's and
God's? One says I can never measure up. But God's measurement lessens my load by assuring me I am wanted, accepted, and of enormous value to Him.

Certainly Your immeasurable love for me, Lord,
sets the standard by which I am measured. Forgive
me for allowing my illness to outweigh that divine
passion. Today I will cease to measure myself by
illness and let You love me. ❧

As the Father has loved me, so have I loved you. Now remain in my love. *John 15:9*

The Living Bible translates this verse as "live within my love." Other versions use "abide in my love."

To abide can mean to bide one's time, to wait. The ill person may declare, "I can't abide this pain one more day" or "I can't abide being sick and helpless." In this sense, abiding means to endure, to bear, to tolerate my illness when all I want is somebody to turn off the switch. Abiding can also signify residing or dwelling, as in "I don't want to abide in this body any longer!" Or it can mean to remain, tarry, stay, or stop for a while. I can choose how I will interpret *abide.*

Although I must abide my body—that is, tolerate physical symptoms—I don't have to abide in my body. I can stop for awhile and abide in Jesus and His love for me. I can take up lodging in Him. Because He abided suffering, He understands my longing for a safe place to abide. His arms are open, waiting to close around me, that I might find rest and remain in Him.

Lord Jesus, I need to once again avail myself of Your loving arms. Remind me throughout today that You love me equally as much as God loves You. Today I will abide in You. ❧

No longer will they call you Deserted, or name your land Desolate . . . for the Lord will take delight in you.
Isaiah 62:4

One afternoon, Abraham Lincoln's children and a playmate ventured into Mrs. Lincoln's carefully kept parlor and made a mess. When Mrs. Lincoln returned and saw the evidence of the boys' misbehavior, she became angry and scolded them fervently. Hearing the commotion, Mr. Lincoln came into the room and defended the boys, which caused his wife to chide him as well.

"But he only laughed," wrote the visiting boy later, "picked her up in his arms, and kissed the daylights out of her. And she clung to him like a girl." Clearly, Lincoln enjoyed his wife. He knew there'd be no reasoning with her, so he simply loved her.

When God hears me griping about one more day with my illness or berating myself because I can't do something or lashing out at Him for causing my pain, he doesn't bother with explanations I won't hear. For the moment, He overlooks my quest for satisfaction and gives me just what I need—an ample dose of His love and mercy.

O God, I want to let You love me like that, but something gets in the way. I'm afraid to enjoy You as much as You enjoy me. Please don't stop compelling me to work through whatever's separating us. Today I will consider that it just might be this illness.   ☞

"No," said Peter, "you shall never wash my feet." Jesus answered. "Unless I wash you, you have no part with me." "Then, Lord," Simon Peter replied, "not just my feet but my hands and my head as well!"   *John 13:8–9*

We were preparing for Easter communion in my husband's hometown church. Our family had always belonged to churches that invited children to participate in the sacred celebration, so I handed a thimble-sized container of grape juice to our preschooler and said, "Jesus loves you, Christian." He looked at the juice curiously, held it up to the light, and generally inspected it. Words were said, prayers prayed, and we all feasted on the symbolic body and blood of Jesus.

When the silver tray came back down the aisle to collect the empty cups, Christian was still busy draining his. His little fingers tried to get at those last few drops, and failing that he poked his tongue deep into the tiny glass. That little taste only left him craving more.

Illness can prevent me from believing that God wants any of me, much less all of me. And He yearns for me to desire all of Him. It's still hard to accept that He loves and wants me so very much.

Dear Jesus, Your cup of kindness is often as hard to drink from as the cup of suffering. I want to come to You with my whole heart, open to anything and everything You have for me. Create in me today the open, accepting spirit of a child.   ❧

Blessed are those who are persecuted because of
righteousness, for theirs is the kingdom of heaven. . . .
Rejoice and be glad, because great is your reward in
heaven. *Matthew 5:10, 12*

Social commentator Malcolm Muggeridge has written, "Indeed I can say with complete truthfulness that everything I
have learned in my seventy-five years in this world, everything that has truly enhanced and enlightened my existence, has been through affliction and not through
happiness."

Can there be blessedness in suffering, in persecution,
in illness? The Beatitudes, these happy keys to the kingdom, are a progression, a step-by-step guide to how God
reconstructs a heart. As illness destroys my outsides, God is
rebuilding my insides. His kingdom is not only some future
reward, but a here-and-now reality in my heart. My illness
may seem like a desert of persecution, a never-ending in-
justice. But persecution is temporary, and the kingdom of
heaven is eternal.

In his book, *The Applause of Heaven*, Max Lucado para-
phrases this beatitude as follows: "Blessed are those who
manage to keep an eye on heaven while walking through
hell on earth."

O God, again I need Your help with my eyes.
This time would You give me ones that recognize
heaven in me and on earth? Today I will look for
You in this hell of illness. ❧

He himself gives all men life and breath and everything else . . . so that men would seek him and perhaps reach out for him and find him, though he is not far from each one of us. For in him we live and move and have our being.   *Acts 17:25, 27–28*

Cruising nomadically, motorcycle gangs make many people uneasy with their stereotypically hard-driving and rough-talking "hog" jockeys and "old ladies." In yet another instance of looks being deceiving, these groups often include vacationing accountants, convention-bound war veterans, and retired couples. What they all have in common, though, is a love for the open road and especially for their Harley-Davidson motorcycles. "A Harley isn't something you have," observes one owner, "it's something you live and breathe."

I may know that five hundred pounds of metal can never be the essence of a person or satisfy his spirit. But I may not understand that living and breathing illness day after day, for years on end, can stunt my spirit, leaving no room within me for rejuvenation through God's Holy Spirit. The essence of my being is not illness. My substance is God Himself.

O God, my days all too often emphasize the illness that is in me over Your divine Spirit Who inhabits me, too. Come and live in me today, breathe in to me and become my very being.

The Lord is my shepherd, I shall not be in want.
Psalm 23:1

In *A Shepherd Looks at Psalm 23*, Phillip Keller outlines the tender care that a conscientious shepherd takes with his sheep. They are coaxed through the valleys where water is cleaner and fresher to the high ground where grazing is choice and sweet. The flock is guided and kept on the right path, protected from pests and predators along the way, and constantly watched over and sought out if lost.

Keller writes that our view of God "is often too small—too cramped—too provincial—too human. And because it is we feel unwilling to allow Him to have authority or control—much less outright ownership of our lives."

Without Him, I run the risk of having a less-than-caring owner, one who allows me to drink diseased water, forgets to feed me, and leaves me alone to fend off danger. With God as my Good Shepherd, I need not worry about acquiring more or better things or gaining a healthier or more attractive body. I have all I need under His care. I am safe. It is enough.

My Shepherd, You know me and You love me. You gave Your life in order to protect me. You provide me with all You have. Today that will be enough for me.

He makes me lie down in green pastures, he leads me
beside quiet waters, he restores my soul.   *Psalm 23:2–3*

Every summer for more than thirty years, children growing
up in the cramped and polluted environment of New York
City have had the opportunity to visit small towns and
sprawling farms in surrounding communities. These Fresh
Air Kids, as the charitable organization is known, are invited into homes to spend several weeks absorbing Amish
farm life in Pennsylvania, exploring the mountains of Western Maryland, or just enjoying the simple pleasure of a
quiet chat on a porch swing.

An oasis is provided for children who might otherwise
buckle under the pressures of city living, and relationships
are forged that endure time and distance.

God provides just such respites for me, refreshing oases
within the ongoing atmosphere of chronic illness. He calls
me out of pain into tranquil, verdant pastures and away
from fear to lie beside cool, calm water. Knowing my soul
will become weary from illness, He prepares a place for me
to find restoration. In Him, refreshment is always available.

Tender Shepherd, like a sheep, I often wander away
from the real refreshment I can find in You. I'm
easily distracted by false promises of rest and relief,
only to find they are mirages, not true oases. Today
I will head toward You.   ☙

Even though I walk through the valley of the shadow
of death, I will fear no evil, for you are with me.
Psalm 23:4

Sheep ranchers are familiar with animals becoming "cast,"
turned over on their backs, unable to get up again. It can
happen to any sheep, but more often to those whose heavy
fleece, weight, or pregnancy change their bodies' center of
gravity. Once cast, a sheep will flail about in fear and frustration, trying to right itself again. But struggling only
causes body gases to build up and cut off blood circulation.

Buzzards, vultures, and other predators spread a shadow
of death over the defenseless animal. No matter how hard
it tries, without the shepherd's intervention, the sheep cannot pull itself up. The situation is hopeless.

As long as the shepherd is nearby, however, looking out
for every wayward sheep and curious little lamb, no animal has anything to fear. The shepherd will search for his
sheep and set each one upright again.

Lord Jesus, the shadows of illness circle me every
day, and I often feel paralyzed by them. My soul
becomes cast down by fear and anxiety, by hopelessness and pain. Come to me in my darkest valley
and lift my spirit today.   ✿

Your rod and your staff, they comfort me.   *Psalm* 23:4

The Christian life is laden with paradox, or seeming contradictions. One of the most mysterious is that when I am comfortable I do not grow, and, paradoxically, discomfort or illness can bring the most growth and freedom. I can lose everything I believe necessary to happiness, including my physical health, and find that which is truly necessary—God Himself.

But, in the interest of comfort and absence of pain, I am prone to resist and even deny these opportunity-filled difficulties. Eugene Peterson maintains that suffering need not push me off the edge of a life that feels out of control, but rather toward the center of life and God. "The aim of the person of faith," he writes, "is not to be as comfortable as possible but to live as deeply and thoroughly as possible—to deal with the reality of life, discover truth, create beauty, act out love."

In David's day, a shepherd used the same rod that controlled his sheep to defend the vulnerable flock. The same staff that held them back when they wanted to run off was used to rescue lambs stuck on a mountain ledge or trapped in a gully. Even in paradox, I can find comfort.

Lord, there's so much I don't understand. I wake up sick and think that if You really loved me, You'd get me out of this. Help me to accept the paradoxes of life today and find in them truth, beauty, and love. ☙

AUGUST 14   *Never Alone*

And there were shepherds living out in the fields
nearby, keeping watch over their flocks at night.
Luke 2:8

Nighttime can be the loneliest part of any twenty-four
hours. For those who are chronically ill, it may be physically painful as well. And the combination can be especially tormenting. If I awake in pain, I can't always count on
television to distract me or lull me back to sleep. There
may not be anyone else around to keep me company, and if
there is I may do my best not to wake them, too.

With pain and sleeplessness as my only companions,
the night may be when I feel most alone. But feeling isn't
always believing. In Jesus' day, well-tended sheep were
never left alone to face wolves or thieves or attacks of pain
in the night. Shepherds took turns staying awake and
guarding the flock, or even nursing a small or sick lamb
through the dark, lonely evening.

While earth's shepherds watched their flocks, a Heavenly Shepherd entered the world to care for His sheep.
He came at night, assuring me of continued companionship even in the longest, darkest hours.

O sympathetic Shepherd, thank You for being my
companion and my friend. Today I will consider
Your ever-faithful and comforting presence.
Tonight I will sleep soundly in You.   ✣

He causes his sun to rise on the evil and the good,
and sends rain on the righteous and the unrighteous.
Matthew 5:45

A former "Army brat," who attended base elementary schools, Carol remembers watching films of concentration camps and becoming fascinated by the evil of which man is capable.

When she was older and learned of the necessity of Christ's sacrifice on her behalf, it all made perfect sense to her. "Basically, I don't trust mankind," she says. "But I do trust God and man together. Some pretty exciting things can happen." Philosophically, she adds, "I figure if we miss stuff like being in a concentration camp in this life, we're pretty lucky. I'm genuinely surprised—and deeply grateful to God—when nice things happen."

It was this depth of understanding and acceptance that carried Carol through the shock of being told her health problem had a name, Ménière's disease, and that it would not be going away. Yes, she gets discouraged. But the blinding rage or nagging doubt and despair that many chronically ill people experience were not an issue with Carol. She tends to spend more energy expressing prayerful gratitude for the many good things in her life.

I confess, Lord, that, even though both exist in
Your world, I am more inclined to see the negative
than I am to look for the positive. Teach me the
secret of a happy, grateful heart. Today I will
examine my life for reasons to thank You. 🐦

AUGUST 16   🐦   *Penetrating Words*

The unfolding of your words gives light; it gives
understanding to the simple.   *Psalm 119:130*

In *My Friend, the Bible*, John Sherrill's personal account of
his deepening trust in the power of Scripture, he writes,
"Every problem we face can take us one step away from
God, or one step closer." He relates his fear that cancer had
returned to his body and how that fear kept him from hearing the words of the Bible. He read them, but nothing pen-
etrated because he was afraid to listen. When he finally did,
the comfort and understanding he sought was there in a
book that is alive and dynamic, continually unfolding.

Being ill can make me feel downright simple at times,
out of touch with sophisticated people around me. But God
says He will give me understanding when I open, or un-
fold, His words. The Bible addresses me and what I am experiencing right now, today. It will continue to speak each
day that I open it—thereby opening myself to its penetration and power.

Wise and wonderful God, penetrate my life and my
body with Your very being. Create in me a craving
to read and study and learn more of You through
the Scriptures today. Thank You for giving me a
Word that is alive, vital, and constantly new.   🐦

> Surely he took up our infirmities and carried our
> sorrows, yet we considered him stricken by God. . . .
> But he was pierced for our transgressions . . . and by
> his wounds we are healed.   *Isaiah 53:4–5*

Chronically ill Christians and Vietnam veterans have much in common. Just as many U.S. citizens were embarrassed by homecoming vets during the 1960s and '70s, many in the Church today are embarrassed by the presence of Christians who continue to suffer.

America resented being reminded of an "inhumane" war. The Church doesn't want to be reminded that God cannot be controlled and many people are not healed. Some vets were ignored out of ignorance and self-righteous horror. Some Christians don't want to be reminded of seemingly unanswered prayers, deepening doubts, and acute disappointment.

Consequently, they may ignore me and others who are ill among them. Then I may doubt myself and God and feel like an outcast for being sick. "At such a time," writes Jack Hayford, a minister who believes in the miraculous healing power of God, "wisdom doesn't wrestle; it learns to rest. . . . Faith's focus isn't ultimately upon its productivity, but upon its Source—God Himself."

Merciful God, I am reminded that people thought even Jesus was being punished by You. I am reminded that my sin is forgiven and my body will one day be whole. I am reminded that my wounded soul can experience healing today and be a living reminder of Your love.   🐦

> But you are a chosen people, a royal priesthood, a
> holy nation, a people belonging to God, that you
> may declare the praises of him who called you out of
> darkness into his wonderful light.   *1 Peter 2:9*

It was a fairy-tale wedding. Miss Diana Spencer disappeared into the Gothic cathedral, and Diana, Princess of Wales, emerged. A horse-drawn carriage transported the prince and his bride to their palace, where they stepped out onto a balcony and kissed for all to see. Every schoolgirl, and not a few of their mothers, dreamed about what it would be like to live as a royal princess. But this prince was mortal, and it wasn't long before life in the royal palace began to sour for Princess Diana.

In God's kingdom, "every little girl is a princess," insists Christian author George MacDonald, "the daughter of a king." I am indeed descended from Royalty—the King of Kings. His Son, the Prince of Peace, chose me and lifted me out of the darkness of common living into the light of life. Nothing—no hurt from the past, no sin of the present, no illness of the future—will keep His love from me.

And, because I am chosen, I can serve Him and others out of the depths of His love for me.

> I love You, Lord. Today I will honor You and
> declare Your praises. Your love for me fills me to
> overflowing and makes me feel just like the royal
> servant I am.   ☞

Who will bring any charge against those whom God
has chosen? It is God who justifies.   *Romans 8:33*

"Do you want to trade this trip for the rest of your summer?"

Nancy's husband was referring to an upcoming week at
the beach with her Sunday school class. They both knew
from previous experience that the unairconditioned facili-
ties where the group would be staying would not bode well
for her asthma. Although Nancy didn't want to miss out on
the fun, or disappoint her friends in the class, she decided
not to go.

That weekend, when Nancy's husband and son went
camping, she threw herself into nonstop chores around the
house. She planted and weeded, shopped and cleaned, all
the while chasing after her four-year-old. By Saturday night
Nancy was exhausted and wheezing. Not until she was
forced to go to bed did she begin to think about her fren-
zied behavior. "Am I somehow trying to justify my existence," she thought, "if not to God, then to myself? Am I
trying to make up for my inability to go to the beach?"

In this case, self-justification means denying reality and
acting *just as if* I'm not sick. Or acting *just as if* God's justifi-
cation is not enough. But God brings no charge against me.
It is His love that forgives my inabilities.

God, forgive me for usurping Your place and
setting myself up as the one who justifies. Today
I will resist the urge to try to prove myself to
anybody, least of all to You.   🐦

There, by the Ahava Canal, I proclaimed a fast, so
that we might humble ourselves before our God and
ask him for a safe journey for us and our children, . . .
and he answered our prayer.   *Ezra 8:21, 23*

A newspaper article highlighted ways arthritis sufferers
could make travel more pleasant by advance planning. Aspects included being realistic and flexible, locating appropriate transportation and hotel accommodations, and
choosing the right travel insurance and travel agents.
"Begin a trip or outing well rested," was the first tip. The article continued with suggestions for preventing joint stiff-
ness and fatigue, for getting help when needed, and for
sensible packing and luggage handling.

My journey through life with illness can be similarly
planned, by following Ezra's example. As they began their
return to Jerusalem from bondage, his company stopped to
pray. Ezra "knows the way is long and lonely. Dangers
abound," comments preacher H. A. Ironside. "A safe con-
voy is surely needed, and where shall such be found but in
the living God?"

I can appeal to my heavenly Travel Agent in advance
and depend on Him to see me safely through whatever
may lie ahead.

I don't want to be caught, O living God, without
having talked to You about my plans in advance.
Perhaps the biggest danger I face is losing touch
with You as I travel. Today I will look to You,
inviting You to guide and protect me.   ৯

For we do not have a high priest who is unable to sympathize with our weaknesses, but we have one who has been tempted in every way, just as we are— yet was without sin. Let us then approach the throne of grace with confidence, so that we may receive mercy and find grace to help us in our time of need.
Hebrews 4:15–16

"Come on back," the nurse said. "She's awake." I followed her through the familiar odor of sodium pentathol and stood over my fifteen-year-old daughter, seeing instead a helpless infant. "I woke up and didn't know where I was," Aura said plaintively as one large tear slid down a blood-stained cheek. Several procedures had been performed, and the two impacted wisdom teeth were out.

My voice was strong as I talked softly, reassuring Aura she was safe. But the antiseptic smells and the sight of my child's bloody, swollen face were getting to me. I began to feel lightheaded and strangely sick as I reached for a stool. Memories of my own oral surgery, waking up in the same position with the same eerie feelings, spun around me. The idea of someone I had spent my life protecting going through that same pain and fear was almost more than I could bear.

Is this how Jesus feels? I thought, when He looks down on my suffering?

You do understand don't You, Lord? You've been through it all. You would no more leave me alone or refuse to comfort me than I would deny my child the same. Today I welcome Your mercy and grace. ☞

> If we had forgotten the name of our God or spread
> out our hands to a foreign god, would not God have
> discovered it, since he knows the secrets of the
> heart?. . . Redeem us because of your unfailing love.
> *Psalm 44:20–21, 26*

Living with a chronic illness is trying enough. But when
the person involved is in the public eye, those trials can be
greatly magnified. For more than fifteen years, comedian
Richard Pryor kept his multiple sclerosis a secret from the
press and all but his closest friends. When walking started
to become a problem for him, and it was apparent that
something was wrong, Pryor finally had to admit his actual condition to the world.

The same was true of former Mouseketeer Annette
Funicello, who went public about her multiple sclerosis
after five years of keeping it secret.

I may not want people to pity me or fuss over me. I may
fear that they won't understand the true nature of my illness. But I don't have to worry about keeping anything secret from God. I needn't fret about His reaction to any
aspect of my life. He knows everything about me. He expects me to be imperfect and He loves me unfailingly just
the way I am.

> O God, You Who know all the secrets of my heart,
> keep me from forgetting how wide is Your mercy
> and how deep is Your love. Save me from the temp-
> tation to try to fool You the same way I fool others.
> Today I will hold no secrets from You.   ☙

Now it is God who has made us for this very purpose
and has given us the Spirit as a deposit, guaranteeing
what is to come. . . . We live by faith, not by sight.
2 Corinthians 5:5, 7

A relaxing oceanfront vacation is only hours away from my
home. But to reach the beach, I must cross the four-mile-
long Chesapeake Bay Bridge, where I often feel apprehen-
sive. What if the structure collapses hundreds of feet above
the choppy salt water? What if I panic halfway across?

But I move ahead on my will, not my feelings. I can see
the massive expanse of wire cables, steel girders, and con-
crete pilings, and I trust it to keep me and millions of others from tumbling into the bay below. That is, I *think* I'm
putting my faith in what I see. In actuality, my faith lies in
the builders of the bridge, the professionals who designed
and constructed it. I'm putting my life into hands I've never
seen or touched.

God asks me to do the same thing with Him—to trust
Him Whom I've never seen to carry me safely and securely
over the deep and troubled waters of chronic illness. He
asks me to go on my will, not my feelings—to move ahead
into each day believing His unseen Spirit goes before me
structuring my life.

Lord, my faith falters more often than I like to
admit. I believe the sight of my diseased body more
than I have faith in the promise of Your power.
Hold on to me today, especially when I lose sight
of You.

I have been crucified with Christ and I no longer live,
but Christ lives in me. The life I live in the body, I
live by faith in the Son of God, who loved me and
gave himself for me.   *Galatians* 2:20

"You can't tell me what to do. I have my rights!" This state-
ment has become increasingly popular as the American ex-
periment in democracy moves well into its third hundred
years. The Declaration of Independence, which liberated
the colonies from the rule of the English monarchy, proclaims the right to "life, liberty, and the pursuit of happiness." The United States Constitution's Bill of Rights
guarantees freedom of worship, speech, and press and the
rights to petition the government and to a speedy trial by
jury, among others.

It can be difficult for Americans to understand the concept of having no rights with God. My life and my rights
were nailed to a cross at Calvary. I have no right to expect
anything from God, because all things are freely given;
otherwise, they would cease to be gifts. I have no real right
to expect happiness, liberty, or even life. I have, in fact, no
inalienable right to be healthy and free from pain and suffering. I am no longer my own. I belong to Jesus Christ.

Most Holy Son of God, thank You for the heavenly rights You gave up to restore my right to
approach God and to live in the faith of His love
for me. Empty me today of my desire for "rights"
and fill me instead with a longing to be Your
willing servant.   🔊

AUGUST 25   *Transformed*

Do not be conformed any longer to the pattern of
this world, but be transformed by the renewing of
your mind. Then you will be able to test and approve
what God's will is—his good, pleasing and perfect
will.   *Romans 12:2*

More so each year, it seems, the world is saying, "If it hurts,
take a pill. If it's unsightly, cut it off. If it disrupts my life,
get rid of it. If it eludes me, keep seeking an answer."

Going against the flow of popular opinion and modern
thought can lead to loneliness and misunderstanding. The
"mind transplant" God offers won't always make life easier,
but it will make it better. God doesn't ask me to transform
myself or to fight the tide alone, as transformation is not
my doing, but His.

My body has been transformed from healthy to sick
against my will, but God will not change my mind without my permission. Through the renewing, I can arrive at
a different level of understanding of God's desire for my
life. He can bring me to appreciate that His will is indeed
good for me, can be pleasing to me, and will be perfected
in me.

Lord Jesus, I consent to Your revitalization of my
intellect and powers of reasoning. Throughout the
process, help me to remember that it's not my body
You're changing, or my behavior or my feelings,
but my will. With it, I choose to worship You
today.   ❧

He has made everything beautiful in its time. He has also set eternity in the hearts of men; yet they cannot fathom what God has done from beginning to end.
Ecclesiastes 3:11

It must have been a hard-driving, time-conscious Type A personality who invented the fax machine, someone impatient waiting even for the mail.

I may become impatient waiting on God to make me better or happier or more comfortable. Surely I won't have to cancel my vacation plans, I may think, or, Surely I'll feel better by Easter, or, Surely God doesn't want me to go on like this much longer.

God, however, is not limited by the finiteness of time. Perhaps it's not so much my waiting on God as it is His waiting for me to catch up with Him.

During her encounter with tuberculosis and the ensuing struggle to try to pin God down, Catherine Marshall relates that she finally "hit bottom." "And there," she writes, "I met God at the place where He had been waiting for me all along; where I knew that I wanted Christ's presence in my life more than I wanted health. Never mind healing, I wanted to be certain that God wasn't dead, that Jesus Christ lived, that He was real, and that I had been received by Him."

O infinite and unfathomable God, You used Catherine Marshall's life, and I know You are using mine. Free me from this inner timetable that I might recognize the beauty of Your timing in my life. I will meditate on living today and eternity received by You.   🕭

As the rain and the snow come down from heaven,
and do not return to it without watering the earth . . .
so is my word that goes out from my mouth: It will
not return to me empty.   *Isaiah 55:10–11*

Country-gospel singer Dottie Rambo once had such intense chronic back pain that she sent a letter to all her friends asking them to "pray that if God is not going to heal me, that He will take me home." Over time, she underwent one back surgery after another. Her hips were fused, a rib was removed, and Dottie had to learn to walk all over again. "I was on enough medication to kill a three-hundred-pound man," she says.

Dottie still lives and works in pain. She has discovered, though, not just how to cope, but how to handle all of life in the midst of suffering by immersing herself in the Word of God.

No matter where I may be on the scale of discouragement, I can always depend on God to know the precise Words with which to water my parched spirit. When I bury His Word in my heart, it will bubble up just when I need the comfort, the grace, or the power. The written utterances of Almighty God are life to Dottie Rambo just as they can be to me.

Say the Word, Lord, and I am lifted. Say the Word
and I am comforted. Say the Word and I am
empowered to meet another day. Today, Lord God,
I will store Your living, flourishing Word in my
heart that I may have life in You.   ❧

When a king's face brightens, it means life; his favor is
like a rain cloud in spring.   *Proverbs 16:15*

Being a lupus patient means Jackie is especially sensitive to
the weather. Extremes in temperature, humidity, or baro-
metric pressure make it difficult or impossible for her to
function. The sun itself is a singular enemy. Exposure to
sunlight causes a reaction in lupus sufferers, usually a facial
rash. Jackie must always wear sunscreen and stay out of ul-
traviolet rays whenever possible. She even had her car windows tinted. And picking blueberries in the shade for just
an hour causes her face to break out the next day. Consequently, Jackie welcomes cloudy days. Clouds mean she
can be outdoors and move around more freely.

For many other people, cloudy days may be unpleasant.
But God uses sun, rain, clouds, cold, heat, storms, and darkness of night. He brings all kinds of weather into my life
at just the right hour for my optimum growth. And when
cloudy weather rolls in, it just may hold the freedom I need
to relax and be refreshed in Him.

My Lord and my King, Your favor brightens my
day and means life to me. Thank You for tending to
all my needs in every kind of weather. Today Your
face shining on me will be all the sun I need.   ☞

> There is a time for everything, . . . a time to weep and a time to laugh. *Ecclesiastes 3:1, 4*

"Laugh and the world laughs with you; / Weep, and you weep alone." These words of Ella Wheeler Wilcox are more than a hundred years old, but they're still relevant for Christians today. Even though the Bible says tears are normal and to be expected, many followers of the empathic Christ don't want to weep with those who suffer. A friend's pain may be a reminder of something that needs attention in one's own life. Just like the world, the Church may laugh with me, but disappoint me and leave me alone in my time of tears, whether I'm weeping out of pain, out of joy, or out of awe.

Jesus Himself never renounces His love for me. He's in for the long haul, the good times and the bad. Not only does He weep with me, He may even provoke tears, knowing that they can cleanse and heal. He wants it all—my laughter and my tears, my joy and my pain, my gladness and my sadness.

Laugh, and Jesus laughs with me. Weep, and . . . Jesus weeps with me, too.

Thank You, Jesus, for the release that tears bring. Thank You for entering into my world today, for walking through life with me and feeling what I feel. Help me to be the same for others, free to laugh and weep at all the right times. ꙮ

But the more they were oppressed, the more they
multiplied and spread.   *Exodus 1:12*

Just as in the days of the ancient Hebrews, oppression is
still a vehicle for growth today. Under the cruel dictator-
ship of Idi Amin, citizens of the African nation of Uganda
converted to Christianity in record numbers. Since everything else was stripped from them, their only hope was in
Jesus Christ. People walked for days just to sit on the
ground outside an overcrowded mud hut church and listen
to forbidden Bible teaching. Hundreds of thousands of
Ugandans lived in the terror of physical and political oppression, only to experience a spiritual freedom they never
knew was possible.

Am I allowing my suffering in illness to bring me closer
to God and to others? Or is mine the habit of pulling away
from God, and from others, when bad things happen?
Maybe I'm waiting for God to heal me, and *then* things will
be better between us.

But not all healing is physical. My circumstances or my
body may turn on me, but God is always for me. My illness
can be an opportunity to have a depth of fellowship with
God I may have never before imagined.

God in heaven and God of the earth, there are
days I feel tyrannized by this illness. It surrounds
me and oppresses me, body and soul. Thank You
that in Christ my spirit is unfettered today, ever
free.   🌿

I pray that you, being rooted and established in love, may have power, together with all the saints, to grasp how wide and long and high and deep is the love of Christ. *Ephesians 3:17–18*

"When things happen to us which disappoint us," writes Peter G. van Breemen, "we are inclined to complain 'How can God permit this?' We begin to doubt the love of God. It takes courage to believe in God's acceptance no matter what happens to us. . . . God's love is infinite. We can never grasp it, never get hold of it, much less control it. The only thing we can do is jump into its bottomless depth. And we do not like to jump. We are afraid to let go."

I saw it on a T-shirt: "Because I'm the Mommy, that's why." In the family hierarchy, a child may respond with a defiant, "You just don't love me!" But mature wisdom tells us that Mom does indeed love the child and that is why she stops him from playing in the middle of a busy street or prevents her from socializing at the corner bar.

No matter how unfair my life's circumstances may look or feel, I can be sure that God is watching out for me, and in His merciful control saying, "I love you, child."

Most holy God, knowing that I can never fully comprehend the extent of Your providential love, I bow to Your judgment today. I bow, though, when what I really want to do is jump. Please melt my fear of being loved and help me let go and take the plunge.

> In the land of Uz there lived a man whose name was
> Job. . . . The Lord said . . . "There is no one on earth
> like him; he is blameless and upright, a man who fears
> God and shuns evil."   *Job 1:1, 8*

Growing up with an overly critical and dictatorial father
caused me to strive for perfection in everything I did.
Achieving excellence, I reasoned, would keep me safe from
criticism. As a young homemaker, I fussed over the house
and food for dinner guests, always using our best wedding
china and silver. I thought I wanted to make others feel
special. I know now I was also attempting to protect myself
from fault-finders.

A friend once told a mutual acquaintance that her family would be visiting us for dinner. "Well, good luck!" came
the snide reply. For this acquaintance, I was too perfect.

I learned then that there's no such thing as perfect, that
there would always be something about me some people
could criticize.

Nobody living today is perfect. On accepting that fact,
I may think God is punishing me through illness. But Job
was totally blameless, undeserving of all that was about to
happen to him, and he suffered. Job neither caused nor de-
served tragedy and illness.

> O perfect God, unlike Job I am neither upright
> nor blameless. But You are neither critical nor
> dictatorial. Free me from the fear that I have done
> something to cause You to strike me with illness.
> Today I accept myself as the work of Your gentle,
> loving hands.   🐾

"Does Job fear God for nothing?" Satan
replied. . . ."Stretch out your hand and strike
everything he has, and he will surely curse you to
your face." *Job 1:9, 11*

Job's life had been proceeding splendidly until Satan entered it. "What would happen," Satan taunted God, "if your perfect servant Job's happy circumstances came to an end? Let me make him miserable and see what he does then."

Satan is like a kindergarten bully. One child plays quietly, building a block tower, until suddenly his peaceful play is violently interrupted. The bully, intent on destruction, comes out of nowhere gleefully kicking over the carefully built tower, spilling blocks everywhere. Ultimately, the teacher will help pick up toys, dry tears, and restore order in the classroom. Play has been only temporarily short-circuited.

In the spiritual realm, God controls evil. Satan does exist and he can frustrate my life with illness, but he has no authority to destroy me.

"We underestimate God and we overestimate evil," writes Eugene Peterson. "We don't see what God is doing and conclude that he is doing nothing. We see everything that evil is doing and think it is in control."

Thank You, Almighty God, for reminding me that
Satan's power to wound is limited. Instill in me
today the peace that comes from knowing Who's
really in charge. 🜉

Then he fell to the ground in worship and said. . .
"The Lord gave and the Lord has taken away; may
the name of the Lord be praised."   *Job 1:20–21*

Job's seven handsome sons and three beloved daughters
were swept up and killed in a tornado. All his considerable
wealth disappeared within one twenty-four-hour period.
Not only were his means for today stripped away, but so
was his hope for the future—his family. Suddenly and
without warning Job possessed nothing.

Did he drink himself into oblivion? Lose himself in trying to build another fortune? No, Job fell to the ground and
worshiped God! Certainly Job responded out of the shock
of grief, but could his faith also have been on autopilot,
programmed out of habit and tradition? His life had been
lived following religious rituals. Perhaps Job's first response
to this overwhelming tragedy was to do the expected religious thing. Perhaps he didn't feel the inner permission to
get angry or question God. Perhaps Job was relating to
God with his head and not his heart.

God always wants to hear my honest and heartfelt responses to life's difficulties. He can take it.

O God, You know my heart and You love me
anyway. Forgive me for trying to deny or suppress
"unacceptable" responses to my illness. Today I
fully give You my suffering and my heart and all
that is in it.   ✶

"Skin for skin!" Satan replied. "A man will give all he has for his own life. But stretch out your hand and strike his flesh and bones, and he will surely curse you to your face." *Job 2:4–5*

Flesh and bones, there's the crux of the matter. If all Job's other troubles didn't do him in, surely never-ending illness would.

Job apparently withstood the first of Satan's challenges. "Now let's see what he's really made of," Satan sneered. God gave the go-ahead for Job's body to be attacked, but not so severely as to kill him. Soon Job was covered with open sores. Swollen and unrecognizable, he was tormented by nightmares, sleeplessness, and depression. His blackened, feverish skin, covered with maggots, peeled right off.

Did Job ever wish Satan would just finish the job? I have endured headaches so bad I didn't care how many drugs I took—or in what frequency or combination—so long as they ended the intolerable pain. If the drugs killed me, at least the torture would be over.

Thankfully, I'm still here. And, thankfully, we have Job as what Henry Gariepy calls, in his book of the same name, a portrait of perseverance.

How grateful I am, Lord, that today I can rely on You to provide me with all I need to persevere through physical pain and spiritual drought. Save me from muttering curses under my breath. 🜪

He replied, "You are talking like a foolish woman.
Shall we accept good from God, and not trouble?"
Job 2:10

"Curse God and die!" Job's wife seemingly turned against him. Has this woman been maligned over the years? She lost everything, too, and had to watch her beloved husband suffer and writhe in overwhelming misery. Her suggestion may be the first hint of sanctioned suicide in the Bible. But Job was not comforted. He philosophically reasoned that illness and trouble are no respecters of persons. Suffering is part of the human condition and common to all, just as all are bound by natural laws like gravity.

When handed a brightly wrapped present, I excitedly accept it. Wordlessly, I'm saying, "I'll take it." Job responded to God's offerings, invitingly wrapped or not, with "I'll take it, God." Job knew the Giver and felt safe in accepting the gift.

Having been widowed several times, Christian writer Elisabeth Elliot knows about loss. "Resignation," she says, "is surrender to fate. Acceptance is surrender to God."

Dear God, I don't always welcome Your gifts. The festively wrapped ones are easier to accept than others. Keep me from resignation today as I surrender myself and my illness into Your care. ❧

> When Job's three friends . . . heard about all the
> troubles that had come upon him, they set out from
> their homes and met together by agreement to go
> and sympathize with him and comfort him.   *Job 2:11*

"Nobody knows the trouble I've seen. Nobody knows my sorrow," are the familiar words of a spiritual.

Job's friends heard about his troubles and hurried to his side. In stunned silence, they sat with him in an ash pile for an entire week. They even tore their clothes and rubbed dirt into their hair. But these symbolic gestures could never equal what Job himself was experiencing. Identification with another's suffering can never be total.

Garfield, the self-indulgent cartoon cat, when confronted with his owner's stubbed toe, uncharacteristically comforts Jon and is thanked in return for caring. Walking away, Garfield shrugs, "Hey, it's not like it happened to me."

There is Someone, though, Who knows the trouble I've seen, Who knows my sorrow. He knows the name of my illness and experiences every one of its symptoms. With Jesus Christ, it is like it happened to Him.

Others can only sympathize with me in illness, but
You, O empathic God, put Yourself in my place
and into my body. Today I thank You for the pure
friendship that comes out of shared suffering.   🐾

> After this, Job opened his mouth and cursed the day
> of his birth. . . ."What I feared has come upon me;
> what I dreaded has happened to me." *Job 3:1, 25*

All that he loved and valued had vanished, and his wife was in total despair. Job suffered constant physical pain, and his closest friends said nothing for seven days. Unable to bear it any longer, Job finally spoke.

What came out of his mouth then? Did worship rise to the heavens? There was nothing wrong with Job's eyesight, and he saw his friends' healthy bodies. He knew they would return to intact families and tents. When he'd been healthy, Job had withstood suffering and praised God. It's the physical pain that wore him down and out.

Job asked why five times here, calling himself "bitter of soul." Angry at God and at himself, Job experienced what he had feared. He used to offer burnt sacrifices each morning for his children, lest they "curse God in their hearts" (Job 1:5). Now it is he who curses God. Job knew what Jesus later said, that out of the heart come the things that destroy relationships (Mark 7:21).

Fortunately for Job, and for me, God is in the business of healing hearts and restoring relationships.

Lord, it's easy to be bitter when all I see in my future is more illness. I'm scared, though, that bitterness will sabotage my relationship with You. Today I choose to keep in mind that even cursing God was paid for on the cross. ✍

Showing Mercy

Then Eliphaz the Temanite replied . . . "Consider now:
Who, being innocent, has ever perished? . . . As I have
observed, those who plow evil and those who sow
trouble reap it." *Job 4:1, 7–8*

"We hand folks over to God's mercy," wrote George Eliot,
"and show none ourselves."

In contemporary terms, Job's three friends were his support group. They were from Edom, an area known for the
wisdom of its people. Perhaps this reputation swelled their
heads. First, Eliphaz told Job that the innocent do not suffer, that Job must have done something to bring disaster on
himself. He went so far as to say he had a vision in which
God told him Job was being disciplined for sinning. That's
as cruel as telling a woman who's just miscarried that God
is punishing her for the abortion she underwent at fifteen.

Eliphaz continued with, "If I were you, this is what I
would do. . . ." This type of religious talk has been dubbed
"toxic faith." It can be, and often is, lethal. Having an illness
that never goes away can bring me into contact with counselors just as well-meaning and misguided as Eliphaz. Their
message is only toxic, though, if I allow it to seep into my
soul.

O just and merciful God, give me the courage to
guard my soul today from that which pollutes Your
words of love and hope. Keep me from the guilt of
adding to another's pain in Your name. I want to
share the mercy You show me.

Then Bildad the Shuite replied:". . . Ask the former generations and find out what their fathers learned. . . . Surely God does not reject a blameless man."
Job 8:1, 8, 20

Prosperity theology teaches that if I do what God wants, then God not only will but must reward me. Health and wealth are within my reach so long as I follow a divine formula. A vibrant relationship with God, allowing for the free choices of created beings and the existence of unseen forces, is reduced to a formula. If I'm sick or poor, then I have failed to follow the proper procedure. No room is left for the possibility that God is either more than or different from what was factored into the equation.

Job's friends missed this opportunity to stretch their concept of God. They were bound by the teachings of former generations. If a man such as Job, "the greatest man among all the people of the East" (Job 1:3), blameless before God, could end up like this, then their whole religious system was in trouble. They chose to diminish Job rather than expand God. Even today, an ongoing, unhealed disease still raises many questions.

And still today the God of Creation rejects no man or woman, no matter his or her failing or weakness.

I'm so glad that You, O God, are too large to fit into neat man-made boxes and that my questions neither threaten nor contain you. Today I will consider no question too hard to ask.

Then Zophar the Naamathite replied ". . . If you put
away the sin that is in your hand and allow no evil
to dwell in your tent, then you will lift up your face
without shame; you will stand firm and without fear."
Job 11:1, 13–15

Once again, one of Job's friends deigns to speak for God.
Zophar thinks Job just isn't getting it and calls him a
phony: "If you were truly upright as you claim, all this
never would have happened to you." So far all the discus-
sion has centered on what may have caused Job's unfortu-
nate state of affairs.

In *When Bad Things Happen to Good People*, Rabbi Harold
Kushner makes this point: "The question we should be asking is not 'Where does the tragedy come from?' but 'Where
does it lead?' "

I can fume and fuss, trying to explain the hows and
whys of my illness, but that only sends me into cerebral
overdrive. There are so many different voices vying for a
hearing inside my head, especially if I know people like
Job's friends. I need to be able to differentiate among the
voices, to recognize the voice of God when I hear it.
Throughout all this, God had been listening to and loving
Job, consoling him through silence.

Most holy God, thank You that through Jesus Christ
I can lift up my face without shame today. That I can
stand firm and without fear in Your presence today.
Thank You for the silent voice in the midst of illness
that leads me into Your arms.   ✍

If only there were someone to arbitrate between us, to lay his hand upon us both, someone to remove God's rod from me, so that his terror would frighten me no more.   *Job 9:33*

Job felt totally alone. In many ways his wife and friends had reinforced his sense of estrangement from God. Maybe they're right, he thought. Maybe he was guilty of some unknown sin because his appeals to God weren't getting anywhere. He cried out for someone, anyone, to bridge the apparent chasm between him and God's favor. Job wanted an arbitrator, someone else who could make the connection that eluded him.

Job couldn't look into the future and see Jesus Christ. He felt abandoned in his despair. But I can look back to the cross and the finished work of Christ. I can be comforted today by God's presence through His Spirit. And I can see ahead to the final redemption when illness will be exchanged for glory.

Billy Graham has preached that as Jesus hung on the cross, both arms outstretched, one hand firmly held the hand of God. With His other hand, Jesus reaches out to me. The connection has been made. Daily and eternal access to God are mine.

O righteous God, I admit I am often frightened by the thought of Your holiness compared to my sinfulness. Thank You for Jesus, the Bridge between us, Who dissolves my fear and redeems my illness. Today I will take hold of His hand.   ❧

Does it please you to oppress me, to spurn the work of your hands, while you smile on the schemes of the wicked? Do you have eyes of flesh? Do you see as a mortal sees? Are your days like those of a mortal?
Job 10:3–5

Job thought he knew God and understood God's ways. But his physical and emotional pain gave birth to the most severe of all traumas, spiritual agony.

"Who are You, God!?" Job cried in his torment. Certain he has not sinned against God, Job could not explain his situation. He related to God as if they shared a business interest. "I've kept my end of the bargain, God," Job argued. "I've been perfectly obedient. Why haven't You held up Your end?" Job presents God with question after question, without realizing he is the one being tested. At this point, Job would rather have died (Job 10:18) than examine himself.

Socrates said that the unexamined life is not worth living. It's possible that, like Job, I spend far too much energy examining God and not enough looking inside myself. Each day I live with illness, though, makes it increasingly difficult to ignore the issue of self-examination, even though I need not fear it. For God already knows what's in my heart and loves me anyway.

O God, forgive my superficiality which can slowly lead to spiritual arrogance. You are God; I am not. Today I will take a good look at our relationship and not fear being known by You.   *&*

You are worthless physicians, all of you!   *Job 13:4*

All Job could see in the future was more adversity, and his friends didn't disappoint him in that regard. Professor and author Robert Veninga believes that "friendships have an immense power to heal a broken spirit." The converse is also true: Friendships can kill a broken spirit.

"Sticks and stones," they say, "may break my bones, but words can never hurt me." The truth is, though, that words can hurt. In some ways words are more effective at wounding than stones or sticks.

God made it clear from the beginning: Job had nothing to be chastised for. He was blameless. No matter what my illness, no matter what my friends may say, no matter how much discomfort I endure, no matter how long my illness lasts, I, too, stand blameless before God. Jesus Christ is the greatest of all Physicians and the closest of all Friends. Through Him I am declared the righteousness of God. It is in those words of friendship that I can find healing.

O great and glorious Physician, today I will not allow my broken body to break my spirit as well. I will feed my friendship with You. Teach me to speak only words that carry hope and healing.

Though he slay me, yet will I hope in him.   *Job 13:15*

A child hopes for a bike for his birthday. A young woman stores her dreams in a hope chest. In Scripture, hope refers to a sure thing, something I can rely on. I can be confident that that in which I place my hope will indeed appear.

Job's hope was his confidence that a trustworthy God was in control, no matter what the future held. Finally, Job came to what must have felt like the end of himself. He left his friends and their concepts of God behind, along with his own vented anger and bitterness. When Job had nothing left that he could do, he collapsed into God's grace.

My illness can increase my hope because it forces me to stretch my faith. Hope won't erase illness, but it can change my reaction to it.

"It's not what happens that matters," said the famed stress researcher, Hans Selye, "but how you take it." The nurse of a dying AIDS patient quotes him as saying, "I would gladly choose AIDS again if it meant getting to know Jesus Christ."

Dear Jesus, You are my Hope. Thank You that I can have confidence in You, not wishes and dreams, no matter what my illness holds for today.   🐦

If a man dies, will he live again? All the days of my
hard service I will wait for my renewal to come.
Job 14:14

Job had been thinking about dying. Now he wanted to
know what happens after death. Job dared to hope for
more than the common belief of the time, that life ends
with death. He was still patiently hoping in God. While his
friends were mired in tradition, Job chose to think maybe,
just maybe, what he believed then would not necessarily
define what he would believe forever. What if, Job
thought, God is bigger than we have dared to imagine?
Job's life had changed. Was his God adequate to accom-
modating this change? More importantly, would Job accept a God Who existed beyond the limits of religious
explanation?

Chronic illness can feel like a living death. Will I ever
truly live and enjoy all God offers again?

American statesman William Jennings Bryan wrote, "If
the Father deigns to touch with divine power the cold and
pulseless heart of the buried acorn and make it burst forth
from its prison walls, will He leave neglected in the earth
the soul of a man made in the image of his Creator?"

O gracious God and heavenly Father, thank You
that I don't have to wonder about eternity like Job.
Today I will consider the words of the One Who
has secured all my tomorrows: "Whoever lives and
believes in me will never die."   🐼

Where then is my hope? Who can see any hope for me?   *Job 17:15*

The patience of Job is commonly misunderstood to mean that Job meekly accepted all that came his way. The truth is that Job accepted nothing without a fight. He experienced depression, suicidal fantasies, rages at God, and seductive temptations to call it quits.

Throughout it all, though, Job did not give up. He retained a patient hope that his friends did not have. They chose not to go in search of the real God, the One it takes time and suffering to get to know. Much like his ancestor Jacob (Gen. 32), Job wrestled with God and wasn't about to let go until God in His fullness satisfied his soul.

In the subtitle of her book, *Living With Chronic Illness*, Cheri Register refers to life with illness as "days of patience and passion." Job allowed his own passionate feelings expression, patiently hoping in God to be larger than anything he might think or feel.

Henry Gariepy writes, "Life with Christ is an endless hope; without Him, a hopeless end."

O Lord, how grateful I am for the unshakable confidence that is mine today in Christ Jesus, in Whom I patiently hope.   🐦

I know that my Redeemer lives, and that in the end
he will stand upon the earth. And after my skin has
been destroyed, yet in my flesh I will see God. . . .
How my heart yearns within me! *Job 19:25–27*

Poet and translator Stephen Mitchell describes Job this
way: "He has faced evil, looked straight into its face and
through it, into a vast wonder and love."

Job had crossed over the bridge. The mediator he
sought had been made known to him. But how? Spirituality
isn't taught; it's caught. Just as parents pass values on to
their children by example, so God can be known only
through time spent in His presence. Job had been on a
quest for the center of the One, True God, and with Him
diligence does not go forever unrewarded.

In the face of evidence to the contrary, Job continued to
go against religious teachings and his own narrow view of
God. He came to desire God Himself and all that knowing Him might bring. Job's misery made it impossible for
his faith to remain stagnant. He found himself at the lowest
point of his life, the same point where he discovered his
greatest hope. It had been so all along, but Job had to find
that out. He had reached his point of no return.

O God, You always have something new for me.
Thank You for the anticipation I feel in Your
presence. Today my heart will look up in hope. ❦

If only I knew where to find him; if only I could go to his dwelling!   *Job 23:3*

"Who are You, God?" became "Where are You, God?" Job knew his Redeemer lived, but he couldn't make contact with Him. God was silent, and Job was suffering the most acute form of loneliness—separation from God. But he kept on asking and searching for a God who would make a difference in his life.

Job had been as penitent as he knew how and even managed to praise God at intervals during his suffering. Where was this Being to Whom he had given himself?

The emotional pain of loneliness is a sign, just as physical pain is, that something is missing or out of balance. Job was still not in right relationship with God.

In his torment, Job didn't know some of the things I can know. I know where my Redeemer dwells: He inhabits His Word; He resides in prayer; and He occupies my heart through His Spirit. He is never far away. If illness is preventing me from finding God, I may be like someone who keeps looking for eyeglasses that are perched on her head.

My Redeemer and my God, sometimes I can't find You. Teach me how to recognize Your loving presence. Today I will concentrate on believing that You are with me in everything I do.

How I long for the months gone by, for the days
when God watched over me, when his lamp shone
upon my head and by his light I walked through
darkness! Oh, for the days when I was in my prime.
Job 29:2–4

The good old days. For Job, they were the time he was
rich, respected, and righteous. "Those days are gone now,"
he mused, talking as if to fill the throbbing void created by
God's silence.

Job indulged in that great human pastime, self-pity.
Men who used to come to him for counsel now mocked
Job. He recalled the way things used to be and mourned.

Martin Luther said, "I have had many things placed in
my hands and I have lost them all; but whatever I have
placed in God's hands I still possess."

Could it be that Job, whose "many things" included a
spotless reputation before God and man, for all his religious busyness, had been reluctant to place his heart into
God's hands?

"The good old days" may mean "When my body was
healthy and whole" or "When my mind was quick and
clear" or "When God watched over me." With illness
looming daily, it's easy to forget that God is still paying attention to me, still taking care of me the way He always
has, still loving me.

God, I don't want to possess anything, even
memories, if it means forfeiting any part of my
relationship with You. Today my memories will be
of Your acts of faithfulness. ✒

And now my life ebbs away, days of suffering grip me. . . . I cry out to you, O God, but you do not answer. . . . I stand up in the assembly and cry for help.   *Job 30:16, 20, 28*

Job was coming to the end of his tether. He said things to God and learned things about himself he might never have said or learned had it not been for his tragedies. He exposed thoughts and feelings too scary to reveal before.

He confronted the question I face today: Who can I trust to see me without all my protective barriers? Job stood up in the assembly and cried for help. But, more than that, Job trusted God to see him as he truly was—alone and vulnerable.

Cheri Register comments on this type of vulnerability. "Illness offers a rare chance for intimacy," she writes, "an opportunity to examine the essential human fate you share without the patina of social convention."

Job saw his illness as a chance for intimacy with God, an opportunity to do away with layers of religious convention, an opportunity to drop anything that limited his access to God. Job's suffering simply allowed no room for playing games.

God of the real and the unreal, today I am ready to get real with You. I'm tired of feeling embarrassed in Your presence because I am weak. My own life is dying. Please fill me with Yours.   ☿

Surely no one lays a hand on a broken man when he
cries for help in his distress.   *Job* 30:24

No matter what Job had been through so far—family
tragedy beyond comprehension, financial ruin, an unsup-
portive spouse and friends, physical affliction—he continued to believe that his God was not only just, but
approachable and compassionate as well. Until he was told
otherwise from the mouth of God Himself, Job's faith
would remain in One Who hears and cares. After the ter-
rible shaking his life had taken, Job was barely hanging
on. With everything and everybody else gone, all he had
to hang on to was God Himself. He simply could not believe that the God he knew would disappoint him.

"Faith like Job's cannot be shaken," wrote Rabbi Abraham Heschel. "Faith like Job's is the result of having been
shaken."

Being chronically ill means I have been shaken from the
security of my physical abilities and the good health I may
at one time have taken for granted. But God will not break
my spirit when He is all I have to hang on to. "A bruised
reed he will not break," said the prophet Isaiah (42:3).
God's hand of comfort is the only one He extends to me.

Lord, I flinch if another person raises a hand to me.
But I can always expect gentleness and healing
from Your offered hands. Help me to absorb more
deeply into my spirit today the immeasurable
depth and breadth of Your tender love.   ☙

Have I not wept for those in trouble? Has not my soul grieved for the poor? Yet when I hoped for good, evil came; when I looked for light, then came darkness.   *Job* 30:25–26

Job examined his life once again. He agreed with God's finding—no sin here. Still, he felt compelled to list all his moral and religious accomplishments. Long-held beliefs and traditions are difficult, often impossible, to break, and it had not yet completely sunk in for Job that although the source of all suffering is sin, not all suffering is related to specific acts of sin.

Since his trials began, Job's picture of God had grown tremendously, but that did not leave him immune to the very human feelings of guilt and self-doubt. This was Job's last stand. Without realizing it, Job stood on the threshold of entering into God's holy joy.

"Before joy is discovered," writes Robert Veninga in *A Gift of Hope*, "self-reproach must be surrendered." Job was almost ready to run up the white flag.

No matter how much my illness may stretch my faith, I will never outgrow God-given reactions to life, God, and myself.

Why is surrender to You so hard, God? Why can't I let go of wanting to be perfect in my own eyes? Please help me to receive Your unbounded love for me today.   ❧

So these men stopped answering Job, because he was
righteous in his own eyes.   *Job 32:1*

"Our sense of sin," said Thomas D. Bernard, "is in propor-
tion to our nearness to God." Job was drawing ever nearer
to God, beginning to feel the warm breath of God's holiness. Job's mind had not uncovered any broken laws or
unatoned-for sins, not even secret sins hidden in his unconscious. Job's head was clear, but his heart was on the
verge of melting. The spiritual seesaw he had been on was
beginning to balance itself.

Since Job had not yet come to the place where God
dwelled, he had not yet come to realize that existing in a
sinful world made him part of that world. His understanding had not yet grown to the point of accepting that a fish
in a pond can't help but be wet. Job wavered between questioning his own righteousness and affirming it.

This is the same balance that, as a chronically ill Christian, I may struggle to maintain—if I base my understanding of God on the fluctuating state of my health. But God
and His love for me never waver.

O holy God, the only righteousness I can claim is
that of Jesus Christ, Who lived and died yesterday
that I might know the inexpressible joy of Your
love in the midst of ongoing illness today.   🐦

God is greater than man. Why do you complain to him that he answers none of man's words? For God does speak—now one way, now another—though man may not perceive it.   *Job 33:12–14*

One person's perception may differ from another's. Two people may attend the same stage play and each come away having heard two different stories.

God is speaking to me today. Maybe not always in audible words, but He is here communicating with me nonetheless. It's possible I've decided that God will speak only through my complete and total physical healing. But, whether I acknowledge Him or not, He is speaking. Whether I hear Him or not, He continues trying to reach me. Whether I'm well or not, God is loving me.

Some days it may seem as if my illness is so loud that I can't hear above it, when actually God may be communicating with me through the pain. God speaks when all else is silent. He speaks through the hands of those who care for me and through written words. In the end, God's ultimate Word was sounded at Calvary, the place where illness and disease were absorbed into Himself.

Lord, please fine-tune my hearing today that I might fully perceive You with my heart and with my soul.

Men cry out under a load of oppression. . . . But no
one says, "Where is God my Maker, who gives songs
in the night. . . ?" *Job 35:9–10*

Enter Elihu. This is not the first question he used to chal-
lenge Job's view of God. He declared the magnitude of
God and continued to wear away at Job's ever-thinning ve-
neer of moral superiority. Elihu threw Job's own words back
at him. Remember when Job said essentially the same thing
to his wife?

God was using Elihu to prepare the ground of Job's
heart to hear and receive what He would soon have to say.
Job's own dark night of the soul would soon be over.

Joni Eareckson Tada writes, "We aren't always responsible for circumstances. . . . We are responsible for the way
we respond to them." That's my response-ability. However
intense my illness may be today, God gives me the ability
to respond to Him with songs in the dark, lonely nighttimes of illness. All songs aren't joyous; some are melan-
choly. God's songs are custom crafted. The one He com-
poses for me will be just the melody I need to proceed
through illness with a song in my heart.

O Master Musician, create in me today ears to hear
the music that plays its most beautiful of melodies
only in the night. Teach me to appropriate the
ability to respond in harmony with You. 🐖

But those who suffer he delivers in their suffering; he speaks to them in their affliction.   *Job 36:15*

If God delivers those who suffer, why am I still sick? Amy Carmichael, a turn-of-the-century missionary to India's poor, was bedridden for decades. She wrote, "Triumph is not deliverance *from*, but victory *in* trial" (italics added).

Perhaps the most visible contemporary example of deliverance while still in trial is Joni Eareckson Tada. A diving accident in 1967 left her a quadriplegic, paralyzed from the neck down. Twenty-five years later, Joni is still in a wheelchair and in need of constant care. But she is married, drives a car, runs a nonprofit organization, writes best-selling books, travels and speaks on behalf of the handicapped, and supports herself through the sale of her paintings and records.

Suffering cannot be avoided; my illness is with me every day. But it can be transcended, as Joni's has been. God will take my yielded pain and deliver me into a joy that is found only in Him.

My Rock and my Redeemer, thank You for the promise of freedom in You regardless of the circumstances of my illness. May I come to accept the truth of deliverance *in* instead of constantly looking for deliverance *from*.   ₮

How great is God—beyond our understanding!
Job 36:26

God is not accountable to us. He owes me no explanations for my illness. I may be made in the image of God, but that does not mean He is no more than a magnification of me. God is sovereign. He can do what He wants, how He wants, when He wants. But His sovereignty always includes loving identification with me, His created child.

In *Your God Is Too Small*, Bible translator J. B. Phillips writes, "The God who is responsible for the terrifying vastnesses of the Universe . . . [is] interested in the lives of the minute specks of consciousness which exist on this insignificant planet."

These could have been Job's words when God finally got through to him. Job felt utterly useless. He was disgusting to look at. He could produce nothing. His life was bereft of meaning and all he could think about was his own physical and psychic pain. Yet Almighty God took notice and tenderly cared for Job just as He does for me in spite of my inabilities—or maybe even because of them.

"Although Job almost gave up on God," writes theologian David L. McKenna, "God never gave up on him."

O God Who art higher than the heavens and wider than the seas, teach me the way of true humility today. ❖

Then the Lord answered Job out of the storm.
Job 38:1

Out of what storm did God answer Job: out of Job's diatribe, out of his inner turmoil? If God could reveal Himself out of the storm, then He must have been in it with Job to begin with.

God does not leave me alone in the storm of pain and disease. God does not always calm the storm; sometimes He calms me in the middle of it. He comes alongside of me, taking my hand in His, calming my spirit by the presence of His.

The English writer A. A. Milne has given joy to countless numbers of children and adults with his stories about a naive, lovable bear named Winnie the Pooh. Pooh Bear and his friends learn about life and its idiosyncrasies through their adventures and relationships with each other. One of Pooh's friends is Piglet, who one day approached Pooh from behind:

"Pooh!" he whispered.

"Yes, Piglet?"

"Nothing," said Piglet, taking Pooh's paw. "I just wanted to be sure of you."

Everlasting God, the act of placing my sick, trembling hand in Yours today fills me with tranquility of soul. I will spend my day focusing on how near You are to me, never any farther away than the length of my arm.   ⊁

Then Job replied to the Lord:. . . "Surely I spoke of things I did not understand. . . . My ears had heard of you but now my eyes have seen you." *Job 42:1, 3, 5*

One day my children wanted to know, "Mom, have you ever stolen anything?" "Yes," I answered honestly, after some thought. And I told them about an incident that happened decades ago. Today, though, it continues to come up in family conversations when it's to one of the kid's advantage to remind me of my reckless youth.

Can one be too honest in answering? I'm often like a kid with God, demanding He answer me. If God actually explained all the mysteries of the world, especially the mystery of pain, would I receive His answers as my children do mine? Would I distort them for my own purposes, rewrite them, or simply not believe Him? In His mercy, God does not always give me the answers I seek. Instead He offers the Answer.

"Here at Dachau," says Christian Reger, who spent four years in that German concentration camp during World War II, "I learned something far greater than the 'why' of life. I learned to know the who of my life." Job came to that same knowing. So can I.

Unsearchable God, would I even comprehend Your answers if one were dissected and placed before me? Today I will rest from having to know the why of my illness. I will keep my mind instead on the Who of love. ✿

After Job had prayed for his friends, the Lord made him prosperous again.   *Job 42:10*

God scolded Job's self-righteous friends and told Job to pray for them while Job was still miserable and in need himself.

Billy Graham believes that "God sometimes causes us pain so that we may pray for others"—so that we may know how to pray for fellow sufferers. Suffering did not negate Job's usefulness to God.

In *Portraits of Perseverance*, Henry Gariepy writes, "It is the going on when life is difficult that makes a person great, that builds character, and enables that person to be *used of God*" (italics added).

Job had been dragged to hell and back again. After he prayed for his friends, Job's wealth and family were restored. The Bible says he "died old and full of years." It does not say he lived those years free from illness and disease. What is known for sure is that Job's faith survived the assault, not only intact, but stronger and deeper than ever.

When a trial is yielded to God, its outcome will always benefit me—and others along with me.

Most holy God, I want so badly to believe there is purpose in my pain. Use me. Draw me into intercession today. I will pray for others that they may see Your merciful hand in my life.

> But one thing I do: Forgetting what is behind and
> straining toward what is ahead, I press on toward the
> goal to win the prize for which God has called me
> heavenward in Christ Jesus.   *Philippians 3:13–14*

Henry Gariepy tells the story of an old missionary and
then-president Theodore Roosevelt traveling on the same
ship from Africa to America. At the African port, throngs
of people cheered the world leader, while the missionary
boarded unnoticed and alone. His wife was dead, their
children were grown, and his life had been spent in the
cause of Christ in a foreign, hostile land.

During the voyage, President Roosevelt enjoyed the
finest stateroom and the best of treatment. Upon the ship's
arrival in San Francisco, crowds awaited the president, and
a red carpet was laid out for him. Bells and whistles
sounded as hundreds applauded and waved banners. But
the missionary disembarked unheralded.

Alone in a small hotel room that evening, he prayed,
"Lord, I don't want to complain, but I just don't understand.
I gave my life for You, and it feels like no one cares."

"And, in that moment," Gariepy writes, "it seemed that
the Lord reached down from heaven and laid his hand on
the old missionary's shoulder and said, 'Missionary, you're
not home yet.' "

Because of You, Lord Jesus, I can be sure there will
be an abundance of triumphant health and glorious
rejoicing at my eternal homecoming. For now,
though, help me to recognize the prizes You have
placed in my life today. 🙶

Let us hold unswervingly to the hope we profess, for he who promised is faithful.   *Hebrews 10:23*

Probably because of persecution, some members of the Christian community had withdrawn from the fellowship. The author of Hebrews encouraged them to come back in, to persevere and not give up, to hold confidently to their faith in Christ, to continue believing not only in God's promise to save them from the power of sin, but also in His ability to provide strength within the oppression.

The Greek word *echo*, translated as *hold*, means steadfast adherence. It means fastening myself to something and not letting go. In English, an echo is something I cannot throw away. It keeps coming back to me like a resounding boomerang no matter how far I may try to throw my voice.

When illness flares, I may try to toss my hope in God back to God. But because of *His* faithfulness, not mine, He just holds on to my hope for a little while and safeguards it until I'm ready to hope again. He knows each time I may hold on to it a little longer than before.

Faithful and immovable God, thank You for fastening Yourself to me and never letting go—no matter how angry or discouraged I get over this illness. Today I will reclaim some of that hope You're holding on to for me.

OCTOBER 3 ☞ *Standing Still*

Do not be afraid. Stand firm and you will see the
deliverance the Lord will bring you today. . . . The
Lord will fight for you; you need only to be still.
Exodus 14:13–14

With Pharoah's chariots closing fast behind them and the
vastness of the Red Sea spread out before them, it appeared
the Israelites' newfound freedom from slavery would be
short-lived. "What have you done to us?" they cried to
Moses. "Have you brought us to the desert to die?"

"Stand firm," Moses replied. He didn't mean not to
move their tents and animals, but rather that they should
remain secure in their belief in God's saving power. "Still
your hearts," he was saying. He wanted them to take on
an undisturbed attitude, one of defenseless quietness in the
Lord, trusting Him to direct and deliver. And deliver God
did—right through those deep waters of the Red Sea.

There may be times that seem as if God has freed me
from the bondage of illness only to have it return, perhaps
with what feels like more of a vengeance than before. "Do
not be afraid," is God's word to me. "Don't panic. Don't lose
heart. Still your soul and watch for the deliverance I will
bring you today. I will fight for you."

Lord God, when it's my body that's hurting, it's so
hard to still either my mind or my heart. When my
body attacks me today, help me to remember that
You feel my pain and will come to my aid. ☞

He has sent me to bind up the brokenhearted, . . . to comfort all who mourn, and provide . . . the oil of gladness instead of mourning, and a garment of praise instead of a spirit of despair. *Isaiah 61:1–3*

In biblical times, the oil from the olive trees that grew plentifully in Palestine was a staple. It was burned for warmth and light; and food was cooked in it and seasoned by it. Olive oil was also used in ceremonies of worship, consecration, and anointing, and it was employed medicinally as a healing balm. Shepherds carried oil to pour on the heads of their sheep, to protect them from pests, snakes, and parasites. Oil was so much a part of the fabric of life that perfumed varieties were utilized in the burial ritual. Each of its functions brought some form of comfort to the user.

Even today, olive oil is considered one of the most healthful fats, and oil of many kinds is still essential for comfortable living. Twentieth-century machines won't run without it, nor will twentieth-century bodies. So God continues to supply me with the oil that I need by sending Jesus who provided the oil of gladness—a never-ending, all-purpose supply that warms, seasons, illuminates, consecrates, anoints, heals, protects, and preserves.

Cover me today, tender Shepherd, and consecrate my suffering. When Your hand of anointing touches me, my despair turns to praise, my sadness becomes gladness, and my fear melts away.

OCTOBER 5   🐦   *Transfused with Joy*

About the Son he says, ". . . your God has set you
above your companions by anointing you with the oil
of joy."   *Hebrews 1:8–9*

"The secret of Jesus," writes Sherwood Wirt, "was—and
is—His inner joy," radiant and overflowing. "This kind of
joy cannot be compartmentalized. It suffuses the whole of
existence. . . . It [is] a clear, bubbling unpolluted delight in
God and God's creation, His redemption, His new creation, and His promise of eternal life."

Scripture teaches that Jesus was aware of the suffering
that lay ahead of Him. In fact, if I count His removal from
the glory of heaven to a temporary home on earth surrounded by sin, Jesus was already suffering. How, then,
did He possess all this joy in the middle of it?

Author Barbara Johnson says "Joy is God living in the
marrow of your bones." When the oil of God's joy circu-
lates throughout my insides, what's happening to me from
the outside can be endured. Because Jesus and the Father
were one, God's joy ran through His human veins. I cannot
conjure up joy, delight, or exultation in God. But I can
allow Him to transfuse my spiritual marrow with Himself
and His joy.

Since You, O God, are the One Who delights in
me, You give me the capacity to delight in You.
Anoint me today with the oil of Your joy, that I may
find purposeful perseverance in today's pain.   🐦

❧ *Validation Enough*

Jesus answered, "Even if I testify on my own behalf, my testimony is valid, for I know where I came from and where I am going. But you have no idea where I come from or where I am going. You judge by human standards." *John 8:14–15*

Years ago, during the time when her asthma was being diagnosed, Nancy had a short conversation with a relative who was a nurse. Nancy was describing the frustration and anxiety of being chronically ill. "All you need is a couple of kids," was the terse reply, making Nancy feel as if her asthma symptoms were nothing more than the manifestations of a housewife's boredom. She felt dismissed and unimportant. The professional credentials of a nurse were intimidating, and Nancy began to wonder if the woman were right.

Feelings of inadequacy crept in. Nancy's validity as a human being was in doubt in a society where parking lot tickets are validated more often and easily than people. Even the term often used for those who are chronically incapacitated—invalid—questions my personal worth. As if, because I am ill, I am not real, authentic, genuine, or enough.

But like Jesus I can know where I come from and where I am going. The empathic judgments of my merciful Heavenly Father are validation enough.

Gracious and loving God, true legitimacy comes only from You. Forgive me for the many times I buy into human standards and see myself as lacking. Today I will remember that being made in Your image is as valid as anyone can be. ❧

OCTOBER 7 🦽 *No Barriers*

All have sinned and fall short of the glory of God,
and are justified freely by his grace through the
redemption that came by Christ Jesus. God presented
him as a sacrifice of atonement.   *Romans 3:23–25*

Sometimes the world erects obstacles, limiting the physical
movement of someone who is ill. Stairs can keep me from
the second floor if I have emphysema or another breathing problem or a heart condition. Curbs can prevent me
from crossing the street if I depend on a wheelchair. Un-
thinking drivers can deprive me of access to public places if
they park illegally in designated handicapped spaces.

Romans 3:25 is known as the heart of the Gospel. God's
good news is that because of Jesus Christ and His atoning
sacrifice, all barriers between God and man have been removed. Through Jesus, my sin is atoned for; I am at one
with God. The only barriers between me and God now are
the ones I erect.

God "presented" His Son as a sacrifice so that sin and its
effects, illness included, would not intrude on our eternal
intimacy. "The redemption that came by Christ Jesus" is
not an intellectual concept or religious doctrine but a relationship with God Himself. Access to God is not dependent on the health of my body but on the exercise of my
faith.

Lord Jesus, reveal to me any attitudes of my
heart that keep me from maintaining at-one-
ment with You. Thank You that I don't have to
worry about getting around any barriers to
approach my God.   🦽

OCTOBER 8   *Secret Places*

My frame was not hidden from you when I was made
in the secret place. . . . Your eyes saw my unformed
body. All the days ordained for me were written in
your book before one of them came to be.
Psalm 139:15—16

My husband spent much of his childhood playing alone in
the woods, pretending to be Hopalong Cassidy or sitting
quietly in a cherry tree listening and watching. It was welcome relief from the constant activity of a household of
nine children, seven of them sisters. He retreated to a place
where no one could find him; where he could find himself.

Children have a fascination with secret places, whether
theirs is a playhouse, a hayloft in the barn, the field over
the hill, or the solitude behind their own closet door. Anywhere they can escape. Adults continue this pursuit by
going on vacations and silent retreats or disappearing into
novels and TV.

But there is no place so secret that God cannot find me.
I can retreat into my pain and suffer silently, not wanting to
bother anyone, thinking no one will notice. But God no-
tices, and He is not bothered by any concern in my life. I
never have to pretend pain away or try to hide from God.
He knows all my secret places.

Even as a speck in the womb, Lord God, I was not
hidden from You. Forgive me for the times I try to
get away from You along with all the others. Today
You are invited into all my secret places.   *

OCTOBER 9 ❧ *God's in Control*

The Lord reigns, he is robed in majesty . . . and is
armed with strength. The world is firmly established;
it cannot be moved.   *Psalm 93:1–2*

Many people find amusement-park rides too terrifying to
enjoy. Being that much out of control is overwhelming. But
they can simply choose to stay off the ride.

Nothing is that simple for those who are chronically
ill. An illness I cannot control keeps me from managing
other areas of my life as well. I may find myself poked and
prodded, pinched and peeked at, not really sure what's
going on and, perhaps, feeling a little humiliated. Health-
care providers may do things to me and say things about
me that I don't understand. My own body rebels against me
and I cannot understand that, either. It's not always easy to
be served and waited on and cleaned up after. What are
they thinking? I may wonder. Am I still loved and respected?

Jerry Bridges, author of *Trusting God*, writes, "If there is a
single event in all of the universe that can occur outside of
God's sovereign control, then we cannot trust Him." This
includes lying helpless in a hospital bed, dependent on others for my very life. God knows. God cares. God's in control of it all.

Knowing that Your strong hand stretches out to
catch me even before I fall, O God, settles my
fearful soul today. I may feel as if I'm whirling out
of control, but You are here with me, holding all
things together. ❧

"Bring the whole tithe into the storehouse, that there may be food in my house. Test me in this," says the Lord Almighty, "and see if I will not throw open the floodgates of heaven and pour out so much blessing that you will not have room enough for it."
Malachi 3:10

Married to an unbeliever, my grandmother tithed, or gave ten percent, of her grocery money (the small amount for which she alone was responsible) to her church. "God has never let me down," she often told me, "even when things were bad." I've followed her example and I, too, have found God to be overwhelmingly faithful.

What would happen, then, if I were to tithe my meager amounts of emotional and physical energy by depending on God to meet the need when I make even a small effort on His behalf? I may not have much stamina to give, or perhaps I can't depend on consistent strength, but I can depend on God to work through me. "I am learning," says one young woman with multiple sclerosis, "to depend more on God and less on my own abilities."

Being ill does not exempt me from being useful and important to God. He is behind me all the way, multiplying all that I hand over to Him and being consistently faithful to His word.

Almighty God, You don't care how much or how little I have to give, You just want me. I will test You today by yielding what energy I have to You. Today I am Yours. ❧

OCTOBER 11   *Faith Has Its Rewards*

And without faith it is impossible to please God,
because anyone who comes to him must believe that
he exists and that he rewards those who earnestly
seek him.   *Hebrews 11:6*

I read the words and think I believe them. But, more often
than not, what I really believe is that without *health* it is impossible to please God—because I must have displeased
Him terribly to be "rewarded" with this illness. Besides,
people become displeased with me, even though they try
to hide it, when I cite my illness and bow out of a commitment.

But the scripture says only that I must believe that God
exists and that God rewards those who earnestly seek him.
It doesn't say anything about the physical aspect of my
being. It's referring to my senses, my spiritual nature, my
soul's thirst for God. It means I conclude from His action in
my life and all I see around me that God does indeed exist
and that I believe His promises to love and care for me.

Faith in God is what will carry me through illness and
through life. God rewards with the power to endure.
When I allow myself to be carried, that is when God is
pleased.

Carry me, merciful God. Teach me to judge Your
love for me not by the circumstances in which I
find myself, but by my faith in Your promises.
Today I will get to know You better that I might
trust You more.   ✢

OCTOBER 12 ❧ *A Steadfast Spirit*

Create in me a pure heart, O God, and renew a
steadfast spirit within me. . . . Restore to me the joy
of your salvation and grant me a willing spirit, to
sustain me.   *Psalm 51:10, 12*

Some people find airplane travel extremely stressful. Some
don't like being out of control, while others suffer from
motion sickness. Whatever the concern, it becomes im-
material once the plane has taken off. It is not going to return to the ground just because I may be having a panic
attack. There are no emergency brakes for passengers on
airplanes, so there's no turning back. Attendants may try
to calm me or otherwise help me cope with life thirty thousand feet in the air, but the flight continues.

And so it is in illness. I may feel out of control and be
weary of dealing with symptoms and inabilities. I may be
frightened and angry. I may yearn to go back and do things
I did before I was sick. But there is no turning back; I cannot change my situation.

But just as a suffering traveler has flight attendants and
others with him throughout the trip, I am not left alone
in my struggle. If I ask Him, God will provide whatever
strength, peace, and spiritual motivation I need to continue. God's steadfastness will see me through.

Chronic illness is frightening and spiritually
fatiguing, Lord, but I can be steadfast because
You are. Restore me to the sustaining joy of
Your salvation and create a willing spirit within
me today.   ❧

Christ Jesus, who died—more than that, who was raised to life—is at the right hand of God and is also interceding for us.   *Romans 8:34*

The message, an advertisement for a local law firm, blares shrilly from the television set: "If you have a phone, you have a lawyer!" The commercial goes on to depict and describe any number of tragic situations to which the viewer might someday fall victim. "Remember," an announcer coos as he repeats the convenient toll-free number, "we're only a phone call away."

Chronic sufferers don't need televised reminders portraying all the painful things that can happen. Chronic illness is distressing enough as it is. What I need are reminders of God's care for me in the midst of it. God's primary medium of communication, the Bible, directs me to Jesus Christ as my advocate. This same Word also reassures me that prayer is a direct line to my Heavenly Lawyer. Jesus is always before the throne of the Father, interceding on my behalf, defending me when I sin, and asking God to help me out in my times of trouble.

If I have Jesus Christ, I have the ear of God.

Precious Jesus, how do I begin to satisfy the exorbitant cost of Your intercession on my behalf? Today I will begin to repay You by picking up the receiver and listening for Your voice at the other end of the line.

The Lord is my light and my salvation—whom shall I fear? The Lord is the stronghold of my life—of whom shall I be afraid? *Psalm 27:1*

Glenna remembers being embarrassed about her condition and afraid to go out in public. After her seizure-induced concussion, looking up at the numbers in an elevator made her head swim, and she feared humiliating herself by falling into strangers. She bent down to talk to a child in church one day and almost toppled right over into the next row of seats.

She was also afraid to tell people (especially Christians) that she was sick, afraid of what they might think of her. What if somebody asked about her illness? She didn't like explaining symptoms and feelings they couldn't possibly understand. Some days it was just easier to stay home and hide from them all.

I may hide my embarrassment and shame by lashing out at the very ones who love me and want to help, instead of directing my anger at the illness itself. God is not ashamed of me or humiliated by me or any aspect of my illness. He loves me so much just the way I am that He shines His light on me so everyone can see that I'm His.

God, I don't want to be held hostage by others' opinions of me. Today, when fear causes feelings of embarrassment, I will hide in the safe and secure stronghold of Your love.

Submit yourselves, then, to God. Resist the devil, and he will flee from you. Come near to God and he will come near to you.   *James 4:7–8*

Writer Aleksandr Solzhenitsyn tells the story of a Russian felon meeting up with a Baptist preacher. They have both been imprisoned in Siberian gulags for many years, and the criminal wants to know how the cleric maintains his sanity with such obvious peace and joy. "You pray to be delivered from the gulag," replied the clergyman. "I pray for the strength to survive within it."

In *When You Can't Come Back*, his account of the loss of his pitching arm to cancer, professional-baseball player Dave Dravecky speaks to the same issue. "In America," he writes, "Christians pray for the burden of suffering to be lifted from their backs. In the rest of the world, Christians pray for stronger backs."

Both the suffering prisoner and the afflicted ball player understand the lesson of submission to their God and bowing to His judgments. They know that nearness to God requires obedient surrender. But they both also trust that in drawing near to God, God will draw near to them, providing the courage needed to see them through.

Lord, You don't tell me to resist suffering and
it will flee, but you instruct me to withstand the
temptation to flee from it. And then You promise
to stay close by me today and all my days.   *ba*

As the mountains surround Jerusalem, so the Lord
surrounds his people both now and forevermore.
Psalm 125:2

Jonathan Hager, a German immigrant who in the eigh-
teenth century founded the town where I live, built his
family an intriguing house. Known as a house-fort, the
three-story structure was erected out of twelve-inch-thick
stone walls so that it would not be vulnerable to fire—from
either within or without. The foundation was built over the
source of a natural spring, which ensured a supply of clean
water. When word came of an approaching enemy, Hager
would move all his livestock into the cellar, where a permanent water trough had been dug. Because this was the
spring's source, and water flowed away from the house, no
enemy could poison people or animals inside. Hager
planned ahead and surrounded his family with protection
so lasting that it still stands 250 years later.

God surrounds me and He knows everything about my
vulnerabilities in illness. He provides and protects. God is
with me, for me, under and over me, behind and before
me, and dwelling within me.

With Your stalwart, protective, and refreshing
presence surrounding me, Lord God, how can I not
persevere through any aspect of this illness today?
With You around me, I have all I need. ❧

He is the image of the invisible God. . . . By him all things were created. . . . He is before all things, and in him all things hold together.   *Colossians 1:15–17*

My love of jigsaw puzzles is a legacy from the times in my childhood when adult relatives would spend long, quiet hours with me scanning the top of the dining room table for pieces of blue sky or a farmer's rake. Sometimes, when we were almost finished, especially if it was a large puzzle that had been worked many times, we'd realize one or more pieces was missing. And we couldn't put the picture together without all the pieces.

Even with all the pieces a completed jigsaw puzzle will fall apart when it's picked up, when I try to get a handle on it, so puzzle manufacturers make a clear coating to brush over the finished product. When it has dried, it holds all the pieces together invisibly, turning a thousand-piece dilemma into a one-piece creation.

Being ill can feel like pieces are missing out of my life. I may even unconsciously continue to search for intangible ones. But even when I can't feel or see it, God holds my life together, allowing me to get a handle on the puzzle of pain and suffering and find my missing peace.

Thank You, Lord Jesus, for being a picture of God to me, for reassuring me that You care about every part of my life, no matter how insignificant. Today I will believe that You are holding it all together.   🐟

Jesus answered, "It is written: 'Man does not live on bread alone, but on every word that comes from the mouth of God.' " *Matthew 4:4*

As a lupus patient, Jackie suffers from intermittent stomach pain. To keep her discomfort to a minimum, she's learned to take her own food along when attending picnics or potluck dinners. Salads and casseroles often contain distress-inducing ingredients, as do sodas and juices made with tap water. So Jackie tucks a piece of ham into a plastic bag, grabs her bottled water, and heads out to enjoy herself.

Three or more times a day a sick person may need to put much thought and effort into the food on her plate. "How will eating this affect my illness?" "How will not eating that hurt or help me?" "What penalty will I pay for cheating just a little today?" "Whom will I offend by refusing their food, and therefore their hospitality?"

God doesn't let me wonder when it comes to the spiritual food I need for healthful living. I'm to feast on His Word, savoring His sweetness and allowing Him to fill me up from head to heart. I need never worry about ill-effects from consuming the Word that is my true bread.

Give me this day, Lord, my daily bread. Feed me and fill me with the food of life, which is the knowledge of Your amazing grace and healing love. Today I come to You for true nourishment. 🜂

So that we should no longer be slaves to sin . . . you have been set free from sin and have become slaves to righteousness.   *Romans 6:6, 18*

Chronic illness can be a cruel master. It's always on my back, dictating what I can and cannot do or be or feel. Illness can beat me up and order me around. In most cases, I have to do what my illness wants, not what I want. My choices are few.

But Paul makes it clear that in Christ I have been set free from slavery to illness and sin. I am now a slave to Christ. Illness does not govern my life; Christ does. Paul's readers would have been familiar with the then-common practice of slavery. If an owner chose to, he could legally free a slave out of his love and affection for that man or woman. When that happened, most of the former slaves never looked back. But occasionally one returned to his master out of loyalty, respect, and caring. As a Christian, I have chosen to be Christ's slave.

A slave is one who is wholly subject to, devoted to, or under the influence of an entity outside of oneself. I can live seemingly enslaved within the confines of chronic illness because I am, in reality, a love slave to Jesus Christ.

Gentle Master, I know that sin and illness do not own me, but some days I need more reminding than others. Today I am free to come under Your tender influence and devote myself to Your loving care.   🐦

OCTOBER 20   *Another Reality*

> Now we see but a poor reflection as in a mirror; then we shall see face to face. Now I know in part; then I shall know fully, just as I am fully known.
> 1 Corinthians 13:12

Autumn has always been my favorite season. Like Goldilocks at the three bears' house, I find something wrong with all the others. Spring is too wet and humid. Summer is unbearably hot. Winter comes in a close second to autumn, but the kaleidoscopic colors and crisp weather make fall just right. It's almost as if I can see God moving a giant heavenly paintbrush over the trees, shrubs, and sky.

But although I love fall, fall, unfortunately, does not love me. Those millions of brilliant leaves eventually drop off their trees and form a decaying carpet that holds billions of tiny mold and mildew spores, to which I'm allergic. To me, everything *looks* wonderful in autumn. But in reality there exists an unseen catalyst for months of headaches and fatigue yet to come.

Things aren't always what they seem with illness either. My suffering on earth is not all there is to the reality of life and living. There is more beneath the surface of my singular experience. The mysteries of God abound. Yet of one thing I can be sure. One day I will know God as fully as He knows me today.

Lord Jesus, I cannot wait to see Your face! Thank You for letting me know there's more to my existence than all that I see and feel today.   &

God is our refuge and strength, an ever-present help
in trouble.   *Psalm 46:1*

"Don't leave home without it." American Express' advertis-
ing slogan is worth remembering. When traveling, there
are many things most people would hate to leave at
home—a familiar pillow or plenty of clean underwear, for
example. But, for people who must always take into consideration a chronic illness, medicines and other health-
management provisions can top the list. Professionals urge
all travelers, sick or well, to keep medications with them
while flying, to take extra written prescriptions and an
extra pair of eyeglasses, and to wear a medical alert bracelet
and take other precautionary measures to ensure an enjoy-
able trip.

Leaving home, where things are familiar and life feels
somewhat safe, for an unknown environment can produce
anxiety in the most hardy. I may even wonder if God travels with me or if I'll be able to make the same intimate contact with Him wherever I go as I do at home. But God is
ever-present. He and His powerful love exist everywhere
at the same time. No matter where I may go, I need never
fear leaving home without God at my side.

My Refuge and my Strength, when I forget that
You are with me and lapse into fear or loneliness,
please remind me that You never travel far away
from me. Today I will worship You, thanking You
for Your ever-present concern in my life.   ❧

This is how we know what love is: Jesus Christ laid down his life for us.   *1 John 2:16*

Before advanced technology, sacrifice was the only thing that warned underground coal miners of dangerous gas. A caged canary was carried with the men, and as long as the little bird was singing, all was well. But if the canary's song suddenly stopped, it was time to beat a hasty retreat. A bird's death alerted the men and gave them a chance to escape lethal danger. The canary's chirping, then, was a sound of safety and security. With it in their ears, they could go about their work free from worry about an invisible killer.

"Security becomes courage to live when the question of love is settled," assert John and Paula Sandford in their book *Healing the Wounded Spirit*. When I'm convinced of God's love for me no matter what, I can live freely. I am no longer worried about my performance now or my destiny later. In spite of experiencing the fear and doubt inherent in chronic illness, the sure knowledge of God's chronic and sacrificial love gives me courage to continue.

With the greatest of all love songs ringing in my ears, Lord Jesus, I am filled with courage today. Thank You for setting me free. Thank You for continually reminding me of how very much You do love me. &

People brought all their sick to him and begged him
to let the sick just touch the edge of his cloak, and all
who touched him were healed.   *Matthew 14:35–36*

"Many people," writes theologian John R. W. Stott, "visualize a God who sits comfortably on a distant throne. Such
a view is wholly false."

God is not far away. Through Jesus Christ, He is close
enough to touch me and to be touched. God has always
known what man only recently observed: that when babies
are not held and cuddled and touched, they fail to thrive
and often die, and that adults need a minimum of twelve
good touches a day for emotional health. For lack of touching, then, marriages can die. If a human touch can impart
so much, how much more central to health is a touch from
my God?

Jesus touched souls by forgiving sins, and He wrought
physical healing by touching bodies. Jesus never withdrew
from touching people, whether lepers, Samaritans, or sinners. His touch of love was available to all, even though
Jesus did not heal every sick person who lived during His
three-year ministry and all the bodies He did heal eventually died. It was and is the touch itself that's important.
What happens because of it is always healing.

If You love me and touch me, God, then why am I
still sick? Help me to understand a love so deep
that it insists on an unusual depth of healing. And
even though I don't understand, Lord, today I will
reach out for You.   ❧

"Sir," the woman said, "you have nothing to draw with and the well is deep. Where can you get this living water?" *John 4:11*

To put it mildly, chronic illness is draining. I'm forced to continue tapping a rapidly depleting well of energy and emotion. Constantly trying to keep my balance between sickness and health can sap me of strength, hope, faith, and love—love for God, for others, and for myself. I may even feel, as the Samaritan woman did, that my inner well is too deep and too empty to be reached, much less satisfied.

The woman Jesus encountered was also drained, she from continually looking for love, always with the wrong man. Jesus not only met her longing, but He filled her parched soul by respecting her enough to trust her with the revelation that He was Israel's long-awaited Messiah.

Jesus Christ will reveal Himself to me as well, no matter how emotionally or physically enervated I may be. He has an overflowing bucket of living water on a rope so long that it will descend as deep as my need. Jesus reaches out to and into me with the only water that can fill me up and restore my needy soul.

Thank You, mighty God and heavenly Father, for revealing Yourself to me through Your Son then and Your Holy Spirit now. Touch the deepest part of my tired soul today that I might be filled with all the love You know I need. ☞

And my God will meet all your needs according to
his glorious riches in Christ Jesus.   *Philippians 4:19*

"Mommy, will I have a vanity in heaven?"

What a question from a five-year-old! Her desire for a
frilly little makeup table continued to be thwarted on earth,
so I guessed her vision of a heavenly paradise included one.
But could I actually tell her that God has a beautiful new
room waiting for her there complete with a lace-skirted
vanity and makeup mirror? What about denying self and
only admiring God?

"If a vanity is what you need," I finally replied, "that's
what God will have for you." She seemed satisfied with that
answer, believing, in her childlike faith, that even a vanity
was not beyond God.

If God gave His only Son, Jesus Christ, to provide for
my entry into heaven, won't He surely meet all my other
needs as well?

"If Jesus comes when I'm playing," her little sister
wanted to know later, "will He let me come inside and get
my blankie first?"

"Whatever is essential in your life, child," the resurrected Christ tells me, "that's what I have already provided
for you."

Glorious God, I know that you will meet *all* my
needs, today's as well as tomorrow's. Please help me
to really believe that today and to stop worrying
about how You're going to accomplish it again
tomorrow.   ☞

Your Father knows what you need before you ask
him. This, then, is how you should pray: "Our
Father. . . give us today our daily bread."
Matthew 6:8–9, 11

Those who are chronically ill cannot go back to the way
they were before illness struck. And, because their condition is chronic, there is minimal hope of a lasting remedy in
the future. All I have is today. Longing for yesterday and
fearing tomorrow only strip me of what I have in today.

"It isn't the experience of today that drives men mad,"
wrote Robert J. Burdette. "It is the remorse for something
that happened yesterday, and the dread of what tomorrow
may disclose."

It's easier said than done, of course, living in the present. When I suffer, it's human nature to focus on when the
pain will end or to ask why things couldn't have stayed as
they were. That's why Jesus tells me to ask God only for
what I need today. He knows that any other approach
would drive me slowly mad. My present moments, though,
are the ones through which God daily proclaims His love
for me.

Dear Father, please give me the portion of peace,
the fragment of faith, and the measure of pleasure I
need for this day. Show me the love I am missing
by glancing back and looking forward, when You
are right here beside me today. ☙

To one there is given through the Spirit the message
of wisdom, to another the message of knowledge by
means of the same Spirit, to another faith by the same
Spirit, to another gifts of healing by that one Spirit.
1 Corinthians 12:8–9

Carol, who hadn't suffered a Ménière's attack in a year,
flipped on the TV while she ironed. A Christian program
was airing an interview with a woman who had been physically healed. Carol, not usually so emotional, was touched.
Sharing the woman's joy, she cried. Then the hosts of the
show prayed for their viewing audience. A man was being
healed of back pain, they said, and God was restoring
someone else's breathing. Then, much to Carol's astonish-
ment, they said, "God's touching a woman with an inner
ear problem. She loses her equilibrium, but she can be assured she's healed."

Carol believes that God still heals today, both miraculously and medically. "If this was for me, then I want to
thank God for it," was her response to the words from the
TV. "But if I have another attack someday, then I'll know
the healing was for someone else."

My reaction may not be as acquiescent as Carol's. What
I can know is that God has more than one avenue of healing and that the end result is not my responsibility.

Spirit of God, please help me to grasp the message
of the knowledge of Your love. Fill me with wisdom
and with faith today as I continue in the struggle to
come to terms with my illness. ❧

"But I will restore you to health and heal your
wounds," declares the Lord, "because you are
called an outcast, Zion for whom no one cares."
Jeremiah 30:17

Whether in a hospital or at home in a sickbed, it's natural to
feel alone and like an outcast, like someone who doesn't fit
in with all the healthy people. I may even feel that no one
cares or understands. But even when I'm indulging in a bit
of self-pity, God deals kindly and tenderly with me. His
bedside manner is never harsh or impatient.

"The sort of physician I appreciate," writes J. I. Packer in
Rediscovering Holiness, "takes the patient into his or her confidence and explains his or her diagnosis, prognosis, and
treatment. Not all physicians behave this way, but the best
do—and so does the Great Physician of our souls, our Lord
Jesus Christ."

God spends whatever time and effort is needed to explain my true spiritual condition. It may take me a long,
long time to come to even some small comprehension of
my soul's chronic need for His saving grace. "Under God's
care," Packer says, "we are getting better, but we are not yet
well."

Most holy of all Physicians, I come to You for
restoration today. Heal my wounded spirit and
renew my confidence in Your timetable. Thank
You for being so sensitive to all my needs.   &

> He will wipe every tear from their eyes. There will be no more death or mourning or crying or pain, for the old order of things has passed away. *Revelation 21:4*

After thirty-five years of smoking cigarettes, my fifty-one-year-old mother was diagnosed with lung and brain cancer. She asked for prayer and anointing with oil. The elders gathered and read from Mark chapter 5 about the woman who had been sick for twelve years. "Daughter," Jesus told the woman, "your faith has healed you. Go in peace and be freed from your suffering."

For almost a year, as she suffered valiantly, Mother believed Jesus' words were for her. The doctors had given her two months; she lived for eleven, convinced that the cancer would not cause her death. But she was wrong.

My mother died from the cancer, and many might think God had failed her. But what most other people couldn't see was that the bitterness she had held toward my father for years had been healed. She was able to let it go, to forgive, and God flooded her with the peace He had promised. And now, as He also promised, she is free from all suffering.

Sometimes, Lord, I ask for one kind of healing and You give me another, better kind. Thank You for disclosing just what kind I can expect in eternity with You. The thought of that future day when pain will be absent and glory will surround me sustains me today. ☙

The grass withers and the flowers fall, but the word of our God stands forever.   *Isaiah* 40:8

"But you promised!" It's a refrain every parent hears at least once. I wasted many hours of my own childhood feeling bitter over what I perceived as broken promises. I vowed then that I'd never make my children a promise I couldn't keep. But, even as much as I respond "We'll see" instead of "I promise," they still hear a commitment. And for us humans, many unanticipated circumstances can negate a promise made in the best of faith.

God knows all His plans from the beginning of the world to its end. Nothing is unforeseen with Him, and He has taken everything into consideration before giving His word. I have the option of saying "I changed my mind" after making a promise. But God doesn't allow Himself such an option with me. His promises are unable to be called back. They are irrevocable, utterly dependable.

Author Paula Reeve says, "Faith is . . . remembering that in the kingdom of God everything is based on promise, not on feeling."

You don't promise me health or a life free from pain, God. But You do promise never to leave me alone in that pain. You don't promise comfortable living, but You do promise the gift of the comfort of Your love. Today I will believe the gift and promise of Your love.   🐦

He who dwells in the shelter of the Most High . . .
will not fear the terror of night, nor the arrow that
flies by day, nor the pestilence that stalks in the
darkness, nor the plague that destroys at midday.
Psalm 91:1, 5–6

In spite of all the fun and frivolity, some Christians avoid
Halloween because of its occultic beginnings. Originating
in Ireland in the fifth century B.C. and later adopted by the
Romans, October 31 was known as All Hallows Eve. The
spirits of people who had died in the previous year were
believed to return on that date to claim a person's or an
animal's body to inhabit for the next twelve months. Only
then could those spirits proceed peacefully into the after-
life. Dressing as witches, demons, or other devilish spirits
was seen as a way to appear uninviting so that the real spirits would pass on by.

Because of the fear of spirit possession, people readily
accepted a lie from Satan, the father of lies (John 8:44).
He continues that lie today, trying to instill fear in me—
about the meaning of death and disease, about the significance of pain and suffering, and, most of all, about the
powerful extent of God's love for me.

Most high God, today I will take up residence in
the shelter of Your love and not fear the terror of
Halloween nor the plague of chronic illness. With
You surrounding me, I need not fear any disturbing
darkness nor any lying arrow.   &

> I will make a covenant of peace with them; it will be
> an everlasting covenant. . . . My dwelling place will
> be with them; I will be their God, and they will be
> my people.   *Ezekiel 37:26–27*

While hiking in the Swiss Alps in 1948, George de Mestral became annoyed by the burrs that clung irritatingly to his clothes. He wondered if it might not be possible to develop a fastener based on this interaction between burr and fabric. What is now known as Velcro was conceived. Useless in its separate components, this nylon locking tape is inordinately strong when pressure bonds the pieces. Velcro is not only used to fasten clothing and to anchor gear in gravity-free space vehicles, it is also employed to seal the chambers of artificial hearts. Decades of research has developed virtually indissoluble Velcro.

If I allow God to fit Himself to me and use the pressures of my life, there exists an eternal bond between us, a connection that illness cannot break. This eternal connection, or covenant, is a promise from God. According to United States law, a contract may or may not be reduced to writing, whereas a covenant must always be in writing and under seal. When God places His seal on my heart, we become an indestructible team.

Thank You, Lord God, for keeping the promises
You make. Thank You that I can depend on You to
dwell with me always. Today I will concentrate on
fastening myself to the peace of Your presence.   ☙

God is love. . . . There is no fear in love. But perfect love drives out fear, because fear has to do with punishment.   *1 John 4:16, 18*

It is God's love that is perfect—complete, whole, in need of nothing. The quality of my perfectly human love will always be found lacking. When I have absorbed the indefinability of God's immeasurable love, when I have accepted that God loves me and treasures me, when I believe there is a bond between us that cannot be broken, that is when my fear is driven out. Fear is consumed and taken over by an inexhaustible supply of perfect love.

Ralph Waldo Emerson wrote that "knowledge is the antidote to fear." When I *know*, not just in my head but deep in my soul, that God can do nothing else but love me, that is when my fear of rejection by God is dissolved. It can also be when the poisons of my many other nameless fears also begin to find healing, including my fear of what illness may bring in the future or the fear that God is somehow punishing me with this illness.

The Amplified Bible puts 1 John 4:18 this way: In God's perfect love "dread does not exist." Love "turns fear out of doors *and* expels every trace of terror!"

I know You love me, Lord. Help me in the not knowing. When I forget Your mercy today and fear that my illness is condemnation from You, drive out the dread and replace it with Your perfect love.   ☞

NOVEMBER 3 ✣ *Knowing Jesus*

Then you will know the truth, and the truth will set you free. *John 8:32*

Sir Francis Bacon is credited with coining the expression "Knowledge itself is power" over four hundred years ago. The tendency today is to think of that sentiment as pertaining only to schooling and education. If I absorb enough head knowledge, the world tells me, I will know more than the other guy, thus exerting power over him and freeing myself from fearing his control of me.

God's knowledge of truth is different from the world's. God's truth is how very much He loves me. God's truth expressed itself in the human form of Jesus Christ, Who is Himself the Truth. Knowing Jesus sets me free to appropriate the power inherent in the One Who is Truth.

Paraphrasing Bacon, Ralph Waldo Emerson stated, "There is no knowledge that is not power." If that is so, then true power comes from the knowledge of the love of Christ: power to accept God's acceptance of me, power to bring against this illness, power to deny myself and make wise choices and decisions, power to live with illness and bear up under it, power to endure.

When I look at my body, Lord Jesus, I feel powerless. But when I look at You—the Way, the Truth, and the Life—I am set free to accept the truth of being loved for Whose I am. Today I will listen to You and believe the Truth when I hear it. ✣

> In him we were also chosen, having been predestined according to the plan of him who works out everything in conformity with the purpose of his will, in order that we . . . might be for the praise of his glory. *Ephesians 1:11–12*

Americans are fortunate to live in a democracy where, at least in theory, government exists to serve the people. To that end, political elections are held every year about this time. Candidates vying for federal, state, and local offices work hard to convince voters that they are the best qualified for the job. An election, then, is a contest; somebody wins and somebody else loses.

The biblical doctrine of election means that God chose me before I chose Him. I came to Him only because He first pursued me. I pray to Him only because He first calls me to prayer. I never have to worry about winning a contest for God's favor. I don't have to campaign for His acceptance or worry about how my image as an ill person will affect His vote. The election is over, and because of the atoning death of Jesus Christ, everybody wins. The only thing left now is the victory celebration.

Because of You, Lord God, I am lovingly hounded into heaven. I'm so grateful that You continually strive with me and for me. Thank You for choosing me out of Your unfathomable love. Today I will sing the praise of Your glory! 🐾

NOVEMBER 5 ❧ *Giving*

It is more blessed to give than to receive. *Acts 20:35*

Those who are chronically ill can get used to receiving, being chronically catered to. Jackie, who has lupus, says, "I used to think that because I was sick, I couldn't do anything." Then Jackie read about an ill young man who declared, "If you give, you get."

The onset of a scary and confusing illness had caused Jackie to forget this previously experienced truth. Changing her outlook, Jackie stopped focusing on the negative, the things she couldn't do, and began to look for something, anything, she was able to do.

Housecleaning was a problem, but Jackie could handle laundry. She and her grown daughter struck a bargain. They traded clean clothes for clean bathrooms. Soon, the self-esteem of both mother and daughter soared. Besides fresh laundry, Jackie was also giving her daughter the joy of helping.

I may not be physically able to do what Jackie did, but if I'm well enough to read this book I can form a smile or make a phone call. And I can pray.

Lord, I know there's something I can give, to others and to You. Show me one thing today, however small, that I can do to make a difference in someone else's life. I want to stretch myself and feel the getting in the giving. ❧

NOVEMBER 6 ❧ *True Need*

For he will deliver the needy who cry out, the afflicted who have no one to help. He will take pity on the weak and the needy and save the needy from death. *Psalm 72:12–13*

In *Waking from the American Dream*, theologian Donald McCullough calls America a "can-do culture," one in which we believe "our dreams can be realized with enough hard work and positive thinking. But at one time or another, in one way or another, we wake up to reality. We learn, often with great pain, that we can't always have what we desperately want." McCullough asserts that God gives me what I *need*, not necessarily what I *want*. The dream is what I think I need. Waking from it, I'm able to see that God has already provided me with what He knows I need: "to be loved by hands that will never let [me] go." I want happily-ever-after living. God knows I need the assurance of a happy hereafter living with Him.

Not every problem in life has a remedy, and nobody knows this better than the chronically ill. Simple-sounding religious remedies can be enticing, but they're almost never what I really need. What I need, and what God provides, is an ever-open ear, an infinite measure of His love, and an unending supply of hope.

O God Who hears the cries of the needy, help me to recognize my own true needs today. Give me the courage to lay myself bare before You and receive all that You have already provided for me. ❧

Delight yourself in the Lord and he will give you the
desires of your heart.   *Psalm 37:4*

A wave of contentment washed over me as I watched my
husband and two little girls construct a wooden swing set.
As it took on the form of two connected A's, a feeling of
safety grew within me, as if I'd come home. It wasn't until
months later that I understood what had been stirring inside me that day.

We had recently moved from a small townhouse to this
house on two acres of land with a driveway where two cars
were parked. Our third child had just been born, and now
there was this swing set. It was all so "fifties"—something I
hadn't experienced as a child growing up in the real 1950s.
Until I was ten, there were never two cars in our driveway
because my parents frequently separated in anger. There
wasn't even a driveway. My only backyard was at my
grandparents' house, and it didn't really feel like mine.

It wasn't until long after the dream came true that I realized God had granted me a desire buried so deep I hadn't
even known I wanted it. He had been giving me what I
needed long before I knew I desired it as well.

One other thing. Our new address was Miracle Drive.

Lord, as I take delight in You, Your desires for me
become my own. Thank You for today's assurance
that I don't have to see it or feel it happening to
believe that You know about and are responding to
all my deepest needs.   ✍

NOVEMBER 8 ❧ *Salt*

You are the salt of the earth.   *Matthew 5:13*

The church I grew up in emphasized witnessing to others. The term implied I had to do something—knock on doors, talk to strangers, bring a friend to church, and behave better than any ten-year-old could be expected to. I had to force myself to do or be something so attractive that others would be attracted to Jesus.

But Jesus says I *am* salt. I don't have to do anything to *become* salt. In Him, I exist as salt. Practically speaking, salt preserves food and cleans wounds. It brings out the flavor of food, and it creates thirst.

I can be salt on the earth as I live with this illness and continue to learn how to manage it each day. As others watch my reactions to what they may see as the unfairness of illness, they learn of God.

Whether I understand it or not, my illness does have great purpose. I can create a thirst for God in others. I can be a living witness to a God Who has cleaned up my life and preserves me through the daily-ness of illness. I can be the salt that brings out the best in others.

Thank You, most holy God, for being salt to me. Thank You for meaning and purpose in the midst of illness. Today I will be open to anyone who might need a little spice in life.   ❧

> Blessed is the man who trusts in the Lord. . . . He will
> be like a tree planted by the water. . . . It does not fear
> when heat comes. . . . It has no worries in a year of
> drought and never fails to bear fruit.   *Jeremiah 17:7–8*

When witnesses take the stand in a courtroom, they give a firsthand account of events by relating their personal experiences.

When Jesus told the disciples, "Go ye into all the world and be my witnesses," (Acts 1:8) He was asking them to tell about their own encounters with Him, the Risen and Living Lord. He said the Holy Spirit would come and give them power to do that. As it turned out, when the Spirit did come, the power they received was to speak many different languages. They didn't have to go "into all the world," but only open their mouths right where they stood to testify to the authority and strength of God.

"Witnessing is not a spare-time occupation or a once-a-week activity," says Dan Greene. "It must be a quality of life. You don't go witnessing, you are a witness."

By trusting in God through the heat and drought of illness, I will bear fruit. God waters me with His Spirit, and through the painful struggles of my life I testify to the power of God in me.

Today I will trust You, Lord, to use my woundedness to witness to Your loving and powerful presence in the lives of all people.   ❧

Find rest, O my soul, in God alone; my hope comes from him.   *Psalm 62:5*

In some middle-class American suburbs, carefully tended landscaping and precisely manicured lawns can be a tip-off that healthy retirees live there. More than many others, retired people tend to have more time, and possibly money, to devote to weeding flower beds, mowing and watering grass, pruning trees, and edging sidewalks. They have left a career behind and retired from a lifetime of work for pay. Now, in true American-dream fashion, many are taking it easy. Taking a rest from fighting traffic, fighting finances, and fighting the world of work.

No one can retire from being chronically ill. The fighting continues as long as I live. I can't save up a little health and energy each day and put it into a retirement fitness account to draw from later on. But as a Christian I have something much better. I can retire—or withdraw from focusing on illness and rest in God—anytime I want. I don't have to wait until I'm sixty-five. God alone is my hope no matter my age, no matter my job or financial status, no matter my illness. In Him, I will find rest.

God of my past, present, and future, thank You for the hope that comes from banking on You. Yours is the only rest that makes a difference in my life. Today I will withdraw and spend some of the hope You have put in reserve for me.   ✦

I will turn their mourning into gladness; I will give
them comfort and joy instead of sorrow.
Jeremiah 31:13

Facing a lifetime of chronic illness involves a great deal of
grieving. For some, the process lasts only months. For others, years are required before they finally come to a place
of accepting the frailty of their bodies. Some never reach
this point. They remain forever angry at God and bitter
about their lot in life. It needn't be that way, though, because God gives me the gift of grief. Allowing it to follow
its natural course can only bring healing into my life.

Grief, says the Reverend Leigh Early, "is a process by
which we are allowed to value the loss, and be healed of
the loss, so that our life can go on. Just as the body knows
how to heal a cut, so the spirit uses the process of grief to
heal the injured parts of our soul. It is as if grief is the scab
that permits healing."

Coming to terms with sickness, then, promotes health.
What's been going on under the scab of my grief will eventually be exposed as gladness and joy, even though scars
of mourning and sorrow remain.

God of my gladness and God of my grief, thank
You for the gift of mourning and the opportunity it
gives me to explore my suffering and Your role in
it. Today I will not fear being scarred by grief. I will
glory in the healing that comes from knowing You
love me.

> Every good and perfect gift is from above, coming down from the Father of the heavenly lights, who does not change like shifting shadows.   *James 1:17*

Not all chronic illnesses are the same. Not all involve constant physical pain. Not all display symptoms other people notice. Flare-ups can occur without warning, as in asthma or Ménière's disease. Even within the same illness, symptoms can change daily, or hourly. With lupus, for example, the physical effects can be stomach pain one day and joint aches the next. Each day can deliver new difficulties and new losses, precipitating unexpected changes in outlook and schedule. And with these fluctuations come small daily griefs. Each day illness tosses something different at me, I must come to terms with that unanticipated new circumstance.

Never knowing just what tomorrow will bring can be unduly disturbing if I'm not aware that God Himself never changes. His love for me and protection of me is not transient, arbitrary, or fluctuating. His love is not only as fixed as my illness, as deep as my suffering, and as high as my joy, it is more fixed, deeper, and higher still. God's boundless love for me never changes.

Father of the heavenly lights, thank You for the dependability of the light of Your love in my unpredictable life. Today I will follow its beacon as I make my through the maze of illness.   ☙

That is why, for Christ's sake, I delight in weaknesses,
in insults, in hardships, in persecutions, in difficulties.
For when I am weak, then I am strong.
2 Corinthians 12:10

The gold chain holding my grandfather's railroad retirement pin was fragile, and it broke easily. I wore it around
my neck every day, and it often got caught in my clothing. If I pulled on it accidentally, a weak spot in the delicate
links would give way. After taking it to a jeweler several
times and having the broken ends soldered together, I noticed that it never broke in the same place twice. Once broken and repaired, one small area was stronger than the
entire rest of the necklace that had never been broken.

"The world breaks everyone," wrote Ernest Hemingway,
"and afterward many are strong at the broken places."

If I let Him, God will invade this weakness of illness and
make me strong in the area I feel the most vulnerable. In
Him, my life can have a powerful effect on others for
Christ's sake.

Simone Weil wrote, "The extreme greatness of Christianity lies in the fact that it does not seek a supernatural
remedy for suffering but a supernatural use for it."

Lord, I am weak today; make me strong. I am
hurting today; heal my sadness. I am broken today;
mend my grief. Living with illness is hard, Lord; lift
me up. Take my suffering and use it today.   ɫ

Then Jesus cried out, "When a man believes in me, he does not believe in me only, but in the one who sent me. When he looks at me, he sees the one who sent me." *John 12:44–45*

Some say that after spending years together, a pet and its owner can grow to resemble one another. A similar idea is applied to married couples. If they are together long enough, it's said, each can take on the other's mannerisms, style of speech, and even appearance. And, of course, many children look, act, and sound like one or both parents.

Jesus said He looks just like His Father in heaven. To look at the Son was to see the Father. Jesus spent a great deal of time in conversation with God. He pulled away from the crowds on a regular basis to immerse Himself in God's company. And He said He didn't do anything that didn't originate with God.

As God's child, I, too, can immerse myself in Him. Through spiritual osmosis—a gradual process of absorbing God's Spirit into mine—I may even begin to resemble the One with Whom I spend so much time. Despite my outer appearance, others will not see someone who is sick. They will see God in me.

Holy Father, thank You for revealing the depth of Your love through Jesus Your Son. Draw me into Yourself today and continue the work of loving me into someone who resembles You.

NOVEMBER 15   *Dis-ease*

Jesus Christ is the same yesterday and today and forever.   *Hebrews 13:8*

Along with the exhilaration of crisp weather, the aroma of burning leaves, and the brilliance of azure blue skies, autumn brings apprehension and uneasiness for Nancy. Her asthma is usually more active during the cold winter months. With winter looming before her and the threat of more frequent and more severe breathing difficulties, Nancy often experiences anxiety and a general feeling of dis-ease. Just anticipating what might happen tomorrow intensifies her stress load and reduces her overall comfort level. She begins to live fearfully in tomorrow, which limits her capacity to live joyfully in today.

As the holiday season with its built-in tensions approaches, like Nancy, I may become that much more uneasy by worrying about what turn my illness will take. But if Jesus was there for me yesterday, what makes me think He won't be there for me tomorrow? If His comforting presence and healing power have evidenced themselves before, certainly they will again.

Jesus, my Messiah, save me today from dis-ease, from the ever-widening trap of feeling anxious and troubled and outside the scope of Your love. My body and my emotions may change, but You remain ever the same in love and mercy and power.

NOVEMBER 16 ❧ *Jesus My Rock*

Trust in the Lord forever, for the Lord, the Lord, is the Rock eternal.   *Isaiah 26:4*

Charles Spurgeon told a story of the dying woman visited by her Welsh pastor. "Are you sinking?" the clergyman asked her. "Why no," the woman replied weakly. "If I had been standing in sand I might sink, but I'm standing on the Rock of Ages and there is no sinking here."

A rock implies stability and safety, strength and reliability. It is a secure place in the midst of surrounding deep waters. It keeps me anchored and surely fastened. Even the smallest rock endures long after I am gone.

In ancient times a tribal lookout would climb to the top of a rock to get a broader perspective. For that reason, the Old Testament refers to God as the Rock. The New Testament uses the same imagery when describing Jesus Christ as a sure foundation.

The elusiveness of many chronic illnesses, and the incessancy of most, requires a rock to stand on. I need the changelessness and permanence of a Rock I can trust never to sink beneath me. No matter how high or how low I may go, God is always rock solid.

Lord God, sinking is something I know about. Sometimes I wonder if I've sunk so far that I've disappeared out of Your sight. Thank You for today's assurance that, in spite of my fears to the contrary, I can never sink while standing on the Rock Eternal.   ❧

Let the beloved of the Lord rest secure in him, for he shields him all day long, and the one the Lord loves rests between his shoulders.   *Deuteronomy 33:12*

For Jackie, trying to collect Social Security disability benefits has been a long and anxiety-filled process. For most of her fifty-one years, she's worked and paid into the system, but now she finds lupus prevents her from performing a steady job. There are too many days when pain and fatigue keep her glued to the sofa, too many times she can't remember simple information or directions. But to the Social Security Administration she appears healthy enough— no missing limbs, no paralysis, no infection. Even with a lawyer and a congresswoman on her side, she has not yet received the benefits she needs.

"Why can't they accept a doctor's word that I'm sick?" Jackie wants to know. "If I'm too sick to work, I certainly don't have the energy for a lengthy, drawn-out dispute with them."

Americans have dubbed it "social" security and have come to rely on an arm of the government for protection in times of trouble. But God, of course, is my only security in life, social or otherwise. In Him, I am protected. In Him, I can rest secure.

Lord, please melt my anxieties today. You know I am ill, and You know what all my needs are, especially the ones that aren't being met. Today my security will rest in You and You alone.

> If we live, we live to the Lord; and if we die, we die to
> the Lord. So, whether we live or die, we belong to
> the Lord. *Romans 14:8*

For the Christian, life is a process of living and dying, death
and resurrection, a series of losses and gains. This is especially true for the chronically ill Christian, who experiences
little losses and deaths, small gains and resurrections, every
day.

No matter what my circumstances—life or death, sickness or health, acceptance or denial—I belong to God.
Throughout my lifelong battle with sin, I am His. On the
job, I am His; without a job, I am His. Married, I am His;
single, I am His. Up and about, I am His; bedridden, I am
His.

Because God doesn't change, if I belonged to Him yesterday, I still belong to Him today. If I belong to Him
today, I will belong to Him tomorrow. If not even death
can cancel our relationship, then surely illness won't either.
I belong to God. I am His.

> Lord of the living and the dying, how can I
> understand a love that does not go away? I can't
> even understand the utter reliability of belonging
> to You. Give me the courage and strength to die a
> little to myself today so that more of You may live
> in me. ❧

In love he predestined us to be adopted as his sons
through Jesus Christ, in accordance with his pleasure
and will—to the praise of his glorious grace, which
he has freely given us in the One he loves.
Ephesians 1:5—6

"Everybody pray for me tonight," my daughter announced
as we put dinner on the table. Everybody? Since when did
this very private teenager include the whole family in
something as intimate as prayer? Ah, yes—the school play.
It was that time of year again, and auditions started tonight.
Alex's talent and training had gotten her the lead in last
year's production, and all her friends assured her it would
happen again. But she was still nervous and frightened.

Later I stopped by her room on my way out to a meeting. Bending over, I spoke softly, "Just remember, you never
have to audition for this family."

"Aw, Mom, you always say such corny stuff," she
replied. Maybe so, I thought, but her smile said otherwise.

My place in God's family is just as firmly set. I wasn't
born into it. Rather, I was adopted, specially chosen. I
never have to audition, worrying that my illness will prevent me from getting the part. My adoption into God's
family never depends on what I can or cannot do, but on
what Jesus has already done.

Jesus, my Brother, thank You for the surety of my
place within Your family. Today I will worship You
and revel in the love of our Father. ❧

Cast your cares on the Lord and he will sustain you.
Psalm 55:22

Concerned when her sixteen-year-old son attended his first heavy-metal rock concert, Carol flashed back to what life was like when his older brother, in a typical twenty-year-old identity search, became engaged in a fight with alcoholism. She was afraid that because the disease had manifested itself once in her family, it could happen again. "You get real paranoid," Carol says, "scared of what might happen." She recognizes that these same feelings also affect her outlook in her struggle with the uncertainty of Ménière's disease.

Because I may have had a frightful experience with a certain procedure or drug, I may fear that my body will react the same way again. My illness may have taken a sudden painful turn and I may worry that I'll have to relive the same nightmare in the future.

But worrying, carrying around a heavy load of cares, won't keep anything from happening. All it does is weigh me down and grate on the peace God's given me for today.

As Ralph Waldo Emerson put it, "What torments of grief you endured/From evils which never arrived!" God will take care of me and sustain me through whatever my illness may hold for tomorrow.

Take my cares, Lord. Wrench them from me if You have to. Today You have my permission to strip me of any care or worry that threatens my physical and emotional serenity in You. Thank You for the promise of sustenance throughout the process.   ❧

There is one body and one Spirit—just as you were
called to one hope when you were called—one Lord,
one faith, one baptism; one God and Father of all,
who is over all and through all and in all.
Ephesians 4:4–6

President Ronald Reagan was known for his quick wit and
indefatigable good humor. Even after suffering a critical
bullet wound at the hands of a would-be assassin, he managed to get off a one-liner. Lying helpless on the operating
table, immediately before he was anesthetized, Reagan
looked up at the surgeon and quipped, "I sure hope you're a
Republican."

"Mr. President," the doctor replied, "today we're all Re-
publicans."

A common tragedy brought a nation together then just
as a common hope in Jesus Christ unifies the Church
today. Denominational lines are invisible to a God Who
willingly sacrificed His Only Son and ripped the temple
curtain in two so that all could approach Him freely.

Neither does God see the divisions people create between political parties, between the well-behaved and the
rowdy, the talented and the dull, or the sick and the well.
Our collective hope in Christ is exactly that—*in* Christ.
Not in the state of my health or lack of it.

My Father and Father of us all, thank You for the
place You created for me in Your body of believers
and the hope that gives me. Today I will consider
how my illness might benefit others.   🐾

> On my bed I remember you; I think of you through
> the watches of the night. Because you are my help,
> I sing in the shadow of your wings. My soul clings
> to you; your right hand upholds me. *Psalm 63:6–8*

For many people, holidays and occasions such as weddings and funerals bring a gathering of the clan. Families come together and fall into a retelling of old tales. "Remember the Christmas we spent two days driving around in the cold looking for the perfect tree?" someone may laugh. "Remember the time Mama put the milk in the cupboard and the clean dishes in the fridge?" Or, "Remember when Susie was six and we forgot there was no school and sent her anyway?"

Reminiscing can remind me that I'm part of something much bigger than myself. Remember the time God protected baby Moses in the bulrushes? Remember when He empowered young David with just five stones? Remember the wonder of the first Christmas? I have personal collections of memories of God, of all the times He preserved me in situations that seemed hopeless. I don't need a sound or pain-free body to recall God's comforting presence in past suffering or His omnipotent might in today's difficulty. I can cling to Him, remembering that His strong right hand upholds me.

> Like the psalmist, I will remember Your deeds
> today, Lord. I will remember Your miracles of long
> ago. I will meditate on all Your works and consider
> all Your mighty deeds. I will recollect my memories
> of You and be encouraged by them. ✦

But he said to them, "I have food to eat that you know nothing about. . . . My food," said Jesus, "is to do the will of him who sent me and to finish his work."
John 4:32, 34

Around this time of year, between Thanksgiving and Christmas, food can become a serious issue in people's lives, whether they're sick or not. While food is necessary for survival, some of it can be good for me and some of it can be bad for me. If I overindulge in the bad and ingest too little of the good, my physical condition will suffer. I may even experience painful consequences.

The same holds true in my spiritual life. If I take in too much unhealthy spiritual food, my relationship with God will suffer. Jesus said that doing His Father's will was what gave Him nourishment. It fed His soul and kept Him going. Giving Himself and providing the way for my salvation was the supreme soul food for Jesus. Acceptance—of this illness and of His finished work on my behalf—is the main course of the banquet He sets out for me daily. It's what nourishes me and feeds my soul.

Lord Jesus Christ, today I will feast at the table of thanksgiving, savoring Your love for me. Teach me to make wise choices for my spiritual and physical well-being.

Here I am! I stand at the door and knock. If anyone hears my voice and opens the door, I will come in and eat with him, and he with me.   *Revelation 3:20*

Many things about a chronic illness create distance between people. One of them can be a family dinner during the holidays. Some chronic sufferers, diabetics especially, must watch their diets vigilantly.

Giving in to certain temptations, no matter how many hours Aunt Sally toiled in a hot kitchen, can have serious consequences. If Aunt Sally doesn't understand this, her coaxing and cajoling may only serve to make me feel guilty and alienated from the very family I need—and during a season when the whole world seems to be pulling together and family warmth and harmony are touted everywhere. In a house full of friends and relatives, I can suddenly feel very alone.

But there is One Who never tries to force me to do anything, much less "enjoy" myself by hurting my body. Jesus is always ready and willing to break bread with me, regardless of the menu. He understands my needs and wants only my welfare. All I have to do is heed His knocking.

O Bread of Life, thank You that I don't have to limit the nourishment I take from You. Today I can have as much of You as I want and then some. Remind me that You are the One Who unites us all— parents and children, doctors and patients, healthy and sick.

So Judah went into captivity, away from her land.
Jeremiah 52:27

Eugene Peterson defines exile as "being where we don't want to be with people we don't want to be with."

I sure don't want to be in a land of illness inhabited by white coats who repeat the same questions, send me for tests, and present me with bills. Chronic illness can feel like exile within my own homeland, especially when others don't want me around.

The people of Judah didn't want to live in Babylon, so they remained apart, not becoming involved in the alien society around them. "After all," they reasoned, "we'll surely be going home soon."

But if I wait for the day I am healed, and put things off until I feel well, then I won't live deeply today: discovering, creating, growing, loving, being the glory of God. I could die in an accident long before my illness catches up with me, and I'd have missed out on all that living.

Peterson goes on to say that "with the pain and in the midst of alienation a sense of freedom can occur"—freedom from man's opinions of me, freedom to pursue God in a way I'd never before thought possible.

Lord, today I recognize You as the God of my exile. Never before have You left Your people alone as outcasts, and You will not start with me. Thank You for the exile You endured in order to rescue me from mine.

But our citizenship is in heaven. And we eagerly await
a Savior from there, the Lord Jesus Christ, who . . .
will transform our lowly bodies so that they will be
like his glorious body.   *Philippians* 3:20

"Illness is the night-side of life, a more onerous citizenship,"
writes Susan Sontag in her book *Illness As Metaphor.* "Everyone who is born holds dual citizenship, in the kingdom of
the well and in the kingdom of the sick."

In some countries it is possible to become a citizen of a
new country while still maintaining all the legal rights and
privileges of the country of one's birth. For example, one
might be born of American parents on foreign soil and thus
be considered a citizen of both countries.

It may seem as if a chronic condition dictates that I always live in the kingdom of the sick, but Paul says I'm just
visiting here. As a Christian I already have dual citizenship.
I have been born here on earth, and I have also experienced a second birth which qualifies me for citizenship in
the heavenly kingdom, where there is no more sickness.

One day I will be welcomed to a homeland where my
citizenship is now and forever, where my lowly body will
be changed for one of glory.

Thank You, Dear Jesus, for providing everything
I need for the journey home. Strengthen me today
as I continue my visit here.   🐦

Consequently, you are no longer foreigners and aliens, but fellow citizens with God's people and members of God's household.   *Ephesians 2:19*

Restoration is about returning someone or something to a former condition, a better state of being. It's what the popular PBS series "This Old House" does to old buildings. It's what contemporary artists do to aged, yet valuable oil paintings. It's what furniture makers do to priceless antique chairs.

It's also what God has done and will do for me as a result of the life, death, and resurrection of Jesus Christ. I have been restored to a spiritually sinless state through His self-sacrifice. And I will one day be restored to a perfect, disease-free body. I am now restored to and reconciled with the family of God Himself. Never again need I feel outside of that family because of my illness.

As a member of His household, I am entitled to all the rights and privileges of God's child, and I can confidently expect His ungrudging attention and loving concern. Illness or no illness, healing or no healing, my full citizenship is completely restored.

Most loving God, I'm learning that almost everyone feels outside Your accepted circle. Thank You for the restoration Jesus provides, that draws us all inside. Today I will focus on what we all have in common, instead of the illnesses that drive us apart.   ❧

NOVEMBER 28   *Overspending*

> Why spend money on what is not bread, and your labor on what does not satisfy? *Isaiah 55:2*

Glenna remembers the Christmas after her first seizure. She was well enough to push herself into doing some Christmas shopping by going along on trips to the mall with friends. But she was not sufficiently healthy to keep track of all her purchases and expenditures for her family of five plus all their relatives and friends.

She was also experiencing a load of guilt over her inability to do the standard Christmas things like making handmade gifts, home-baked goodies, and special decorations. It took less effort to buy a gift than to deal honestly with herself and others about the reality of her condition. Consequently, she greatly overspent that year, and not only monetarily.

I don't have to spend more energy than I have to acquire God's love. He's utterly accepting of me and of what I can and cannot do. He loves me too much to be pleased when I make myself sicker in a vain attempt to alleviate the false guilt of not being able to do more.

Satisfy me today, Lord. I've been trying to please others in order to fill an inner void that this illness has caused. Teach me to spend my energies where they will recognize the most gain—on, in, and with You.

Because your love is better than life, my lips will glorify you. . . . My soul will be satisfied as with the richest of foods.   *Psalm 63:3, 5*

There are those who contend, nutritionists and dietitians among them, that the Western world is addicted to sugar and other empty calories, foods devoid of nutritional value. What is certain is that when I eat these so-called junk foods, my stomach will feel full, while my body continues to beg for the nutrients it needs and is being deprived of. I will experience hunger even though my stomach may not be capable of holding more food. My body will have a continual appetite for that which will not satisfy it until I give it what it needs to thrive. Ingesting sawdust may fill me up, but it can never keep me healthy.

I may have an appetite, too, for more than I possess, and fill my life with things, with people, with a career, even with religion. But none of these will satisfy me and satisfy my need for God. They may even make me crave Him all the more. "Listen," writes pastor and best-selling author Charles Swindoll, "our major goal in life is not to be happy or satisfied, but to glorify God."

God of love and life, I confess that my appetite often runs contrary to Your will. Just as I crave foods that can damage my body, so I often desire things that can spoil our relationship. Teach me to feast on Your love. Today my soul will glorify You.   ❦

"Abba, Father," he said, "everything is possible for you. Take this cup from me. Yet not what I will, but what you will." *Mark 14:36*

It sounds easy enough in theory: "The God Who created me is greater than I am, so I will submit to His wise and loving authority. Because He knows better about everything I do, I will trust His plans for my life."

It looks pretty good on paper, too. But just try living up to the first road test, or the 100th. This pious-sounding ideology waxes quite thin when I'm presented with the prospect of living an unlimited number of years married to this illness. I may want to scream "Enough already!"

Even Jesus recoiled at the thought of submitting to suffering, to crucifixion. As yielded as His heart was to the Father, He still had to grapple His way to what Christian writer Marion Bond West calls "nevertheless living," where "one must travel the dreaded road of fear and deep depression." She continues, "There is no other route and no shortcut. The paradox is that you get there by simply giving up and entering a stage of trust that staggers the imagination."

God, my Father, everything is possible for You. Please take this illness and all its horrors from me. Nevertheless, not what I want, but what You know is best. Today, with Your help, I will yield to You and live in submission to Your will. ❧

DECEMBER 1   *The Light Has Come*

I have come into the world as a light, so that no one
who believes in me should stay in darkness.
John 12:46

Advent is the name given to a Church season, the four
weeks or so immediately preceding Christmas Day. In
Latin, the word means "to come" and it begins the English
word *adventure*. During Advent, the Church waits, expectant
and hopeful.

Many Christians symbolically employ an Advent
wreath, in which five candles representing the God of
Light Who comes into the world of man as Man Himself,
are arranged in a circular bed of greens. Jesus compares His
coming to the turning on of a light in a dark room. On the
very first day of creation, God said, "Let there be light."
Then thousands of years later, He hung a star in the sky so
brilliant that it guided travelers from hundreds of miles
away to the birthplace of the One Who is Light.

God has gone to all this trouble so that I might believe
there's hope for me in the darkness of my illness as well as
in the darkness of evil. I don't have to remain in the dark.
The Light has come.

You Who are the Light of the world, thank You
for coming as a comforting night light when I
need it in the dark nighttimes of my illness. Fill
my heart today with the anticipation of and a new
appreciation for Your illuminating advent into my
world.   🪶

"I tell you the truth, anyone who will not receive the kingdom of God like a little child will never enter it." And he took the children in his arms.   *Mark 10:15–16*

"When are you going to stop acting like a child?" Growing up, a child might hear these words from an exasperated parent. In fact, as a way of relieving tension, I've said the same thing to my own kids. "You're acting like a bunch of children!" I've laughed tongue-in-cheek, giving them permission to be just that.

Somewhere along the line, though, I have lost many childlike qualities and become a grown-up. And the funny thing is, once I'm grown and my parents stop asking their question, Jesus begins to ask His. "When are you going to start acting like a child?" He wants to know. A child says, "Daddy, I don't feel well. Can I have a hug?" A child needs comfort and attention and a safe place to be. A child asks, "Will I be better soon?" while enduring yet another injection. A child waits patiently with trusting eyes, sure his parent knows best. Jesus knows just what He's asking and just what I need because it was as a child that He came to be with me.

O God, You Who are both Child and Father, come and heal the child inside me today. Show me what it is to be a child, Your child. Enfold me in Your arms and lift me to the comfort of Your kingdom. ❧

DECEMBER 3 ❧ *Joy in the Turmoil*

O God our Savior, the hope of all the ends of the
earth and of the farthest seas,. . . who stilled the
roaring of the seas, the roaring of their waves and the
turmoil of the nations . . . you call forth songs of joy.
Psalm 65:5–8

"Somebody fix that angel!" Glenna screamed in exaspera-
tion, frustrated with herself and her life. Because of a
painful family background and now physical illness, control of her environment was vital to Glenna's peace of
mind, and at that moment, a lop-sided Christmas-tree
angel threatened what little serenity she still possessed.

During the first Christmas season after her seizure,
Glenna couldn't get up from a chair and walk across the
room without feeling as if her world were spinning out of
control. So she positioned herself in the living room and
proceeded to try to manage everything and everyone from
there. Being forced to direct activities she could easily have
done herself just weeks before only created more inner turmoil for Glenna—and just as the whole world was singing
about peace on earth.

God knows the frustration and unrest that chronic illness creates within me. He who stills the seas and rumbles
of war wants to do the same for me.

Savior of the nations and Hope of my heart, still
the turmoil within me today. Fill me with peace
and call forth songs of Christmas joy. ❧

DECEMBER 4 ❧ *God with Me*

> The virgin will be with child and will give birth to a
> son, and they will call him Immanuel—which means,
> "God with us." *Matthew 1:23*

How can God possibly comfort and strengthen me in this
illness if He doesn't know just what hurts me? That's what
Immanuel means, not only "God with me," but "God within
me." It's the name of a God Who resides deep down inside
of me and knows, really knows, what hurts me.

Being ill, I may not always allow that degree of familiar-
ity between me and my friends, my family, or even my
spouse. And when I do risk a life of deep closeness with another individual, that person can't possibly experience the
pain and distress of my illness as Immanuel does. He is my
closest, most intimate Friend. He is always with me.

He doesn't have call waiting on His communications
network. He doesn't put me off with a promise to "do
lunch" later. He is never too busy with another of His children to soothe and pay attention to me. For time and eternity, in pain and in joy, the God of Abraham, Isaac, Jacob,
and me is Immanuel.

Throughout this day, Lord Jesus, open the eyes
and ears of my heart that I may experience Your
presence with and within me. Give me the desire
to allow intimacy with You in a way that I have
never known.   ❧

He who did not spare his own Son, but gave him up
for us all—how will he not also, along with him,
graciously give us all things?   *Romans 8:32*

Most people, especially Christians, want to give to others.
At Christmastime it's natural to want to bestow special gifts
on special friends and loved ones. I may go way out of my
way in order to find or make that one-of-a-kind gift for a
treasured friend. I may even sacrifice all year in order to
afford the perfect Christmas present for my child.

When asked what they want for Christmas, some adults
may demure, "I have everything I need. Don't get me anything this year." But if I know of an unfulfilled desire I may,
out of my great love for that person, spare nothing in an attempt to present it to her.

In the same way, God goes way beyond the proverbial
call of divine duty when I ask for the gift of pain-free,
healthy living. He hears the words of my mouth, but He
gives me what even I don't know I want: the gift of an ever-
deepening relationship with Him.

Someone once said, "I asked God for all things that I
might enjoy life. He gave me life that I might enjoy all
things."

Instead of concentrating on the buying and giving
of presents, Lord, I will focus today on recognizing
and accepting the gift of Your presence and giving
it away to those I love.   🐿

DECEMBER 6 ❧ *The Living One*

I am the Living One; I was dead, and behold I am
alive for ever and ever! *Revelation 1:18*

On December 6, 342 A.D., Saint Nicholas, the patron saint
of children, was buried. Nicholas was a bishop renowned
for his generosity to and love of children. The Santa Claus
Americans now know has his origins in the European legend of a bearded Saint Nicholas, dressed in full red-and-
white bishop's robes, making gift drops to children. Even
though he lived and died more than seventeen hundred
years ago, the world still gets excited about St. Nick. His
spirit lives on.

There is also great excitement this time of year about
another man Who lived and died long ago. Only this man,
Jesus Christ, does not remain dead. It's no legend that after
He died, He rose from His grave. There were witnesses
who wrote down what they saw.

Twenty centuries later, it's not just the spirit of the Man
that lives on, but the man Himself lives inside me. With
Him there, the old me may be dead and buried, but the
new me lives on.

O God of all life, help me to see that even in the
death of my health, I have a new life to celebrate.
Please help me to define this new life in illness.
Today I will be gratefully generous as I share that
life with You and others. ❧

Consider it pure joy, my brothers, whenever you face trials of many kinds, because you know that the testing of your faith develops perseverance. Perseverance must finish its work so that you may be mature and complete, not lacking anything.   *James 1:2—4*

J. B. Phillips translates this passage as "When all kinds of trials and temptations crowd into your lives, my brothers, don't resent them as intruders, but welcome them as friends!"

Is it truly possible to view the trial of suffering as a gift? Charles Colson thinks so. Ex-convict and former right-hand man to President Richard Nixon, he was stripped of money, power, prestige, and his freedom in the aftermath of Watergate. He has written since that he found "a far greater gain: knowing Christ."

Joni Eareckson Tada thinks so, too. Since losing most of her physical abilities in a diving accident, Joni has often said in print and in person that her paralysis has drawn her close to God and provided a spiritual healing which she "wouldn't trade for a hundred active years on my feet."

Everything about life is a gift, even pain. God, however, does not dole out diabetes to one and arthritis to another like Santa at Christmas. In God's loving desire for my wholeness, I can consider this illness pure joy because He exchanges my suffering for hope.

As much as I choke on the words, dear God,
today I will thank You for the gift of illness and
all the other gifts You allow into my life to ensure
that I am "not lacking anything."

DECEMBER 8   *Light of the World*

You are the light of the world.   *Matthew 5:14*

At Christmastime, I'm always charmed by the colorful lights strung around a slightly dilapidated old house. Its simple message shines into my heart. At the same time in church, children sing, "This little light of mine, I'm gonna let it shine."

Illness can make me feel as if my light has gone out, that I have nothing of any value to give to others—others who may even expect me to live in a kind of sick person's darkness. But Jesus says I don't have to shine a light; He says I am light. No matter how powerless I may feel because of illness, God is my power source. I can plug into Him any time I want to shine, to warm others in the Light of His love. In spite of illness, Jesus will shine through me, perhaps even more brightly than if I had never been ill.

Lloyd Ogilvie has written, "We want people to look to us and wonder why we are the way we are, and then beyond us to the Light of the World flashing in us."

O coming King, forgive me for the many times I have hidden my light under the bushel of illness and dimmed Your brilliance. Today charge me with Your power so that I may shine before men, that they will see You and not me.   ☙

DECEMBER 9 ❧ *Holiday Blues*

Your sun will never set again, and your moon will
wane no more; the Lord will be your everlasting light,
and your days of sorrow will end.   *Isaiah 60:20*

The message is everywhere. In colorfully extravagant de-
partment store decorations and incessantly happy holiday
carols. Bakeries and restaurants advertise it through a sea-
sonal array of enticing confections. Even food gets happy
at Christmas.

Joy, or at least a kind of frenetic cheer, seems to permeate the season. But where does all this leave someone with
an illness that refuses to take a holiday? On top of the
stress of illness itself, I may now find myself burdened with
added obligations in addition to my own internal expectations for the season. At the same time, I am confronted
with seemingly happy, healthy people everywhere I look.

How many of them are contending with a type of
chronic sorrow, the so-called "holiday blues," which sociol-
ogist Ronald Knapp describes as "a dull ache in the background of one's feelings"?

With the Christ of Christmas in my life, I don't have to
be one whose soul aches. His warm and healing light can
form the background of my feelings.

Lord God, please keep me from being sucked into
a whirlwind of chronic sorrow. Pull me out of the
holiday blues and into Your everlasting light. Focus
my mind and heart on You today. Thank You for
the promise that one day my pain will come to an
end. ❧

Be strong in the Lord and in his mighty power. Put on the full armor of God so that you can take your stand against the devil's schemes. For our struggle is not against flesh and blood, but against . . . the powers of this dark world.   *Ephesians 6:10–12*

It's a familiar sound every Christmas. Even before I see who's ringing the bell, I know what she looks like. She's wearing what appears to be a military uniform, navy blue with gold buttons and braid, complete with jaunty cap and dashing cape. Beside her, an over-sized red bucket sways inside a five-foot tripod. She's the Salvation Army.

Her bell reminds me it's the season of giving. Her uniform reminds me that even as I celebrate the coming of the Prince of Peace, I'm still engaged in a war. The battle with my own unhealthy flesh and blood is but a skirmish in the larger conflict.

But God makes available *His* strength and mighty power with which to fight. I don't have to rely on my feeble capabilities. He provides the uniform and equipment I need. Jesus comes into this dark world to be my Belt of Truth, Breastplate of Righteousness, Shoes of Peace, Shield of Faith, Helmet of Salvation, and Sword of the Spirit as the Word of God in the flesh.

Because You came, Lord Jesus, I have nothing to fear. I am safe in You. Illness, no matter how chronic or deadly, does not have the power to destroy me, even though the battle continues. Today I will remember that You have already won the war. ❧

Do not be afraid. . . . Today in the town of David a
Savior has been born to you; he is Christ the Lord.
This will be a sign to you: You will find a baby
wrapped in cloths and lying in a manger.   *Luke 2:10–12*

A little baby in a feeding trough? What an incongruous
thought. Certainly this wasn't usual, and certainly this particular child wouldn't be hard to find. How many babies
were sleeping in mangers that night?

A sign is something that distinguishes one thing from
another. It can also explain in picture form what is happening. More than any other time of year, Christmas is full
of signs and symbols. An Advent calendar counts down the
days. Closed-circle wreaths, symbolic of a never ending
Presence, are made of foliage known as evergreen. A brilliant star broke into the dark of that chilly night. A soft,
sweet-smelling, sinless newborn lay helpless surrounded by
stinking animals. It was a sign that this baby was different
from all the rest.

The Savior born that night was not just for shepherds
and searching mystics. Jesus comes for all those wise
enough to seek Him. His coming gives meaning and hope
to all who suffer and wait.

Christ, my Lord, invade my world with a love that
is not afraid to confront painful and puzzling
circumstances. Your love wrapped around me today
is sign enough for me.   *

When your words came, I ate them; they were my joy and my heart's delight, for I bear your name, O Lord God Almighty.   *Jeremiah 15:16*

The joy-full Christmas season is a time of anxiety for Nancy, who has asthma. Overwhelmed by holiday details, Nancy postpones her joy. "There's always the possibility I could get sick and not be able to do all the four thousand things I 'have' to do," she says. "I tend to think that once I finish these cookies or plan that dinner, then I'll have the time to let myself be joyful."

Christmas is a celebration of the coming of the Word; it's a time to take delight in Him and be *joyful*—the Hebrew word for which suggests spontaneous expressions of emotion at celebrations.

Nancy is too busy worrying and preparing for the celebration to enjoy the celebration Himself. Like me, she often holds back her deepest desire, to express her delight in the Incarnate God.

A chronically ill person cannot afford the energy it takes to keep a lid on that kind of God-given gladness. In *I Know Why the Caged Bird Sings*, Maya Angelou writes of discovering this truth in her mother: "She comprehended the perversity of life, that in the struggle lies the joy."

Today, Lord Jesus, I choose You. As the Word that became a baby fills my heart with delight, I will no longer postpone my joy waiting for this illness to end. Show me how I can have joy within the daily struggle.   &#128}

DECEMBER 13 ❧ *No Room?*

The time came for the baby to be born, and she gave birth to her firstborn, a son. She wrapped him in cloths and placed him in a manger, because there was no room for them in the inn.   *Luke 2:6–7*

In the months preceding the 1992 Summer Olympics, held in Barcelona, Spain, tourists from around the world were cautioned about the extraordinarily high cost of lodging there. When interviewed, one hotel representative admitted hiking room rates in order to make as much money as possible from the thousands of international visitors.

Could this have been the same atmosphere Mary and Joseph rode into? Then, the entire Roman world was to be counted, and people were commanded to return to their home towns to register. It must have been quite a windfall for innkeepers, and many probably took advantage of people like Joseph. And so, because human nature tends to look out for itself, there was no safe, clean, affordable place in which God could enter His world.

Does my chronic illness so chronically consume the room inside me that there is no place God can enter? Am I so busy looking out for myself and counting the cost of illness that I make no room for God?

Come, little Lord Jesus, and dwell within me today. I need You and I want You here. Help me to move over and allow You the room You need to work through my illness.   ❧

I consider everything a loss compared to the surpassing greatness of knowing Christ Jesus my Lord, for whose sake I have lost all things. I consider them rubbish, that I may gain Christ and be found in him. *Philippians 3:8–9*

One of comedian Bill Cosby's early routines recounted being teased by his older brother when they were children. Russell had Bill convinced that an adhesive bandage on Bill's belly button kept him intact. He told in vivid detail how, if the bandage was removed, air would whistle out of Bill's stomach and he would spin around the room like a balloon that's been blown up and then let go. When it's all over, the balloon ends up flat and empty on the floor.

As comical as it is to imagine a five-year-old staring wide-eyed at his brother's suggestion, it's not funny to think of the same picture in relation to my illness. If my identity, how I see myself, is enmeshed in my illness, then I may believe that if I let go of the illness, there'll be nothing left of me. I may fear losing myself, flying out of control and becoming dimensionless and hollow, like a deflated balloon. If nothing else, illness can give me some sense of who I am. But a far-healthier self is created by knowing Christ and filling myself with Him.

Lord Jesus, teach me how to let go of this illness, to release its hold on me for the sake of gaining more of You. Today I will consider my losses and all that You've filled me with in return.   *

So the law was put in charge to lead us to Christ that we might be justified by faith. Now that faith has come, we are no longer under the supervision of the law. *Galatians 3:24–25*

The Bible can be approached doctrinally or relationally, in the shadow of the tablets of stone or in the light of the cross. If I approach Scripture by wondering what God is telling me to do, I'm on my way to legalism. If, on the other hand, I ask "What is God saying about Himself?" my focus rotates from me to God, from fear of the law to faith in Christ. I step out of the shadows into the light.

In many ways, though, it can feel safer to stay hidden in the dark. There, the law tells me just what to do and how to act and react. I don't have to think, question, or suffer anxious doubts. Everything is neatly contained.

But God started to pierce that container with His light when a God-man-baby was painfully birthed and fell asleep surrounded by cow dung. Through that act, God was saying plenty about Himself. No human condition is removed from His experience. Hope and trust in Christ instead of the law was born that night. Faith had come.

Thank You, O caring Christ, for coming to fulfill the law and fill me with faith. Thank You that I don't have to fight the hopelessness of legalism along with the many things that my illness makes impossible, too. Today I will faithfully fix my heart on You.

DECEMBER 16 🪶 *Long Night*

Neither the pillar of cloud by day nor the pillar of fire
by night left its place in front of the people.
Exodus 13:21–22

Poinsettias bring explosions of crimson to florist shops, offices, stores, restaurants, homes, and color-starved souls. If
cared for properly, this Christmas "flower" will keep its
scarlet leaves well after the holiday and bloom again the
next year.

In order to attain subsequent budding by November
and color in December, a poinsettia must be pruned and
then exposed to sixteen hours of total darkness each day
throughout September and October. But the plant is sensitive and doesn't always come back after such severe treatment, even though this is the only way to achieve con-
tinuous color.

A poinsettia can't begin to understand why it has been
wrenched from a bright bay window and tossed into black-
ness. It doesn't know someone is thinking about it and caring for it. A plant can't see the thrill it will one day provide.
Nor can it grasp the significance of God becoming a helpless infant in order to penetrate the world in the middle of
the night with the fire of His love.

God of the Israelites and God of my life, thank
You for ever guiding me and never leaving me
throughout the long night of illness. Today I will
trust in the hope Jesus Christ provides, hope that
assures me I am blooming just where You have
planted me.   🪶

The wolf will live with the lamb, the leopard will lie down with the goat, the calf and the lion and the yearling together; and a little child will lead them.
Isaiah 11:6

"Lord, make me an instrument of Your peace," wrote St. Francis of Assisi centuries ago. "Where there is hatred, let me sow love. Where there is injury, pardon. Where there is doubt, faith. Where there is despair, hope. Where there is darkness, light. And where there is sadness, joy."

Each of these conflicting emotions and conditions live within me, not just in external relationships. I may hate myself and be unable to receive God's love. I may have been emotionally injured and am now unable to forgive myself for existing. I may doubt myself, unable to accept God's faith in me. I may feel despair over my illness, unable to see any hope in my future. I may be in darkness, unable to feel the warmth of God's light. I may live in sadness, unable to sense the joy God feels for me.

But the wolf and the lamb inside me can live together in peace. The lions of my soul can be tamed, and the fears of my inner calves can be calmed. The child Jesus comes to start the process.

Lord, St. Francis also said it is in giving that I receive and in pardoning that I am pardoned. Empower me to give forgiveness to myself today, thereby receiving Your Christmas gift of peace within.

> You are to give him the name Jesus, because he will
> save his people from their sins.   *Matthew 1:21*

Names are significant in the Bible. They describe a person's character, nature, or reputation. God's names in Jesus—Wonderful Counselor, Mighty God, Everlasting Father, Prince of Peace—are all linked to His identity and essence.

The name Jesus itself is the Greek form of Joshua, meaning "the Lord saves." Jews believed the Messiah (savior) would overthrow their enemies and save them politically, not realizing that He came to save them from missing the true end and scope of life, which is God.

For those who couldn't read or who only heard about God from others, or for those who were so steeped in the law that they missed the love, Jesus was an unignorable message in the flesh.

My name is not Lupus, Asthma, Diabetes, or Crohn's Disease. Jesus has named me His child and His friend. He writes my name on the palms of His hands and in His Book of Life. He saves me from missing out on the lavishly outrageous love of God our Father.

> O wonderful Christ, I am defined by more than the
> sum total of my broken body's parts. Thank You for
> a new future as one who bears the name Christian.
> Today I will praise the name of Jesus. How majestic
> it is in all the earth!   *

The name of the Lord is a strong tower; the righteous run to it and are safe.   *Proverbs 18:10*

William Shakespeare wrote, "That which we call a rose/By any other name would smell as sweet." He meant no matter what label the flower has, it will still tickle the senses. Even though a name may describe a person, place, or thing, it doesn't change its essence, nature, or being.

The life of the chronically ill can be punctuated by smells that are not so sweet: the sterile odors of doctors' offices and hospital corridors; alcohol, iodine, and medicinal rubs; ostomy bags and fresh wounds; bleach, ammonia, and pine.

But Jesus Christ by any other name—whether He's known as Lord or Redeemer or Mighty Savior—is still the strong place of safety to Whom I can run when illness, with all its sights and sounds and smells, surrounds me. His presence in my life will still smell as sweet as ever. No matter what or how I call Him, He hears me and the strength of His name shelters me.

Today, Lord, I pray with Thomas à Kempis, "In place of all the joys of the world grant me the sweet anointing of Your spirit, and instead of the loves of this life, pour in the love of Your name." ☙

DECEMBER 20 ❧ *Contentment*

Keep your lives free from the love of money and be
content with what you have, because God has said,
"Never will I leave you; never will I forsake you."
Hebrews 13:5

Remember the intense emotions of Christmas mornings
past? Waking up to the sight of that one longed-for gift: a
neon-yellow bike, a sweet-smelling doll that walked, or an
expensive stereo set. Or did disappointment and discon-
tent color the remaining school vacation because of the absence of that one special gift? Perhaps the room full of toys
I did have wasn't enough to satisfy me.

"Contentment," someone has said, "is not the fulfillment
of what you want but the realization of how much you already have." Like a child on Christmas morning, I can still
wake each day, expecting to be healed of my illness. If only
God would give me the healing I want, I may think, I
would be content.

The Bible says I already have the best Christmas gift of
all, God Who gave Himself to redeem me and stay forever
with me. And I'd see Him if I'd start considering all that I
do have instead of what I don't.

Jesus, You Who are my Christmas Presence, keep
me free from coveting health. Satisfy me today with
what I have in You. Forgive me when Everything
there is to have isn't enough for me. ❧

You were taught, with regard to your former way of life, to put off your old self,. . . to be made new in the attitude of your minds; and to put on the new self, created to be like God in true righteousness and holiness. *Ephesians 4:22–24*

Lupus forces Jackie to learn new ways of doing things. Celebrating Christmas used to be centered around Christmas Eve dinner. Now illness sends her to bed earlier, so brunch has become a new family tradition. She also found a church with an early worship service. Lack of stamina influences shopping as well, which she now does by catalogue.

Cooking, Jackie's favorite pastime, had to be relearned, too. "I start off with a lot of energy," she says, "but then I get exhausted and my memory goes. So I've gotten more precise and exact, getting all the ingredients out ahead of time, and reading the recipe step-by-step."

Jackie has found that a change in attitude goes a long way in helping her adjust to the changes that illness brings. Instead of being angry about giving up things she once enjoyed, Jackie now eagerly awaits the UPS truck. She still gets to cook gourmet fare for her family. And she finds great delight in worshiping with children on Christmas Eve.

Her illness is teaching Jackie a new philosophy of life— attitude is everything.

God, I want to be like You. Come into my heart and change the attitudes of my mind. Today I will eagerly anticipate Your arrival.

DECEMBER 22 ❧ *Usefulness*

The Spirit gives life; the flesh counts for nothing. The words I have spoken to you are spirit and they are life. *John 6:63*

This time of year many people have a large, fragrant evergreen tree somewhere in their home. Or they may have a well-crafted facsimile. Either one may be brightly decorated and appear fully alive, but the fact remains, no matter how useful for the moment, both of these trees are dead.

In *Out of Solitude,* Henri Nouwen retells a Taoist tale about a carpenter and his apprentice. Walking through a forest, they came across a tall, beautiful old oak tree. The carpenter wonders if his apprentice knows why "this tree is so tall, so huge, so gnarled, so old and beautiful?"

Because the apprentice does not know, the carpenter replies that it is because the tree is useless. "If it had been useful it would have been cut long ago and made into tables and chairs, but because it is useless it could grow so tall and so beautiful that you could sit in the shade and relax."

When we are not preoccupied with our own usefulness, Nouwen says, we can offer a service we had not planned on.

Teach me the difference, Lord Jesus, between doing and being, between spirit and flesh. Help me to see that my usefulness to You is not always measured in doing. Today I will meditate on Your words and allow myself to be shade for those You bring my way. ❧

Shout for joy, O heavens; rejoice, O earth; burst into song, O mountains! For the Lord comforts His people and will have compassion on His afflicted ones.
Isaiah 49:13

The cold winter winds of illness can come on suddenly and send a spiritual shiver right through me. Where did it come from? I may wonder. I was warm and happy just a minute ago.

When the first chill of winter comes to a forest, mice and other tiny creatures scurry in from the cold and bears begin to prepare for hibernation. They find a safe, cozy place and pull a blanket of snow over themselves, resting in its silent warmth.

I can hibernate, too, and wait out the passing winter in God, surrounded by His blanket of comfort. God doesn't pull me in, but I can choose to enter into Him at any time and be protected from the biting chill of an illness that keeps coming around.

When God chose to reveal Himself to the world that first Christmas, He left the comfort of heaven and hibernated for a while in a womb. From the comfort of the Father, Jesus came to comfort me.

O holy Comforter, thank You for coming to me and giving me a place of comfort in my affliction. Today my soul will rejoice and shout for joy! 🕊

But if I do it, even though you do not believe me,
believe the miracles, that you may know and
understand that the Father is in me, and I in the
Father.   *John 10:38*

Much is made about the miracle of Christmas. But what exactly is a miracle: a healing at Lourdes, a weeping statue, the one on 34th Street? Or is a miracle anything occurring outside the accepted laws of science and nature? It is said that the Virgin Birth is a miracle. Could it be every bit as much a miracle to be mentally, spiritually, emotionally, and physically sustained throughout a chronically recurrent physical assault and to be filled with holy joy in spite of it?

John Claypool recognizes the larger, truer miracle. "Listen," he writes, "there is something bigger in this world than we are and that something bigger is full of grace and mercy, patience and ingenuity. . . . Miracle of miracles, you can forgive yourself because you are forgiven, accept yourself because you are accepted, and begin to start building up the very places you once tore down. There is grace to help in every time of trouble."

Little Lord Jesus, I believe the miracle that is taking
place in me today. I do not always feel it, but
because You tell me to, I will believe it. This night
of all nights, I will open my heart that You might
dwell in me as the Father dwells in You.   💐

But while he was still a long way off, his father saw
him and was filled with compassion for him; he ran
to his son, threw his arms around him and kissed
him. . . . So they began to celebrate. *Luke 15:20, 24*

In Christ's birth, God ran to the world and threw His arms
around it, just as He does with me. He's not watching to
see how much work I can do for him or how many hours I
"squander" because of illness. He's not waiting to pounce
on my performance in life. I'm equally as valuable to Him
whether I possess the health and skill to evangelize millions
in a foreign land or whether I can only manage an occasional encouraging phone call here at home. I am wanted
and welcomed because God can't bear to be without me.

In her book *Successful Living with Chronic Illness*, Kathleen
Lewis says, "Chronic illness may give you an edge during
the holidays since, by traveling at a slower pace, you can
more fully recognize and appreciate, treasure, enjoy, and
celebrate precious relationships and all the blessings that
are yours."

There is much to celebrate. No matter what's going on
around or within me today, I can enjoy and feel safe within
a relationship with a Heavenly Father Who treasures and
appreciates me.

Father God, teach me to appreciate, enjoy, and
delight in You in the same way it pleases You to be
with me. Today we will celebrate together! ☞

Thanks be to God for his indescribable gift!
2 Corinthians 9:15

Chuck Close is a world-famous artist making a six-figure income. His life and career were shattered when a spinal artery collapsed. Paralyzed from the neck down, he's now trapped in a body that won't work. With only limited use of his hands, but full control of his creative spirit, Close continues to paint by doing it differently. He devised a wheelchair lift that moves his immobile body to accommodate his work on the oversized canvasses for which he's known.

"There are a lot of things I can't do, but I can still paint," Close says thankfully. Some observers say there's now more feeling in his work, a deeper level of what it is that touches one's soul.

"I am a confirmed believer in blessings in disguise," writes Robert Lynd. "I prefer them undisguised when I myself happen to be the person blessed; in fact, I can scarcely recognize a blessing in disguise except when it is bestowed upon someone else."

Gifts come in many shapes and sizes, colors and patterns, and not only at Christmas. God's greatest gift to me is the unselfish offering of His one and only Son. And through Him I can experience unlimited blessings, regardless of my physical condition.

> Lord God, when I force myself, I see much in my life
> for which I can be thankful. Today my heart will
> rejoice in You for the undisguised gift of Jesus Christ
> and the extraordinary love that made it so.   𐊨

> If you make an altar of stones for me, do not build it
> with dressed stones, for you will defile it if you use a
> tool on it.   *Exodus 20:25*

After they were freed from centuries of bondage in Egypt,
God showered the Hebrew people with one miracle after
another—parting the Red Sea, manna and quail to eat,
water from a rock—before speaking to them through
Moses and the Ten Commandments. At this point God
told Moses not to make altars out of cut stones, but to use
stones as they are found, in the variety of shapes God created them.

In Egypt, Hebrew slaves had been brick makers. One
brick after another, all the same size and shape, all made of
the same mixture. But now—no more bricks.

Freedom from slavery and freedom in Christ carry with
them a respect for individuality. God is a creator and all
His creations are unique, distinct, and different from one
another. God doesn't want me defiling His creation in me
by trying to live up to someone else's formula for living.

Being ill is not my only definition. God doesn't mold
bricks. God creates snowflakes and fingerprints and grains
of sand.

Thank You, Creator God, for making me special
and unique. I need to know that Your love for me is
not dependent on my abilities or lack of them. Fill
me today with the inescapable truth of Your
penchant for lavishing extravagant individual
attention.   ❧

You also, like living stones, are being built into a
spiritual house to be a holy priesthood . . . the people
of God; once you had not received mercy, but now
you have received mercy.   *1 Peter 2:5, 10*

The Creator God and Master Builder takes all the unformed and unchiseled stones He has created and fits them
together into a "spiritual house." This house, or the
Church, needs each and every stone to function as God
would have it. Each stone is distinctive, with its own individual size, shape, and function. God places and adjusts
each one exactly where He wants it to go, where it's a perfect fit and where it will add to the strength of the building.

I am a living stone, and regardless of my physical condition God's Church needs even me. God has created
within me gifts and aptitudes unique to me and, through
His mercy, God has fitted me into His scheme of things.
My illness is a part of my uniqueness, and it does not pre-
clude me from contributing to the strength of the Church.
If I allow God to set me in the mortar of His Spirit, I can
contribute to His work through my pain and suffering.

As the Builder, God sees the building in its entirety. As
a stone, my view is limited. As His priest, I have something
to give to others that will draw them closer to God.

As freely as I have received Your mercy, Lord God,
freely let me give mercy away today.   🔊

> You, however, are controlled not by the sinful nature but by the Spirit. . . . If Christ is in you, your body is dead because of sin, yet your spirit is alive because of righteousness.   *Romans 8:9–10*

In the nearly twenty years Carol has been teaching the Bible, she has gained more than she's ever given. The concept of redemption, of becoming righteous in God's sight, is one that eludes many people. So Carol uses the analogy her children gave her when they brought home a tadpole and placed it and a large rock in a few inches of water.

"What's the rock for?" she wanted to know.

"It's for when the frog learns to breathe," they replied.

Once the metamorphosis from tadpole to frog was complete, the amphibian would need to climb up on the rock to breathe the air its newly developed lungs required.

The process cannot be reversed. A frog can't go back to being a tadpole. It can slide back into the slimy water anytime, but it cannot stay there forever. It has become a frog just as surely as I have become righteous through Jesus Christ.

This is the picture Carol sees when Ménière's disease decides to pay her a surprise visit. "My spirit has been redeemed," she says. "It can't go back. My flesh, on the other hand, still awaits redemption."

> I have been rescued from a sinful nature and delivered to right-standing before God, Lord Jesus, through Your obedience to His righteous law. Today my spirit will crawl up onto Your Rock of Love and breathe the fresh, life-giving air of freedom.

> I am the Alpha and the Omega, the First and the Last,
> the Beginning and the End.   *Revelation 22:13*

The Chinese achieve written communication by pictogram. Oriental characters that may look like letters to the uninitiated are actually little pictures that add up to words and phrases that are language. Their pictogram for crisis is two doors, one portraying danger and the other opportunity.

Indeed, a crisis is a time of choice, a turning point. It can be the moment in which a decision for life or death is made in a medical crisis. It can be the point at which I determine to take a spiritual right or left turn, toward danger or toward opportunity.

Being chronically ill is not a one-dimensional existence. "You can suffer the danger," says Jeri Falk of the Maryland Lupus Foundation, "and yet simultaneously recognize the opportunity that it opens up."

The most important turning point for the Christian who lives with a chronic illness is Jesus Christ Himself, He Who is multidimensional, the First and the Last, the Beginning as well as the End. He is the axis on which my crisis-filled life turns and rests.

Lord God, You are Father and Friend, Comforter and Confronter, the Promiser of a new beginning with You in every tomorrow. Give me the strength I don't possess to choose rightly in the crises of this day and in this illness.   ❦

"For I know the plans I have for You," declares the Lord, "plans to prosper you and not to harm you, plans to give you hope and a future." *Jeremiah 29:11*

Catherine Marshall came into the public eye as the wife of Dr. Peter Marshall, chaplain to the United States Senate. His sudden death in 1949 left her to raise their son alone. She began to write by compiling her late husband's sermons and prayers before choosing to share her own story.

Marshall was not a stranger to suffering. As a young mother, for a period of almost two years, she had been bedridden with tuberculosis. That time was particularly difficult for a pastor's wife. The church she had come to serve was now serving her. Much later, in *To Live Again*, she wrote about her own growing relationship with God throughout illness and grief. She didn't know then that her life would hold another marriage, stepchildren, grandchildren, and a dozen more books.

"God had been in the past," Marshall wrote. "Then He would be in the future, too. . . . Always He had brought adventure—high hopes, unexpected friends, new ventures that broke old patterns. Then out in my future must lie more goodness, more mercy, more adventures, more friends."

God of my past, present, and future, when I can't see what's ahead for me, You can. Thank You for the promise that it will always be something to look forward to. Today I will hope in You.   ॐ

Index

Index to Scriptures

John 3:16, Mar. 20
John 4:11, Oct. 24
John 4:32, 34, Nov. 23
John 6:63, Dec. 22
John 8:14–15, Oct. 6
John 8:32, Nov. 3
John 9:2–4, June 14
John 9:27, Feb. 22
John 10:10, Mar. 17
John 10:28–30, May 19
John 10:38, Dec. 24
John 12:24, July 25
John 12:44–45, Nov. 14
John 12:46, Dec. 1
John 13:8–9, Aug. 7
John 14:2–3, Jan. 12
John 14:6, Mar. 27
John 14:19, Mar. 31
John 14:26, May 16
John 15:1–2, May 12
John 15:9, Aug. 5
John 15:15–16, June 29
John 16:7, June 19
John 16:20–21, Feb. 7
John 16:33, Apr. 16
John 17:23, 26, Feb. 17
John 21:21–23, Jan. 15

Acts 16:25, Feb. 20
Acts 17:25, 27–28, Aug. 9
Acts 20:24, Feb. 15
Acts 20:35, Nov. 5

Rom. 1:5, June 27
Rom. 3:23–25, Oct. 7
Rom. 5:8, May 29
Rom. 5:20–21, June 1
Rom. 6:6, 18, Oct. 19
Rom. 7:15, Mar. 12
Rom. 8:1, Feb. 28
Rom. 8:9–10, Dec. 29
Rom. 8:18, Feb. 11
Rom. 8:22–23, Feb. 6
Rom. 8:26, Jan. 19
Rom. 8:28, June 22
Rom. 8:32, Dec. 5
Rom. 8:33, Aug. 19
Rom. 8:34, Oct. 13
Rom. 8:35, Apr. 27
Rom. 8:38–39, Mar. 2
Rom. 10:11, June 28
Rom. 12:1, June 25
Rom. 12:2, Aug. 25
Rom. 14:8, Nov. 18

1 Cor. 1:27, 29, Apr. 1
1 Cor. 6:19–20, Apr. 9
1 Cor. 10:13, Mar. 1
1 Cor. 12:8–9, Oct. 27
1 Cor. 13:4–8, Jan. 5

Gal. 2:20, Aug. 24
Gal. 3:24–25, Dec. 15
Gal. 5:1, July 5